ALSO BY MARY TAYLOR SIMETI

On Persephone's Island

Pomp and Sustenance

Mary Taylor Simeti

POMP AND SUSTENANCE

Twenty-Five Centuries of Sicilian Food

An Owl Book
Henry Holt and Company   New York

Library of Congress Cataloging-in-Publication Data
Simeti, Mary Taylor.
Pomp and sustenance : twenty-five centuries of Sicilian food /
Mary Taylor Simeti. — 1st Owl book ed.
p.   cm.
Reprint. Originally published: New York : Knopf, 1989.
"An Owl book."
Includes bibliographical references and index.
ISBN 0-8050-1601-5
1. Cookery, Italian—Sicilian style. 2. Food habits—Italy—
Sicily. 3. Sicily (Italy)—Social life and customs.   I. Title.
TX723.2.S55S56   1991
641.59458—dc20   90-48325
                                                          CIP

Henry Holt books are available at special discounts
for bulk purchases for sales promotions, premiums,
fund-raising, or educational use. Special editions
or book excerpts can also be created to specification.
For details contact:
Special Sales Director, Henry Holt and Company, Inc.,
115 West 18th Street, New York, New York 10011.

First published in hardcover by Alfred A. Knopf, Inc., in 1989.

First Owl Book Edition— 1991.

Designed by Dorothy Schmiderer Baker

Printed in the United States of America
Recognizing the importance of preserving the written word,
Henry Holt and Company, Inc., by policy, prints all of its
first editions on acid-free paper.∞

1   3   5   7   9   10   8   6   4   2

Contents

Preface

I learned to cook in Sicily. Fresh out of an American college and living in a small Sicilian town on a volunteer's stipend of $75 a month, I had no alternative. So I put together what I remembered from watching the black cook from Virginia who had nourished me in my childhood and what I learned from my fellow workers at Danilo Dolci's center for community development, and I came up with a motley repertoire of dishes—American, Tuscan, Umbrian, Piemontese, even Swiss and Swedish. I was willing to try anything as long as it was cheap.

Marriage into a Sicilian family did not give my food the focus one might have expected. My mother-in-law's cooking was so circumscribed by her husband's diabetes and her own ill health that it included little that could have been identified as typically Sicilian. Though I enjoyed the elaborate pastas and desserts that she or the other women in the family produced for special occasions, my own celebrations tended toward roast turkey with stuffing, apple pie, gingerbread men, and other props for my precarious cultural identity. Meanwhile, the first spores of feminism were swelling inside me like a potent but as yet unidentified yeast, and the sheer quantity of "maintenance cooking" required in a society in which the whole family eats all three meals at home discouraged me from spending more time or energy in the kitchen than was absolutely necessary.

I came late, therefore, to exploring Sicilian cooking as a regional cuisine, and to grasping its particular characteristics, and I did so by way of a back door. In the early seventies my husband and I restored his family farm and began to spend our summers in the country. It was there that I learned how olives are gathered and pressed into oil and how grapes mature and become wine, and there that I talked to shepherds as they made ricotta and to peasant women who were bottling the year's supply of tomato sauce.

As I entered the world of Sicilian peasants, I discovered that their culture has very little future but a very ancient past. What I learned on the farm rekindled my college love of history and sent me, once freed from the demands of small children, to the former convents and palaces where Palermo's libraries are housed, in surroundings so picturesque that they can almost compensate for inadequate catalogues and irretrievable books.

Weekday mornings at a library, tempered by weekends on the farm, gave me the eccentric vision of food from which this book stems. I discovered that food in Sicily shares in what I have come to regard as the terrible density of Sicilian culture, an insular culture compacted by centuries of foreign conquest and domestic oppression. Although daunting when it immobilizes the island in the face of its ills, this density of history and tradition is fascinating and deeply satisfying when it informs and gives substance to the actions and rituals of every day—to the catching of fish and the gathering of fruit, to the kneading of daily bread and the preparing of festive pastries.

I must confess that I lack the scruples of a proper historian. My bookish browsing has taken me far afield, to pastures and periods I know nothing about, and I have rushed in where scholars would barely dabble a toe, noting coincidences and making connections with only the frail cement of supposition. Scholarly or not, my reading has given me great pleasure and amusement and has introduced my palate to some novel tastes: to the exotic aromas of earlier epochs—ancient Greek, Arabic, and Norman—and to the familiar yet often unrecognized ingredients of more recent times, those of hunger and faith, of pride and jealousy and joy.

I have come to hypothesize that most of the basic ingredients and techniques of contemporary Sicilian cooking were introduced to the island by the end of the twelfth century. At that point there appears to have been a change in dynamics—from a chronological development determined by external forces to a series of parallel developments in which internal economic considerations play the greatest role in modifying and diversifying the Sicilian diet. The structure of this book reflects that change. The first two chapters deal with the period before 1200, with the classical era and what it is possible to reconstruct of Sicilian cooking under the Greeks and the Romans, and then with the innovations that came with the Arabic and the Norman invasions. After 1200 class rather than conquest is the determining factor. Thus the third chapter is about the peasantry: what sustained them during centuries of increasing poverty and was consequently sacred to them. The fourth chapter is dedicated to the food with which the peasantry celebrated, either in festive contrast to their privations or as a daily reaffirmation of their passage to the middle class. Chapter Five explores what food meant to the aristocracy, who were concerned with status rather than survival. Special categories of Sicilian food occupy the last three chapters: the confections and the pastries produced by the island's convents, the food available in the street and on the road, and finally the particular Sicilian passion, ice cream.

The sources for a history of Sicilian food are myriad but indirect. The first cookbook to be written in the Western world, the lost *Art of Cooking* by Mithaecus, was composed in Syracuse in the fifth century B.C. Unfortunately Mithaecus found no imitators until twenty-five centuries had passed. In order to bridge this millennial gap, I have taken passages from the island's chronicles, novels, and poetry, seasoned them liberally with surmise and conjecture, and laced them with excerpts from the letters and journals of foreign visitors. Throughout, however, present-day Sicilian cooking has been my mainstay, the recipes from today's table serving to illustrate the innovative ingredients and the changing culinary fashions of the past.

The recipes are straightforward directions for classic Sicilian cooking, culled from various cooks and cookbooks. A culinary tradition with such ancient roots presents a multitude of possibilities to choose from. The people of one Sicilian town, when speaking of a given dish, may intend something quite different from the people living in a town twenty miles distant. And even when they are agreed as to the outcome, each family has its own method for achieving it. Although my choices may not always agree with the family traditions or travel experiences of my readers, and although I have often been swayed by personal preference or by the desire to prove a point, I hope in the end to have achieved a balanced selection that is representative of contemporary Sicilian cooking.

I have tried all the recipes myself and have converted measurements from grams into cups, tablespoons, and teaspoons, without making any further adaptation to the American kitchen and marketplace, since I have access to neither. Each time I have used an ingredient that I think might pose a problem for people cooking outside Sicily, I have added a note of explanation, but I rarely suggest substitute ingredients unless I am quite sure that the basic character of the dish will not be altered by their use. One exception regards the quantity of salt. Since I use unrefined sea salt from the beautiful salt flats on Sicily's western shore, which is not consistent in its potency, I have almost always left the amount of salt up to the experience and the preferences of the reader.

I must confess that I have been inconsistent in the way I refer to the recipes, using the Sicilian name in some cases (as in *cuccìa* and *farsumagru*, which have no Italian equivalents, or as in *fritedda*, which in Italian—*fritella*—means something quite different) but preferring the Italian form where there is a one-to-one correspondence. I hope thus to make things simpler for my readers, most of whom will have some familiarity with kitchen Italian, and also to express my distaste for restaurant Sicilian, which bewilders the tourist and debases the dialect in much the same way "ye olde tea shoppe" debases Chaucer's English.

For those who prefer to try Sicilian food *in situ* (an attitude I recommend highly), there is an appendix with suggestions as to where some of the specialties can be found. By no means intended as a complete guide to eating in Sicily, this appendix is, like the book as a whole, a reflection of my own personal quirks, curiosities, and passions.

In the bibliography I have listed the various Sicilian cookbooks, particularly those of Anna Pomar and Pino Correnti, that I have consulted in my researches. But I would also like to mention some of the people—family, friends, and acquaintances—who have been so generous in sharing their recipes and their skills with me: first of all my mother-in-law, the late Giacoma Simeti, and then Giuliana Ajroldi, Caterina Maria Bono, Celeste Catalano, Pina and Gabriella Chimienti, Nata and Maria Vica Costarelli, Pamela Fundarò, Giuseppina Giurintano, Angelo La Mattina of Gelato 2, Anna Rappa, Loly Riela, Michela Rocca, Pina and Irene Ruvolo, Giuseppina Sicilia, Maria Taibi, Claudia Zizzo, and the Lombardo brothers of the Panificio San Francesco in Alcamo. I am deeply grateful for their help, just as I am grateful for the unflagging and venturesome appetites of my family.

Pomp and Sustenance

1

Of Ancient Abundance, Epic Appetites

I learnt to cook so well in Sicily that I will cause the banqueters
to bite the dishes and the plates for joy.
                    Alexis of Tarentum, fourth century B.C.

The first foreign visitor to set foot on Sicilian shores was, some say, the
archetypal traveler himself, Odysseus, who circumnavigated the island in a
state of perpetual astonishment at the abundance of its fields. On the east
coast, at the foot of Mount Etna, he saw the land of the Cyclops, so rich that
despite the ignorance of its gigantic inhabitants, who neither tilled nor plowed,
"grain—/wild wheat and barley—grows untended, and/wine-grapes, in clusters, ripen in heaven's rain." To the west, in the city now known as Trapani,

                    . . . he saw an orchard
          closed by a pale—four spacious acres planted
          with trees in bloom or weighted down for picking:
          pear trees, pomegranates, brilliant apples,
          luscious figs, and olives ripe and dark.
          Fruit never failed upon these trees: winter
          and summer time they bore, for through the year
          the breathing Westwind ripened all in turn—
          so one pear came to prime, and then another,
          and so with apples, figs, and the vine's fruit
          empurpled in the royal vineyard there.
          Currants were dried at one end, on a platform
          bare to the sun, beyond the vintage arbors
          and vats the vintners trod; while near at hand

were new grapes barely formed as the green bloom fell,
or half-ripe clusters, faintly coloring.
After the vines came rows of vegetables
of all the kinds that flourish in every season,
and through the garden plots and orchard ran
channels from one clear fountain, while another
gushed through a pipe under the courtyard entrance
to serve the house and all who came for water.

Homer, *The Odyssey*, ninth century B.C.

It is not mere intellectual whimsy to begin a discussion of contemporary Sicilian food with Odysseus. The gardens of Alcinoüs as Homer describes them, with their constant supply of fresh fruit and vegetables, olives to eat and to press, and vineyards to give wine, vinegar, and dried grapes, contain the very essence of Sicilian cooking. The raw materials present in *The Odyssey*, prepared according to the techniques described by later Greek and Roman authors, still dominate the Sicilian table today, a continuity all the more remarkable in the light of the many subsequent invasions. The conquerors who followed the Greeks increased and enriched the range of Sicilian cooking, but they failed to alter its basic character.

Like the mythical gardens of Alcinoüs, Sicily herself became synonymous with abundance. Here the colonists who had set sail from the poor soils and eroded hillsides of archaic Greece found mountains hidden by thick forests, fields covered by volcanic loam of extraordinary fertility, pastures so redolent of spring wildflowers that hounds could not follow the scent of their prey.

Just as their dogs were confounded by this abundance of perfume, so the colonists themselves were also led astray. Corrupted by the climate of plenty, they abandoned the simple, measured, even abstemious diet that had heretofore been the lot and the vaunt of Greeks of all classes, and by the fifth century B.C. Syracuse, the richest and most powerful of the Greek cities on the island, had become the gastronomic capital of the Mediterranean world.

The Greek invasion was from the very beginning an agricultural rather than a mercantile one, and the wealth of the colonies was derived from the production and exportation of agricultural goods—wheat, cheese, oil, honey, and timber to the homeland, fruit and vegetables to the Greek and Phoenician colonies of North Africa, a scant hundred-mile sail to the south. These products were much appreciated at home on the island as well, where they became the basis of a distinguished local cuisine.

The earliest notices of these culinary developments are very fragmentary: Syracuse produced the treatise by Mithaecus and the first school for professional cooks, which was run by a man named Labducus. The master of them all was not a Syracusan, however, but a man from Gela named Archestratus, a gourmet of such refined palate that it was said he could detect a difference in flavor between a mullet caught during a waxing moon and one taken during the waning.

Archestratus traveled throughout the Mediterranean, a fourth-century B.C. Michelin inspector, spreading the gospel of good eating and passing judgment on what the local markets had to offer: five stars to the eels fished off the coast of Messina and to the herrings from Syracuse; three stars to Sicilian tuna caught near Tindari or Cefalù, but five to that of Byzantium.

> And have a tail-cut from a she-tunny—the large she-tunny, I repeat, whose mother-city is Byzantium. Slice it and roast it all rightly, sprinkling just a little salt, and buttering it with oil. Eat the slices hot, dipping them into a *sauce piquante*: they are nice even if you want to eat them plain, like the deathless gods in form and stature. But if you serve it sprinkled with vinegar, it is done for.
>
> Archestratus of Gela, fourth century B.C.

Only fragments of Archestratus's poetry have survived, incorporated into *The Deipnosophists*—*The Sophists at Dinner*, a lengthy compendium of gastronomic thought and practice written six centuries later by Athenaeus of Naucratis, for whom the precepts of Archestratus represented a golden age of moderation. Yet Archestratus's constant exhortations to simplicity indicate that overindulgence and excess were already the rule. One foreigner who visited the court of the tyrant Dionysius in 387 B.C. was so disgusted by the licentiousness and the gourmandizing he found there that he wrote an epistle home to say so:

> And when I came [to Sicily] I was in no wise pleased at all with "the blissful life," as it is there termed, replete as it is with Italian and Syracusan banqueting; for thus one's existence is spent in gorging food twice a day and never sleeping alone at night and all the practices which accompany this mode of living.
>
> Plato, Epistle VII, fourth century B.C.

FRAGMENTS OF THE TEMPLE AT AGRIGENTO, *an eighteenth-century drawing by Houel*

The measuring stick Plato used to judge anyone's lifestyle was undeniably straight and narrow. Still, the self-indulgence and the overeating that he condemned were not unique to the court of Syracuse. The Golden Mean had fallen into disregard throughout the island, and everywhere fabulous banquets were consumed in the shadow of outsize temples. The Olympaeion then a-building in Agrigento was one of the largest temples in the Greek world and inspired the famous epigram, of uncertain attribution but unerring wit, according to which the people of Agrigento "built as if they thought they would live forever, and ate as if they knew they were never to eat again."

Archestratus, who is said to have known Alexander the Great, wrote at the height of the Hellenistic Age; within a century of his death, Sicily became a province of Rome. Although there are no sources that document how this affected Sicilian cooking, it would appear that in culinary matters, at least, it was the Sicilians who won the war. The fame of Sicilian cuisine spread throughout the classical world, and the Sicilian cook became a stock character in classical comedy, as well as a status symbol for the wealthy Roman. *Siculus coquus et sicula mensa*, the proverb went ("a Sicilian cook and a Sicilian table"). It can therefore be argued that Sicilians played a large part in developing the elaborate cuisine of Imperial Rome.

In the light of this reasoning and in the absence of more direct sources, it is both legitimate and helpful to turn for information to a text that never actually mentions Sicily at all, the *De re coquinaria*. Either written by or dedicated to Marcus Gavius Apicius, a renowned gourmet who lived in Rome in the first century A.D., the *De re coquinaria* is a proper cookbook, albeit one intended for professionals who have no need for precise instructions and exact quantities, and it offers a wealth of details about the food of the Roman Empire.

The modern reader tends to be befuddled by an excess of seasoning when reading the recipes of Apicius, each of which contains a long list of spices and herbs that are repeated with monotonous frequency. I am indebted to the edition translated by Joseph Dommers Vehling, a chef by profession and a classicist by vocation, for pointing out the economy and elegance that lie beneath the trimmings and prove this cuisine to be much closer than is often thought to the true "Mediterranean diet."

Then as now, for the Greeks and the Romans as well as for our cholesterol-conscious contemporaries, the Mediterranean diet was based on cereals and legumes. While in Greece and in many other parts of the world barley, millet, and other lesser grains predominated, Sicily's soil and climate were particularly suited to the cultivation of hard-grained durum wheat. It was durum wheat, therefore, that supplied the basis of the Sicilian classical diet, either in bread (Athenaeus credits the renowned Greek bakers with seventy-two different kinds of bread) or as whole grains boiled into a sort of porridge or gruel known in the Roman world as *puls*. This gruel formed the mainstay of the meals for the slaves, for the peasants, and for the soldiers. Thucydides, speaking of the defeated Athenian army held prisoner in the stone quarries of Syracuse, tells us that the daily allowance for each man was half a pint of water and a pint of grain.

For the plebs, gruel was the main and probably the only course, and it is unlikely that it had much more than a little salt and maybe some wild fennel for seasoning. What variety they could hope for came from legumes: chickpeas, lentils, and fava beans. Apicius gives a recipe for a *tisanum*, a porridge of mixed

THE LATOMIE, *the stone quarries in Syracuse in a nineteenth-century drawing by Bartlett*

legumes that was supposedly the favorite dish of Caesar Augustus. One can imagine that this porridge, spiced up with vegetables and with costly silphium into food fit for an emperor, must have been nostalgic eating for Augustus, taking him back to the days when he was just one of the boys, hitting the chow at the *castrum* with the rest of the legionnaires.

> Soak chickpeas, lentils and peas, crush barley and cook with the legumes. When well cooked add plenty of oil. Now cut greens, leeks, coriander, dill, fennel, beets, mallows, cabbage strunks, all soft and green and very finely cut, and put in a pot. The cabbage cook [separately; also] crush fennel seed, plenty of it, origany, silphium, and lovage, and when ground, add broth to taste, pour this over the porridge, stir, and use some finely chopped cabbage stems to sprinkle on top.
>
> Apicius, *Cookery and Dining in Imperial Rome*, first century A.D.

The Romans were also enthusiastic about fava beans, which grow inside thick green pods as much as ten inches long, each pod containing from three to six flattish beans resembling limas both in their shape and in their mealy texture. Green and tender and very sweet when they are young and still the size of a fingernail, fava beans are often eaten raw, with primosale or pecorino cheese. As the beans ripen, the skins lose their color, become tough and slightly bitter, and must be discarded.

The Greeks associated the fava beans with funerary rites—according to Pythagoras the hollow stalk of the fava plant provided a pathway to Hades for the spirits of the dead—and some were loath to eat them. The Romans had no such qualms, and they may have been the ones to introduce *maccu* onto the Sicilian table. *Maccu* is a purée of dried fava beans that has been a staple of Sicilian peasant cooking from antiquity on down. It is something of a rarity nowadays and almost never to be found in restaurants, except on the occasions in which the rich indulge in nostalgia for the "genuine" tastes of a poverty they have never known.

MACCU
(Fava Bean Soup)

Serves 6

1 pound dried fava beans, peeled	Salt and freshly ground pepper
2 quarts cold water	Olive oil
1 bunch wild fennel sprigs, washed and chopped, or 2 teaspoons fennel seeds	

OPTIONAL

½ pound ditalini or other small pasta	4 ripe tomatoes, peeled and chopped
1 small onion, chopped	2 tablespoons olive oil

Soak the fava beans in water overnight, then drain. If you are not able to buy the beans already peeled, buy 1¼ pounds of unpeeled beans, then peel them after they have soaked.

Put the drained and peeled beans in a heavy flameproof soup pot (preferably of terra cotta) together with the 2 quarts water, the fennel (sprigs or seeds), and some salt. Bring to a boil and simmer uncovered for 2 hours or until the beans are completely tender and can be mashed against the side of the pot with a wooden spoon. Stir frequently.

At this point you must decide whether you wish to eat your *maccu* as a simple purée or to have it with pasta. In the latter case, thin the *maccu* with a cup or two of boiling water, then add the pasta. Stir very frequently as the pasta is cooking, since *maccu* thickens and sticks very easily. For an added fillip, sauté chopped onion and tomatoes in oil until tender and stir in at the last minute.

All versions require that you correct the salt and add a liberal sprinkling of black pepper and of olive oil.

Leftover *maccu* can be poured onto a platter and left to harden, then cut into strips, floured, and fried in a little olive oil—a special treat for the peasant families of the past.

———

Wild fennel is just one of the seasonings that modern Sicilians have inherited from the classical world. The "broth" that Apicius calls for in many of his recipes is *garum*, an essence made from fermenting salted fish that was commonly used to flavor Roman cooking. In spite of the rotten reputation that *garum* has acquired over the centuries, Vehling maintains that at its best it was "akin to our modern anchovy sauce."

In the letters written by the Marquis of Ormonde during his Sicilian travels, there is an all too brief reference to a nineteenth-century version of the same: "The flesh [of the tuna] is good, and a sauce called *garum* is prepared from it." Although salted tuna has disappeared, both anchovies and sardines, either in salt or in oil, occur in contemporary Sicilian cooking with much the same frequency and to much the same end as *garum* in the Roman cuisine. In Syracuse, for example, the most characteristic pasta dish is spaghetti with an anchovy sauce. There are many variants of this all across the island.

PASTA CON ACCIUGHE E MOLLICA
(Pasta with Anchovies and Breadcrumbs)

Serves 6

1 tablespoon olive oil	1 cup warm water
2 cups dried breadcrumbs	1 ½ pounds spaghetti
(see note below)	10–12 anchovy fillets
⅓ cup olive oil	1 teaspoon olive oil
2 garlic cloves	1 tablespoon finely chopped
¼ cup tomato extract	fresh parsley
(see below) or ⅓ cup	
tomato paste	

Coat the bottom of a heavy skillet with 1 tablespoon of olive oil. Add the breadcrumbs and toast them over a low flame, stirring constantly, until they are a rich golden brown. Put them in a small serving bowl and set aside.

Put ⅓ cup olive oil in a skillet, add the garlic cloves, slightly crushed but still of a piece. Sauté the garlic until it begins to color, then discard. Add the tomato extract and the water to the hot oil, stirring until the extract is completely dissolved. Simmer over very low heat for about 10 minutes.

Meanwhile, cook the spaghetti in a large pot of boiling water, only lightly salted since both the tomato extract and the anchovies are very salty.

In a separate pan or a double boiler (I always use a small double-handled frying pan that will sit on top of my spaghetti pot), cook the anchovies together with 1 teaspoon of olive oil, stirring them until they dissolve into a cream. This must be done over steam and not over the direct flame, lest the anchovies turn bitter. Add the anchovies to the tomato sauce and simmer 2 to 3 minutes longer.

Drain the spaghetti when cooked *al dente*, reserving a cup of the cooking water. (This is always a wise precaution when preparing pasta with a very concentrated sauce or with breadcrumbs—a few tablespoons of the reserved liquid will correct any eventual dryness.) Place the spaghetti in a large bowl, add the sauce, and mix thoroughly, pouring in a little of the reserved liquid if necessary. Sprinkle with some of the breadcrumbs and with the parsley. Pass the remaining breadcrumbs on the side.

Note: Sicilians use different kinds of breadcrumbs for different purposes. What I call "dried breadcrumbs" are the ordinary crumbs grated from stale bread, crust and all, which can be either purchased or prepared at home. When browned in oil as in this recipe, these become "toasted breadcrumbs." A third variety are what I shall call "stale white breadcrumbs," meaning more specifically the white part of 2-to-3-day-old semolina-flour bread that has been grated, sieved to remove any big pieces, and allowed to dry for a day or two (a barely warm oven can speed this process). If these breadcrumbs are not thoroughly dry, they will become gluey.

––––––––

Purists require that this recipe be prepared using *'u 'strattu*, tomato extract that is obtained from enormous expanses of bright red tomato purée salted and spread out on boards to dry in the sun until it hardens into a very dark red paste with the consistency of clay. The *'strattu* gleaming in the bright summer sunlight, together with the *pennuli*, a sort of thick-skinned cherry tomato hung up in bunches on the wall to keep until December, make bright splotches of red pigment along the whitewashed streets of Sicilian villages, but it is rarer and rarer that you see it nowadays. As far as I know the *'strattu* produced today is marketed only on a very small and very local scale: most Palermo groceries have bowls of it on their counters and weigh it out by the spoonful.

Given the success that sun-dried tomatoes are currently enjoying in the United States, I can't believe that it will be long before *'strattu* crosses the ocean. Until its moment comes, however, those who are curious, and can count on two days of very hot sun, can try making their own.

'STRATTU
(Tomato Extract)

Makes 1 pound

10 pounds very ripe, healthy tomatoes	5–6 sprigs fresh sweet basil
	2–4 tablespoons olive oil
Salt	Coarse salt

Wash the tomatoes, remove their stems or stem ends, and cut them into small chunks. Pass the chunks of tomatoes through a food mill to remove skins and seeds.

Salt the resulting purée to taste, making it just a little saltier than you would make a normal tomato sauce. Wash and dry the basil sprigs and add them to the purée.

Spread the purée on a wooden tabletop in the sun. Don a large straw hat, equip yourself with a good book in one hand and a sturdy spatula in the other, and start stirring. The purée must be spread out, gathered in, stirred, and spread out again fairly continuously for two days, so that the sun can evaporate the water content. If at first the purée is so liquid that it won't stay on the table, you may have to start the drying process in platters, and then transfer it onto the tabletop when the purée has become a little denser.

Put the table on a porch for the night or in some other place where it will have air but no dew can collect on it. If your sun is not very hot, the drying process may take more than two days.

When the extract has become so thick that it can be modeled like clay, remove the basil. Then oil your hands well and pack the extract little by little into a sterilized glass jar, pressing it

down well so that no air bubbles remain. Cover the surface with
a thin coat of oil, and sprinkle with 1–2 tablespoons of coarse
salt. Cover the jar with a piece of muslin and store in a cool
place. Each time you take some extract out, make sure that the
remaining surface is covered with oil.

————

Those who lack the temperament or the climate for making their own
extract can use in its place commercial tomato paste, either the kind imported
from Italy in a tube and known as "double concentrate," or the canned type.
The final results, however, will not be quite the same.

Another version of pasta and anchovies has no tomato in it, thus making
it the older and, in the eyes of some, the more orthodox. It is also delightfully
quick and easy, although if you use salted anchovies, as tradition requires, you
have the messy task of filleting them. To do this, slide your thumb down the
backbone and open the anchovy like a book. Remove the backbone, then wash

SALTING ANCHOVIES, *an eighteenth-century drawing by Houel*

thoroughly under running water to remove the excess salt and any residual scales. In any case salted anchovies are not easily found today, except in street markets, and anchovy fillets in olive oil make an excellent substitute.

This recipe too requires toasted breadcrumbs, which Sicilians are very fond of sprinkling on their pasta in place of grated cheese. One cook of my acquaintance has told me that for fish and vegetable sauces she browns a couple of garlic cloves in the oil in which she toasts her breadcrumbs. To crumbs destined to be eaten with pasta in a pork and tomato sauce she adds a fresh sage leaf.

PASTA CON SALSA DI ACCIUGHE SALATE
(Pasta with Salted Anchovy Sauce)

Serves 6

⅓ cup dried currants
1 bunch fresh wild fennel
  sprigs (optional)
1½ pounds spaghetti or
  bucatini
1 garlic clove
2 parsley sprigs
½ cup olive oil

½ cup pine nuts
10–12 salted anchovies (see
  above) or 20–24 anchovy
  fillets under oil
1 tablespoon fresh oregano
  leaves
2 cups toasted breadcrumbs
  (see p. 12)

Put the currants to soak for 5 minutes in hot water so they soften, then drain.

If fresh fennel is available and you wish to use it, wash it, chop it roughly, and cook it for about 10 minutes or until tender in abundant boiling water. Lift the fennel out with a slotted spoon and use the same water to cook the pasta. Chop the fennel into small pieces. Drain the pasta when it is cooked, reserving some of the cooking liquid.

In the meantime, in a small pan (here too I use one that will fit over my pasta pot) sauté the garlic and the parsley in the olive oil. Discard them when they begin to color, and add to the oil the currants, the pine nuts, and the anchovies. Cook over steam until the anchovies disintegrate, add the oregano, and place the pan over a very low flame, stirring constantly, for just about a minute.

Toss the pasta with the fennel if you are using it, the sauce, and the reserved liquid if needed. Serve accompanied by the toasted breadcrumbs.

————

If nowadays the Sicilians prefer to use pasta rather than whole grains as a vehicle for anchovies, fennel, and other ancient seasonings, they are still passionately fond of something very similar to the sweet gruel of spelt (a particular variety of wheat), which Apicius calls *apothermum*.

> Boil spelt with pine nuts and peeled almonds immersed in [boiling] water and washed with white clay so that they appear perfectly white, add raisins, [flavor with] condensed wine or raisin wine, and serve it in a round dish with crushed [nuts, fruit, bread, or cake crumbs] sprinkled over it.
>
> Apicius, *Cookery and Dining in Imperial Rome*, first century A.D.

The modern Sicilian equivalent is *cuccìa*, a sweet pudding of boiled wheat berries that is made once a year, on Saint Lucy's Day, when only unmilled wheat is eaten and all food made from wheat flour is banned. This observance is said to commemorate a great famine that came to an end on the feast of Saint Lucy, when grain-laden ships arrived in the harbor and the starving populace boiled up the grain without waiting to mill it. The grain in contemporary *cuccìa* requires three days' soaking, however—too slow a process to fit the story of the famine, which is no doubt a Christian myth fabricated to cloak pagan antecedents.

Saint Lucy, whose feast day in the Julian calendar fell on the shortest day of the year, is the protectress of vision and the bringer of light, who reassures us in winter's darkness. The whole grains of the *cuccìa* are seeds, and as such bear promise, too—that of future harvest. The ancient Greeks had something similar, a ritual dish of boiled seeds known as *panspermia*, which they prepared twice a year in honor of Apollo, to mark the coming and the going of the summer sun.

Cuccìa can be prepared in a number of different versions. The most archaic calls for *vino cotto*, a thick, molasseslike syrup made from sieved grape must boiled down to a third of its original volume, which is the "condensed wine" of the Apician recipe, and which, together with honey, was a basic sweetening agent in classical cooking. Later versions require that the soaked and boiled wheat berries be mixed with ricotta cream or with a cornstarch pudding known as *biancomangiare*, and liberally decorated with bits of chocolate, candied fruit, and abundant cinnamon. In either case the result is as sweet and as gooey as only a true Sicilian could wish.

CUCCÌA
(Saint Lucy's Pudding)

Serves approximately 10 to 12

2 ½ pounds whole wheat berries

Small pinch of salt

Soak the whole wheat berries in cold water for 2 or 3 days, changing the water twice a day.

The day before serving, drain the wheat, place in a large saucepan, cover with fresh water, add the salt, and simmer for 6 to 8 hours, or until quite tender. Turn off the flame, cover the pot, and leave it overnight.

The next morning drain the wheat thoroughly and serve it in a large bowl, adding one of the following:

I. WITH *VINO COTTO*

2 cups *vino cotto* (see note)

1 teaspoon ground cinnamon

Note: The provident Sicilian housewife prepares her winter's supply of *vino cotto* in September, during the grape harvest. To do so, she takes clarified white grape juice (see recipe for *mostarda* on p. 226), and boils it down until it is reduced to one-third of its original volume.

Heat the *vino cotto* in a saucepan until it is warm and pour it over the drained wheat berries. Mix well, heap in a large serving dish, and sprinkle with cinnamon.

II. WITH RICOTTA CREAM

2½ pounds fresh ricotta
  (see note)
3 cups sugar
¼ teaspoon vanilla
  extract

1 cup semisweet chocolate
  bits
½ cup diced *zuccata*
  (see p. 94) or candied
  citron

Pass the ricotta through the fine disk of a food mill or press it through a sieve so that it becomes very fine and creamy in texture. (Some people whip the ricotta with an electric beater, but this eliminates the curds completely and gives it what I find to be an unpleasantly oily consistency.) Beat in the sugar and the vanilla, then add the chocolate and the *zuccata* or citron, mixing enough to distribute them evenly. Add to the drained wheat berries and mix thoroughly. (This version is the most popular in my family.)

Note: Sicilian ricotta is always lightly salted, even when fresh. If using completely unsalted ricotta, you must add a little salt to compensate.

III. *BIANCOMANGIARE* PUDDING

¾ cup cornstarch
5 cups milk
1 cup sugar
1 twist of lemon peel

1 cup semisweet chocolate
  bits
½ cup diced *zuccata* (p. 94)
  or candied citron

In a small bowl, dissolve the cornstarch in a small quantity of milk, taking care to smooth out any lumps. Pour this into a saucepan together with the remaining milk, the sugar, and the lemon peel. Cook over a very low flame until thick, stirring constantly and taking care that the milk does not boil. Remove from the heat, take out the lemon peel, and pour the mixture over the drained wheat berries, mixing well. Allow to cool before adding the chocolate and the candied fruit.

The trick with *cuccìa*, I have been told, is to make it at the right moment and in the right quantity so as to avoid having to refrigerate it at any point, as the cold will toughen the wheat berries irrevocably. The right quantity is difficult to determine: most Sicilians feel that since *cuccìa*, like Christmas, comes only once a year, one should make a lot. I am inclined to think that the quantities that I have given will satisfy the appetites of ten to twelve non-Sicilians.

––––––––

Although Homer didn't specify which vegetables Odysseus saw growing in the gardens of Alcinoüs, we can safely assume that together with legumes and onions, both the cabbage and the squash families were represented, as well as artichokes and cardoons, which according to Pliny originated in Sicily. All of these vegetables occupy a sizable part of any modern Sicilian garden, and are often prepared in ways similar to those suggested by Apicius. He gives various recipes for fresh fava beans, which have quite a different taste from the dried ones used to make *maccu*. The contemporary apotheosis of the fresh fava bean is in *frittedda*, which also requires baby artichokes and new peas, plus many willing hands for the shelling. There are those who make *frittedda* any time of year, using frozen vegetables, but the results are inferior, and in any case I feel that *frittedda* should be a celebration of spring.

FRITTEDDA
(Spring Fava Fry)

Serves 6

2 pounds very young peas	½ cup olive oil
2 pounds very young fava beans	Salt and freshly ground black pepper
12 small, tender artichokes	2 tablespoons white wine vinegar (see note)
5 or 6 scallions	
1½ cups water	

Shell the peas and the fava beans, keeping them separate. Slice off the tips of the artichokes, remove all the tough outer leaves, and peel the base. Be merciless, however extravagant it may seem, for one tough artichoke leaf can ruin an otherwise perfect mouthful. Cut the artichokes into quarters. Remove the choke, if it has formed, together with any prickly tips on the inner leaves. Then cut each quarter in three, so as to have very fine wedges.

Slice the scallions and put them in a heavy saucepan with ½ cup water. Cook over a medium flame, stirring constantly, until the water evaporates. Add the olive oil and sauté the scallions for a few minutes until pale golden.

Add the artichokes, ½ cup hot water, and salt to taste. Cover and cook over a low flame for 5 minutes.

Add the fava beans and ½ cup hot water. Cover and cook 5 more minutes.

Add the peas. Cover and cook for 5 minutes more, then sprinkle with the vinegar and some pepper. Correct the salt, and cook over a medium-high flame, uncovered, for 2 to 3 minutes, or until the vinegar has evaporated. Refrigerate for 24 hours and serve cold.

Note: Here and elsewhere in this book, the quantity of vinegar must be considered a rough approximation and not a rule. I use a very strong white wine vinegar that we produce on our farm; most commercial wine vinegars are considerably lighter. Palates vary too, so it is wise to start with a small amount and keep adding until you reach the level of vinegariness that suits you.

In another recipe, which I learned from my mother-in-law and have never found elsewhere, the young beans are boiled, mixed with breadcrumbs, then dressed almost like a salad, and served cold. They would not have been out of place on Apicius's table.

FAVE CON LA MOLLICA
(Fava Beans with Breadcrumbs)

Serves 6

4 pounds fresh young fava
   beans
¾ cup water
¼ cup olive oil plus
   1 tablespoon
Salt
⅓ cup finely chopped fresh
   mint leaves

1 cup stale white bread-
   crumbs (see p. 12)
1 tablespoon white wine
   vinegar (see note p. 20)
Freshly ground black pepper

Shell the beans, removing the skin from any big enough to have turned whitish. Cook with the water, ¼ cup oil, and a little salt, in a covered pot for about 10 minutes or until tender.

Stir in the mint, breadcrumbs, vinegar, a little pepper, and 1 tablespoon of oil. Correct the salt. Serve cold.

———

As soon as the skin of the fava bean begins to whiten and lose its intense green color, it must be discarded. Skinning each bean individually is a very tedious business, just punishment for anyone wanting to serve large fava beans in elegant circumstances. One Saturday in May some years ago a few friends and I decided on the spur of the moment to drive out to our farm for the day. All we took with us was a loaf of fresh bread and a large wedge of primosale cheese.

In the garden we picked young artichokes—the narrow, pointed variety, silvery gray in color and very sweet, which ripen here in the late spring—and we boiled them in salted water. We also picked enormous fava beans, which we removed from their pods and put in a pan, covered with cold water, some salt, and a liberal dose of oregano. Just a few minutes after the beans reached the boiling point they began to swell and split their skins. We drained them, added some olive oil, and shot the tender innards mouthward by pinching them between thumb and forefinger. The silverware remained in the drawer, our plates were heaped with fava skins and artichoke leaves, our fingers and chins were decidedly oily, but for what we lacked in chic we were more than repaid in pleasure.

Squashes occupied several rows in the classical vegetable garden. Apicius's *aliter cucurbitas more Alexandrino*, which is boiled squash in a spicy vinegar sauce, differs little from a modern Palermo recipe with a nicely misleading name.

FEGATO AI SETTE CANNOLI
(Sette Cannoli's Liver)

Serves 6

2-pound piece of Hubbard or other large winter squash	½ cup white wine vinegar (see note p. 20)
⅓ cup olive oil	½ cup sugar
3 garlic cloves, sliced thin	Salt and freshly ground pepper
½ cup finely chopped fresh mint leaves	⅛ teaspoon ground cinnamon

Peel the squash, remove seeds and strings, and cut the pulp into slices. The shape and size of the slices will vary according to the piece of squash you have, but they should be no more than ½ inch thick. Sauté the slices in the oil until tender and browned on both sides. Arrange the slices on a serving plate and sprinkle with the garlic and the mint leaves.

To the same pan and oil in which you fried the squash add the vinegar, sugar, salt and pepper, and cinnamon. Cook and stir over a medium flame until the sugar melts and the sauce thickens. Pour over the squash. Serve cold.

Sette Cannoli is a poor neighborhood in Palermo, where most people could not afford in the past to buy meat: pumpkin got up to look like liver was the best they could hope for. Apicius had no such problems: the elaborate disguises in which food was often served at Roman banquets were the product of extravagant whim rather than bleak necessity. Yet even his recipes reflect care taken to waste no part of whatever was butchered. This preoccupation with meat—its abundance or, more often, its scarcity and the consequent prestige it confers—is a recurrent theme in Sicilian history. The banquet table groaning with bread and roast meat that greeted Odysseus in the palace of Alcinoüs stretches to accommodate many in some eras, but in others it shrinks to exclude all but the most privileged. In later chapters I offer some meat recipes as they fit into the narrative, but I think it can safely be said that with few exceptions meat is a fare that stimulates the culinary genius of the Sicilians much less than it satisfies their sense of status.

Meat loses its primacy very early on in Sicilian history. In *The Odyssey* fish is mentioned only as a desperate alternative to starvation for shipwrecked sailors. But in later centuries the amount of cultivated land expanded at the expense of pasturage and woodlands, and by the time of Archestratus fish had taken precedence over meat in the Greek diet. Most of the fragments of Archestratus's writings that have survived are concerned with fish, a fact that is neither solely fortuitous nor solely economic, but owes something as well to persistent preference. According to Athenaeus, Sicilians six centuries after Archestratus would still "say the very sea on their coasts is sweet, so much do they enjoy the foods that come out of it." They haven't changed their minds much in the intervening millennia either, and today it is still fish rather than meat that provides the basis of the most interesting and unusual dishes on the Sicilian table.

Archestratus divided fish into two categories: tough-fleshed fish, such as sarg or sea bream, which needed to be softened and rendered palatable by fancy treatment, and fish of finer quality, which deserved a simple grilling.

> Whensoe'er Orion is setting in the heavens, and the mother of the wine-bearing cluster begins to cast away her tresses, then have a baked sarg, overspread with cheese, large, hot, and rent with pungent vinegar. For its flesh is by nature tough. And so be mindful and dress every tough fish in the same way. But the good fish, with naturally tender, fat flesh, sprinkle with a little salt only, and baste with oil. For it contains within itself alone the reward of joy.
>
> Archestratus of Gela, fourth century B.C.

The advice of Archestratus demonstrates how very early the Sicilians acquired their taste for vinegar, although by the first century A.D. they preferred it with mint rather than cheese. Apicius gives a recipe for a mint-and-vinegar sauce for sardines that differs little from a sauce that Syracusans use today just as both Archestratus and Apicius intended, to elevate fish of inferior quality. It is most often used with a rather insignificant local fish—nice but very full of bones—known as a *vope*. (According to one source, the Latin name of this species is *Boops boops* and its English name is "brogue," information which I personally do not find very enlightening.) The recipe would adapt itself happily to almost any fish of modest size and flavor.

VOPE ALLA STEMPERATA
(Fish in Stemperata Sauce)

Serves 6

2½ pounds small whole fish, gutted and scaled
½ cup flour (preferably durum-wheat flour)
⅓ cup olive oil
2 garlic cloves
½ cup white wine vinegar (see p. 20)
½ cup fresh mint leaves, roughly chopped
Salt and freshly ground pepper

Roll the fish in the flour until they are well coated, then shake to remove any excess flour. Fry them in the olive oil together with the garlic cloves, which you will remove as soon as they begin to color. Turn the fish until they are browned on all sides. Add the vinegar, the mint, and salt and pepper. Increase the heat to evaporate some of the vinegar, then simmer covered for about 5 minutes.

———

Boops boops exemplifies a recurrent problem in fish cookery: how to identify the beast. Remembering my first encounter with Southern Italian fish on a trip to Puglia in 1961, when almost every fish on the menu turned out to be,

FISHERMEN MENDING THEIR NETS, *a nineteenth-century engraving by Vuillier*

as far as my pocket dictionary was concerned, mullet of one hue or another, I am staggered by the ease and certitude with which contemporary British classicists identify the Mediterranean fish of twenty-five centuries ago.

One fish that presents no problems in identification is the tuna, which has played a major role in the Sicilian diet ever since Archestratus waxed enthusiastic. It has had a significant part in the economy as well, since barrels of salted tuna were an important export for centuries. We owe tuna as we find it in our contemporary salads and sandwiches to Ignazio Florio, the head of the enormously rich mercantile family who dominated Palermo's social and economic life at the turn of this century. Florio was the first to preserve tuna in olive oil and put it in a can.

Shoals of tuna run off the Sicilian coasts each spring and are captured in an elaborate system of anchored nets, then harpooned in a bloody but spectacular rite known as the *mattanza*. Although the classical dramatist Aeschylus describes something similar, the *mattanza* as it is still performed today is Arabic in origin, rather than Greek. (An ominous headline in the papers in the spring of 1986 announced changes in the *mattanza* at the Favignana *tonnara*, the famous tuna fishery that once belonged to the Florios. The article revealed that it was some fifteenth-century Spanish "innovations" that were being eliminated, in order to return to the original ninth-century Arabic pattern of setting out the nets—a delightful example of the Sicilian sense of time.) Little has changed in how tuna is sold since classical times: at the Museo Mandralisca in Cefalù there is a Sicilian Greek vase on which a fishmonger is depicted cutting slices from an enormous tuna lying on his barrow. If this ancient Greek were to exchange his tunic for an apron, he could step right off the vase and into a present-day Palermo street market without attracting anyone's attention.

THE TUNA SELLER, *a third-century* B.C. *Sicilian Greek vase*

Archestratus puts tuna firmly in the category of fish to be grilled, although he fudges on its cousin, *amia*, which is probably what is now called *alalunga* or bonito:

> Wrap it up in fig leaves with a very little marjoram. No cheese, no nonsense! Just place it tenderly in fig leaves and tie them on top with a string: then push it under hot ashes, bethinking thee wisely of the time when it is done, and burn it not up.
>
> Archestratus of Gela, fourth century B.C.

Most modern Sicilians, although they would not disdain a slice of grilled *ventresca* (the best cut from the tuna's underbelly), would nonetheless disagree with Archestratus. Tuna is prepared here according to a remarkable variety of recipes, yet nearly all of them call for some sort of sauce, and vinegar is often a predominant ingredient. One delicious example has the same name as the recipe for *vope* but is somewhat more elaborate.

TONNO ALLA STEMPERATA
(Tunu in Stemperata Sauce)

Serves 6

2 tablespoons olive oil
6 tuna steaks
   (about 2 pounds)
4 garlic cloves, minced
6 ribs celery, chopped
1 cup pitted green olives
½ cup sultana raisins,
   plumped in hot water
   for 10 minutes

⅓ cup capers
⅓ cup white wine vinegar
   (see p. 20)
Salt and freshly ground
   pepper

Heat the olive oil in a skillet that is large enough to accommodate all the fish in one layer. Sauté the fish steaks a minute or two on each side, or until they are lightly browned.

Remove the fish, and in the same oil sauté the garlic and the celery, stirring constantly, until golden. Add the olives, the raisins, and the capers, and cook over a low flame for 2 or 3 minutes.

Remove from the fire and arrange the steaks in the pan, spooning the cooked ingredients on top of them. Add the vinegar and a sprinkling of salt and black pepper. Cook for a minute over a high flame to evaporate the vinegar, then simmer for about five minutes longer, according to the thickness of the steaks. Serve cold.

———

Eastern Sicily boasts another recipe for tuna with vinegar, which is generally known as *tonno alla Siracusana*.

TONNO ALLA SIRACUSANA
(Syracusan Tuna)

Serves 6 to 8

2½ pounds tuna, in one piece	4 large ripe tomatoes,
3 garlic cloves, cut in slivers	peeled and chopped
8–10 whole cloves	Salt
8–10 whole coriander seeds	½ cup white wine vinegar
1 large onion, chopped fine	(see p. 20)
⅓ cup olive oil	1 tablespoon dried oregano

Make small incisions with a sharp knife in the sides of the piece of tuna and stuff each incision with a sliver of garlic, a clove, and a coriander seed.

In a heavy flameproof casserole, sauté the onion in the oil until it begins to soften. Add the fish, turning it to brown on all sides, then add the tomatoes and the salt to taste. Cover and cook slowly for about 20 minutes, turning the fish occasionally. Add the vinegar and the oregano, and cook uncovered for another 15 to 20 minutes.

After allowing the fish to cool, lift it onto a carving board and slice it with a sharp knife. Arrange the slices on a serving platter and spoon the sauce over them. Serve cold.

———

Palermo has yet another similar dish, one more suited to the earliest days of the tuna season, when the weather is still cool.

TONNO AL RAGÙ
(Tuna Ragout)

Serves 6 to 8

2½ pounds tuna, in one piece
5 or 6 sprigs fresh mint
3 garlic cloves, cut in slivers
1 onion, minced
⅓ cup olive oil
½ cup tomato extract
   (see p. 13) or one 6-ounce
   can tomato paste

5 cups water
1-inch piece stick cinnamon
Freshly ground black pepper
Salt, if needed

Make small incisions with a sharp knife in the sides of the tuna, and stuff the incisions with mint leaves and garlic.

In a heavy flameproof casserole sauté the onion in the oil until it begins to soften. Add the fish and brown it on all sides. Dissolve the tomato extract in 1 cup of water, and pour the tomato mixture and the rest of the water over the fish. Add the cinnamon and a little black pepper, and simmer for 50 to 60 minutes. Correct the salt at the end (tomato extract is usually so salty that no additions are necessary).

Tonno al ragù should be sliced and served while hot, and is often and well accompanied by boiled potatoes.

———

TUNA FISHING, *an eighteenth-century drawing by Houel*

Nowadays the honor of grilling is awarded most frequently to the swordfish, which run in the Straits of Messina. Unlike tuna, sardines, and anchovies, which have been fished in quantity for salting and export from classical times right through to the present, swordfish have always been taken in small quantities, destined for a local and highly privileged market. Swordfish was in fact a novelty to the English visitors who included Sicily in their Grand Tour in the eighteenth and nineteenth centuries, and who described the appearance and the flesh of the swordfish in great detail, heartily applauding its similarity to good British beefsteak.

Although Archestratus makes only brief mention of swordfish, the catching of it must be very ancient indeed, since in the eighteenth century the procedure was still governed by a terminology derived from classical Greek.

The taking of the *pesce spada*, or sword fish, is a much more noble diversion: no art is made use of to ensnare him: but with a small harpoon, fixed to

a long line, they attack him in the open seas, and will often strike him
at a very considerable distance. It is exactly the whale-fishing in miniature.
The Sicilian fishermen (who are abundantly superstitious) have a Greek
sentence which they make use of as a charm to bring him near their boats.
This is the only bait they use, and they pretend that it is of wonderful
efficacy, and absolutely obliges him to follow them: but if unfortunately
he should overhear them speak a word of Italian, he plunges underwater
immediately, and will appear no more.

Patrick Brydone, *A Tour Through Sicily and Malta*, 1773

The English today don't think much of swordfish, to judge by the few
lines with which Elizabeth David dismisses it in her discussion of fish in *Italian
Food*. But I was brought up to think of a slice of swordfish as the *filet mignon*
of the marine world, and this is how the Sicilians feel. Around Palermo
swordfish is most often grilled, with a basting of oil and a sprinkling of salt,
just as Archestratus would have wished, or moistened with a light *salmoriglio*
of olive oil and lemon juice beaten up with oregano, salt, and pepper, and
brushed on with a stalk of dried oregano as the fish is grilling. In Messina,
where the best swordfish is caught, they prefer to simmer the fish in a well-
spiced tomato sauce known as a *ghiotta*.

PESCESPADA ALLA GHIOTTA
(Swordfish alla Ghiotta)

Serves 6

1 onion	½ cup capers, rinsed
½ cup olive oil	6 slices swordfish
1 cup plain tomato sauce	(about 1¾ pounds)
(see p. 172)	Salt and freshly ground
2 celery ribs, chopped	black pepper
1½ cups green olives, pitted	

Chop very fine or grate the onion, and sauté to a pale golden
brown in the olive oil in a skillet large enough to accommodate

all the slices of fish in one layer. Add the tomato sauce and the celery, and simmer for 5 minutes.

Chop the olives and capers coarse and add them to the sauce. Simmer for a few minutes longer.

Remove the skillet from the fire and arrange the slices of fish in a single layer, spooning the sauce over them so that they are covered. Return to the fire and simmer for 10 minutes. Salt and pepper to taste. Serve immediately.

Alternative recipes call for black olives rather than green, and for the addition of chopped baby cucumber pickles (not sweet gherkins but the Italian variety, which are very acid). Slices of boiled potato are often served with this dish.

———

Given the frequency with which capers are appearing in these recipes, a word of introduction is in order. Capers are flower buds picked before they open from a beautiful low bush that grows wild all along the shores of central and southern Italy, trailing long sprays of coin-shaped leaves and delicate white and purple flowers across rocky cliffs and hillsides, not to mention over the heads of oblivious tourists in the Forum in Rome. Sicilian capers, of which the most prized are those that come from the tiny island of Pantelleria, are considerably bigger and more intense in flavor than Provençal capers, and they are usually preserved under salt rather than in vinegar. Included in almost every classical list of spices to be kept on hand, capers have a pungent, almost peppery taste that is still one of the most characteristic flavors of Sicilian cooking.

The Messinesi are particularly fond of capers (excellent capers are also produced on the Aeolian Islands, just north of the Messina coast), and almost all their fish recipes call for capers and green olives, a coupling that, like dried currants and pine nuts, is a constant leitmotif in Sicilian cooking (the currants of the Sicilian cuisine, by the way, being of course not berries but the tiny raisins made from the Corinth grape).

It is possible to use either one of these two classic combinations when executing another swordfish recipe, more delicate and more elaborate, which has become very popular in Palermo's luxury restaurants. Here thin slices of swordfish are wrapped into little bundles—a fish version of the skewered and grilled *involtini* of meat that are one of the most common Sicilian second courses. Each cook has his own idea of what the filling should be, so I am including two different possibilities, although, unlike the Messinesi, my personal preference goes to the first.

A SWORDFISHERMAN, *a nineteenth-century engraving by Vuillier*

INVOLTINI DI PESCESPADA
(Swordfish Rolls)

Serves 6

2½ pounds swordfish
1 large red onion
12–15 bay leaves

2 tablespoons olive oil
1 cup dried breadcrumbs
  (see p. 12)

FILLING I

1 cup fresh parsley leaves
5 garlic cloves
3 tablespoons dried currants,
  soaked in hot water for
  5 minutes

3 tablespoons pine nuts
Salt and freshly ground black
  pepper
1–2 tablespoons olive oil

Chop the parsley and garlic together until very fine. Add the currants and pine nuts; chop roughly. Add salt and pepper to taste. Stir in the olive oil, mixing thoroughly.

FILLING II

½ cup pitted green olives
½ cup capers
⅓ cup fresh parsley leaves
½ cup dried breadcrumbs
  (see p. 12)

½ cup grated caciocavallo,
  parmesan, or pecorino
  cheese
2–3 tablespoons olive oil

Chop the olives, capers, and parsley together until quite fine. Stir in the breadcrumbs and the cheese, moisten with the oil, and blend thoroughly.

If your fishmonger is cooperative, have him bone and skin a 2½-pound round swordfish steak, cut it into quarters, and slice each quarter across into 6 very thin slices. What you are aiming for is 24 slices that are roughly 3 by 4 inches and less than ⅛ inch thick. But, given the price of swordfish, it is wise to tolerate considerable irregularity rather than to trim lavishly—it won't show in the end anyway!

Peel the onion, cut it into quarters or sixths, depending on its size, and then unlayer these wedges so that you have pieces of onion that are wide enough to thread on a skewer.

Place a teaspoon of the filling of your choice on one end of each slice of fish, roll it up as neatly as possible, and spear it on a skewer onto which you have already threaded a piece of onion. Follow with a bay leaf, then another roll of fish, then a slice of onion, and so on, until you have 6 skewers, each with 4 rolls of fish interspersed with onion slices and bay leaves. It is a good idea to run a second skewer through, parallel to the first and about an inch distant, so that the fish rolls don't spin about and break as you turn them over the grill. Italian markets sell 6-inch disposable wooden skewers that are ideal for the purpose and more attractive than most metal skewers.

When all 6 servings are ready, moisten them with oil and then dip them in the breadcrumbs (they should be just lightly coated). Grill them gently, either over the coals or under the broiler, for about 8 to 10 minutes. They can also be baked.

————

Swordfish also provides an excellent basis for a pasta sauce. The traditional version is simply diced swordfish simmered in tomato sauce, but Anna Pomar gives a modern elaboration that is so good I am including it here, if only as an example of how Sicilian cooking is evolving with the introduction of new ingredients (in this case mozzarella) from other regions of Italy.

PASTA CON PESCESPADA
(*Pasta with Swordfish*)

Serves 6

2 garlic cloves
½ cup olive oil
4 large, very ripe tomatoes,
    peeled and chopped
1 cup fresh mint leaves,
    chopped, plus a few
    whole sprigs
Salt and freshly ground
    black pepper

¾ pound swordfish, skinned,
    boned, and diced
½ cup water
1½ pounds bucatini
    (a thick, hollow spaghetti)
¼ pound mozzarella, diced

Sauté the whole garlic cloves in the olive oil until they are pale golden. Add the tomatoes, some of the chopped mint, and salt and pepper, and simmer for 5 minutes.

Remove the garlic cloves, then add the diced swordfish and the water. Simmer for about 15 to 20 minutes over a low flame.

In the meantime, cook the pasta in abundant salted water, drain it well, and put it in a large serving dish. Add the fish sauce, the mozzarella, and the remaining mint leaves, mixing well so that the mozzarella melts in the heat of the pasta (you have to move fast!). Garnish with a few sprigs of mint and serve immediately.

Fish and wheat were by no means the only Sicilian fare that the Greek world appreciated. Cheeses imported from Sicily were held in such high esteem that even the dogs of Athens craved them, as Aristophanes testifies:

> —What else could be the matter?
> That grabby dog Chowhound, of course! Jumped into the pantry,
> clamped onto a rich Sicilian cheese and gulped
> the whole thing down!
> Aristophanes, *The Wasps*, fifth century B.C.

It is safe to assume that Aristophanes was talking about cheeses made from sheep's milk, for sheep predominated in Sicily then as now. Normally the herdsmen who raise both sheep and goats do not process the milk separately, but mix it altogether and heat and curdle it exactly as the giant Polyphemus did:

> . . . A practised job
> he made of it, giving each ewe her suckling;
> thickened his milk, then, into curds and whey,
> sieved out the curds to drip in withy baskets,
> and poured the whey to stand in bowls
> cooling until he drank it for his supper.
> Homer, *The Odyssey*, ninth century B.C.

The principal sheep cheese of Sicily is a large pale-yellow drum about eight inches high and ten inches in diameter, its rind patterned with the weave of the rush baskets in which it is molded. If made for immediate consumption it is either unsalted, in which case it is known as tuma, or given a light salting, which sharpens its flavor slightly and earns it the name of primosale. In either case, it has an oily, elastic texture that never crumbles, and it melts quickly and smoothly. If it is heavily salted and aged until it is suitable for grating, it is known as pecorino or *canestrato* and acquires a taste similar to that of a pecorino romano.

Tuma and primosale are quite bland in taste but with a slight whiff of the stable, a suggestion of gaminess that is much more subtle than in a chèvre, for example. Their taste also varies from month to month, according to what the sheep are finding in their pastures. Winter and spring cheeses are far better than those produced in the summer. Sometimes they are seasoned by stirring in whole peppercorns, and although I have never had the good fortune to taste or even see such a thing, my cleaning woman once mentioned that her father, a retired shepherd from the Madonie Mountains, had recently ordered a cheese prepared for him "the way he likes it," spiced with coriander seeds. I don't know of any cheeses on the American market that are equivalent in taste, but as a last resort in cooked dishes I would substitute a good mozzarella.

The shepherds add more milk to the whey that remains from the first round of cheese making, and bring it to a boil again to produce ricotta. (Ricotta is also made from cow's milk, but this is considered an inferior version. I have a hand-lettered sign from an old grocery store advertising "Ricotta from pure sheep!") Fresh ricotta is a very perishable cheese that will not keep in the summer heat unless it is reduced by heavy salting or baking into a small, hard loaf; such must have been the ricotta that was exported to classical Greece. Salted or baked ricotta is also grated onto Sicilian pasta dishes made in summertime with fresh, sun-ripened tomatoes, including that epitome of simplicity and subtlety that is *pasta con le melanzane*. This recipe, which in Catania is known as *pasta alla Norma*, in honor of a masterpiece by one of the more famous native sons, the composer Vincenzo Bellini, looks rather undistinguished on paper. But when the various ingredients—the tomatoes, the eggplants, the oil, the basil, and the salted ricotta—are at their best, their respective flavors combine into one of the world's truly sublime pasta dishes.

PASTA CON LE MELANZANE
(*Pasta and Eggplant*)

Serves 6

2 medium eggplants
Salt
1⅓ cups or more olive oil
2 garlic cloves
3 cups very ripe tomatoes,
  peeled and chopped,
  or 2 cups tomato sauce,
  variation II (see p. 173)

Salt and freshly ground
  black pepper
1½ pounds spaghetti or
  penne rigate
1 cup salted ricotta, grated
1 cup fresh basil leaves,
  chopped coarse

Wash the eggplants and cut them, unpeeled, into ½-inch slices (Palermo style) or into finger-size sticks (more common in the east). Sprinkle with abundant salt and allow to drain for a couple of hours. Rinse well, drain, pat dry, and then fry in 1 cup of olive oil, or more, until golden brown on all sides. Drain on absorbent paper.

Sauté the garlic cloves and the chopped tomatoes, together with a very little salt and the pepper, in ⅓ cup of oil for about 15 minutes, or prepare the 2 cups of tomato sauce.

Cook the pasta in abundant boiling salted water until *al dente*, then drain. Toss it in a serving bowl with half the ricotta, then the sauce and the basil. Put the fried eggplant on top, and sprinkle with the rest of the ricotta.

Note: Cheaper vegetable oils are often used in place of olive oil for frying eggplant, both in this and in other Sicilian dishes. I consider such substitution to be a decadent practice that vastly alters the results. But then I have my own olive grove. Those less fortunate may want to try a combination of 50 percent olive oil and 50 percent corn, peanut, or other vegetable oil.

Salted ricotta belongs above all to the summer; from October to May ricotta is eaten fresh, both as a cheese and as the basis of Sicilian confectionery. We have already met sweetened ricotta mixed with *cuccìa*, and while the renowned cannoli and the *cassate siciliane* with their ricotta cream fillings belong not to the classical but to a later period in Sicilian history, this is the place for a recipe that uses sugar and ricotta in a different fashion. This is a recipe I inherited from my mother-in-law, and it may have in its rustic simplicity some kinship to classical sweets.

VARCOCCHINI
(*Ricotta Apricots*)

Makes 4 dozen

4 cups ricotta
  (about 1¾ pounds)
  (see note p. 18)
¾ cup sugar
1½ cups flour (see note)
4 eggs

¼ teaspoon vanilla extract
Vegetable oil for frying
½ cup superfine sugar,
  or granulated sugar
  ground fine

Allow the ricotta to drain well, then sieve it or run it through a food mill so that it is creamy. Beat in ¾ cup of sugar, the flour, and the eggs, one by one, and finally the vanilla.

Heat 1½ to 2 inches of oil in a pan, and drop the batter, half a teaspoon at a time, into the hot oil (about 370°F.). The batter should puff up into round balls the size of small apricots (about 1 inch in diameter). Fry slowly until they are a dark golden brown all over, then lift out and drain on absorbent paper.

You can grind the granulated sugar to an even finer grain in a mortar (in my household there are always young and impatient volunteers for this job, with which I might otherwise dispense) or in a blender. Sprinkle the sugar over the *varcocchini* and serve them while they are still warm.

Note: The Sicilian housewife normally keeps two different kinds of flour on hand: *farina rimacinata* or *di semola*, which is made from durum wheat and is used for making pasta and bread (more about this in Chapter Three); and *farina* 00, which is made of soft spring wheat. Unless otherwise specified, I have used *farina* 00 in testing these recipes. According to Carol Field's excellent book *The Italian Baker*, the closest American equivalent to *farina* 00 would be one part pastry flour to three parts all-purpose flour. Very careful bakers may wish to go to the trouble of making up such a mixture; I myself would probably settle for all-purpose flour.

Ricotta is used in much the same manner in a cake that also appears frequently on the tables of my husband's home town of Alcamo. This is known as a *pasticciotto*, which I indulge myself in translating as "plump pasty"—sweet and homely.

PASTICCIOTTO
(Plump Pasty)

One 12-inch pastry

BIANCOMANGIARE FILLING

¾ cup cornstarch
5 cups milk
¾ cup sugar

¼ teaspoon vanilla
⅓ cup semisweet chocolate
   bits

DOUGH

2¼ pounds ricotta,
   well drained (see p. 18)
1½ cups flour
   (see note p. 41)

1 cup sugar
2 whole eggs plus 1 egg yolk
½ teaspoon ground cinnamon

1 egg white

Prepare the *biancomangiare* filling, following the procedure given in the recipe on p. 18. Remove from the heat when thickened and stir in the vanilla. Pour onto a dinner plate to cool. Before it is completely cooled, press in the chocolate bits.

To prepare the dough: Sieve the ricotta or pass it through a food mill so that it is creamy. Beat in the flour, sugar, eggs and extra yolk, and cinnamon.

Grease and flour a 12-inch cake pan. Distribute two-thirds of the dough by spoonfuls on the bottom and sides of the pan, using a wet spoon or wet fingers to smooth it into an even layer a little less than an inch thick. Slide the *biancomangiare* (it should be cooled into a fairly firm disk) onto this, and cover with more spoonfuls of the dough. Smooth this layer as well and press the two dough layers together at the edges so that no filling shows. Beat the egg white and brush it over the top of the cake. Bake in a 300°F. oven for about an hour, or until the cake begins to come away from the sides of the pan. (The cooking time will vary considerably according to the quality of the ricotta.) Whether *pasticciotto* is better eaten when completely cooled or when still warm is, in Alcamo, a matter for passionate and tireless discussion.

———

YOUNG SHEPHERD, *a nineteenth-century engraving by Vuillier*

It is always frustrating to read an irresistible recipe only to be told that it is useless to try to reproduce it outside the narrow confines of its birthplace. This might well be said, alas, of almost any Sicilian recipe: the dish will be immeasurably diminished by using ingredients that cannot claim the peculiar intensity of flavor that the island's merciless sun induces. Having said so once, I shall say it no more. Yet, in order to appreciate the corresponding intensity of feeling that such sensations provoke in the Sicilian soul, I beg the reader to indulge me in a rather lengthy quote from Elio Vittorini's unfinished novel *Le città del mondo*.

> The father turned quickly to look at him. "Good boy!" he said. "Sometimes I think you are just a little slow in understanding, and instead you're quick. . . . Try to be that way always, child. And when you eat cheese with your bread, remember that its taste comes from all this that you are seeing and smelling now, and that it is made of all this space and this sun as well as of milk. But now," he continued, "see how the rush basket has been filled and carried away to drain on a stone. There is nothing white left in the pot. We have arrived at that sweet instant in which the mind, which was turning back a little sadly on its traces, discovers another direction it can start off in, one which is perhaps even more attractive. There is only a greenish liquid remaining in the pot, but the heart is moved to glimpse it through the smoke. Watch, Nardo. The boy is once more bent over his work as before, and again he breaks up twigs of heather, once, then once again, and blows on the embers, and fans the fire. . . . Happy youth! Did you see the sparkle in his glance as his eyes sought out the old man through the smoke and the steam? He can't control his delight at the thought of what will soon be his. And it's understandable. I myself, way up here, am watering at the mouth. . . . The old man no, poor thing. By now he feels no desire for anything. He must be without appetite. But it is with a gentle hand that he is adding the milk to the whey in the pot, despite his face, which is sour and bad-tempered. What gestures a shepherd has, how noble and careful, even when he's a blackened old man who no longer gets much enjoyment out of life! Perforce the ricotta must be delicate, then. It gives us with sweetness all that flavor which the cheese will give us with sharpness at the end of its aging. And it gives it to us right away, piping hot. We ourselves could have it within a quarter of an hour, if we were those two. Think of it, child! To have your bread already broken up in the bowl, and to be waiting there around the pot till the first white flowers come floating up through the pale green of the whey cloudy with steam. . . . They're coming, son! Did you see it too? There was a second there when the smoke cleared and I saw a spread of white at the mouth of the pot, stretching from its southern rim to its northwestern."
>
> Elio Vittorini, *Le città del mondo*, c. 1955

Vittorini might be describing the work of the shepherds who live down the road from me, or he might be describing that of Polyphemus—the technique of making sheep's cheese has not changed over the last twenty-nine centuries, and neither, I dare say, has its taste.

HIERON'S ALTAR, *a nineteenth century engraving by Vuillier*

Since Hieron II, the tyrant who ruled Syracuse during the Punic Wars, saw fit to build an altar large enough to accommodate the simultaneous sacrifice of 450 bulls, it seems safe to infer that there were a lot of cows around too, and probably only slightly more hazardous to imagine that the Greek Sicilians were making something similar to caciocavallo, the principal cow's milk cheese of modern Sicily. This cheese is molded into large bricks, as much as two feet long, that have a smooth yellow rind. If eaten when fresh it is somewhat akin to a provola dolce, but with a stronger, saltier taste. When it ages it becomes hard enough to grate, and serves as a year-round accompaniment to pasta (the use of parmesan has spread beyond the very wealthy only in the last quarter century, and even now is more or less limited to the urban middle and upper classes). For grating purposes caciocavallo may be replaced by a parmesan or a romano.

Since, among other things, it is very slow to melt, caciocavallo is a prerequisite for making *formaggio all' argentiera*. This classic Palermo recipe owes its name and its origin to an anonymous and perhaps mythical silversmith who invented this dish in order to hide the fact that he had fallen on hard times and could no longer afford to buy meat for his supper. The smell of its cooking is said to be indistinguishable from that of rabbit. This is an old trick in Palermo, where the poor used to beg scraps of fat from the butcher to put on the fire so as to impress their neighbors—hence the proverb *"Tutto fumo e niente arrosto"* ("All smoke and no roast").

Formaggio all' argentiera provides us with an example of that unusual combination of cheese and vinegar with which Archestratus claims the Syracusans were wont to improve poor fish and ruin good ones. I offer it, however, without making any claims as to its archeological value.

FORMAGGIO ALL' ARGENTIERA
(Silversmith's Cheese)

Serves 6

2 garlic cloves
2 tablespoons olive oil
6 half-inch-thick slices of
   caciocavallo cheese
   (about 2 pounds)

1–2 tablespoons vinegar
   (see p. 20)
2 tablespoons fresh oregano or
   1 tablespoon dried
½ teaspoon sugar

In a heavy, nonstick skillet, brown the cloves of garlic in the olive oil until golden, then discard. Arrange the slices of cheese in the skillet and brown them lightly on each side. Remove the skillet from the fire and sprinkle the cheese with the vinegar, oregano, and sugar. Cover and return to a very low flame for 4 to 5 minutes. Serve immediately. Although sometimes presented as a first course, I think this dish is best served, together with good bread and a salad, as the main course of a light meal.

GROTTOES CUT IN THE ROCK FOR THE BEES, *an eighteenth-century drawing by Houel*

In the 1780s the French artist Jean Houel, *Peinteur du Roi*, on royally subsidized travels in southeastern Sicily, noted that a great many holes had been cut into the rock of the hillsides, and after some thought he decided that these were where the ancient Greeks had kept their bees. The further he traveled, the more pockmarked cliffs he passed (at Pantalica alone there are more than eight thousand of these chambers carved into the sides of the valley), until he finally remarked in his journal, with a note of exasperation, that those Greeks certainly did produce a lot of honey!

If Houel was wrong about the chambers, which are in fact tombs carved in the rock by the Sican and Sicel peoples who inhabited the island during the Copper and the Bronze ages, before the Greeks arrived, he was not so mistaken with regard to the scope of classical honey production. Honey was the primary sweetener of the ancient world, and therefore had far greater

importance in relation to other agricultural products than it has today. And
the Hyblaean Mountains behind Syracuse, where the majority of the rock-
chamber tombs are located, produced a honey that the ancients rated a close
second to that of Mount Hymettus.

> When you make a present of Sicilian combs from amid Hybla's hills you
> may say that they are Attic combs.
>
> Martial, *Epigrams*, first century A.D.

The wild thyme that still covers the hillsides, a dusty gray-green scrub
that hugs the ground and blends into the pale gray soil, breaks into brilliant
purple bloom in June and gives an intense fragrance to the honey—"I sent
cakes redolent of Hyblaean honey"—which is perhaps one first cause behind
the fame for things confectionery that Sicily has enjoyed through the millennia.

As their modern compatriots reserve certain sweets for specific feasts, such
as Easter's Paschal lamb of marzipan, so the ancient Sicilians had some cakes
that were liturgical. Athenaeus quotes Heracleides of Syracuse as saying that
during the Thesmophoria, the annual festival in honor of Demeter and Persephone, "cakes of sesame and honey were molded in the shape of the female
pudenda, and called throughout the whole of Sicily *mylloi* and carried about
in honor of the goddess." Other cakes, however, were simply for pleasure.

> They set before us a cake, the kind that takes its name from Gelon the
> Sicilian. As for me, the mere sight of it delighted my heart, and my mouth
> watered at the prospect of stowing it away. But there was a long delay
> while they were garnishing the cake with dainties—pistachio nuts and
> dates and shelled walnuts.
>
> · Alciphron, *Letters from Parasites*, second century A.D.

It is difficult, on the basis of such slight mention, to do more than guess
what these classical cakes were like. But there are any number of modern
Sicilian pastries that use the same ingredients as those available to the ancients
and that can at least suggest the ancient flavors.

The *mylloi*, for example, might have been somewhat similar to the *biscotti
regina* that are still sold in most Palermo bakeries, although these oblong
cookies coated with sesame seeds are more phallic than female in form. Sicilians
see an intimate relationship among different physiological processes, and never

fail to call attention to it: in the Palermo dialect these biscuits are also known as *strunzi d'ancilu* ("angel turds"). (People from Catania claim that the Palermitani have it all wrong: queen's cookies are a much more delicate biscuit dipped in a white icing, in comparison with which the sesame cookies are mere "chicken turds"!)

BISCOTTI REGINA
(Queen's Cookies)

Makes 3 dozen cookies

3¾ cups flour (see p. 41)
¾ cup sugar
½ teaspoon ground cinnamon
½ cup lard
2 egg yolks

¼ teaspoon vanilla
½ cup milk or less
2 egg whites, lightly beaten
1 cup sesame seeds

Sift the flour, sugar, and cinnamon into a large mixing bowl, and cut in the lard until the mixture reaches the texture of a coarse meal. Add the egg yolks, vanilla, and as much milk as is necessary to hold the dough together. Knead for a minute and then shape the dough into finger-shaped pieces about 1½ inches long. Roll each piece first in the egg whites and then in the sesame seeds so that it is well covered with a layer of seeds. Place on a greased cookie sheet and bake in a preheated 350°F. oven about 30 minutes or until lightly browned.

———

The cake that made Alciphron's mouth water brings to mind a whole range of filled pastries that are to be found under different names throughout the island, especially at Christmastime. The most common of these are fig-filled cookies called *cuddureddi*, a name said to derive from *kollura*, a Greek word for cake or bun. For Sicilian families, the preparation of huge batches of these cookies to offer holiday visitors is a festive occasion similar to that which baking gingerbread men provided in my childhood, and *cuddureddi*, which can be molded into different shapes and sprinkled with colored sugar and other trimmings, offer almost the same scope for creativity. They can be made either with all-purpose flour or with durum-wheat flour. The latter will take a little more milk and will give a coarser, more rustic pastry.

CUDDUREDDI
(Christmas Cookies)

Makes about 2 dozen

PASTRY

3¾ cups all-purpose or
   durum-wheat flour
½ cup sugar
1 teaspoon baking powder

Pinch salt
½ cup lard
½ to 1 cup milk

FILLING

1 pound dried figs
½ cup coarsely chopped
  walnuts
½ cup coarsely chopped
  toasted almonds
½ cup sultana raisins
1 tablespoon grated
  lemon peel

1 tablespoon grated orange
  or tangerine peel
¼ teaspoon ground cloves
1 teaspoon ground cinnamon
2 tablespoons honey
2 ounces semisweet chocolate,
  grated
½ cup *vino cotto* (see p. 17)

Sift together the flour, sugar, baking powder, and salt. Cut in the lard to a coarse-meal texture, and then add the milk little by little, using just enough to make a fairly firm dough. Knead for a couple of minutes and then shape into a ball and refrigerate for at least an hour.

Soak the figs in warm water for 10 minutes, drain well, and pass them through a meat grinder. Mix in the other filling ingredients and blend thoroughly.

Preheat oven to 350°F.

Knead the dough again briefly and roll it out on a floured surface to a thickness of about ⅛ inch. Cut with a pastry wheel into 4-by-5-inch rectangles. Put a generous tablespoon of filling on each rectangle and fold over lengthwise. Moisten and press the edges together, then make a series of ½-inch cuts along the sealed edge. Curve the cookie slightly so that the cut edge fans out and the darker filling shows. Place on a greased cookie sheet and bake for about 20 minutes.

You may prefer to cut the dough into 3-inch squares, put a teaspoonful of filling in the center of each square, and lift up the four corners to meet on top of the filling, making a little basket. Moisten the corners and pinch them together firmly. Bake for about 15 minutes.

———

In Palermo the *cuddureddi* take a more elegant, urbane form: a ring-shaped pastry that may be anywhere from 6 to 16 inches across and is sprinkled with *fastuca*, a bright green scattering of chopped pistachio nuts. The filling is the same, but the pastry is often richer.

BUCCELLATO
(Christmas Ring)

Makes one 16-inch ring

PASTRY

3¾ cups flour (see p. 41)	1 whole egg
3 tablespoons sugar	1 egg yolk
Pinch of salt	1 tablespoon grated
½ cup lard	orange rind
¼ cup sweet butter	½ cup white wine or less

FILLING

1 batch *cuddureddi* filling	1 egg white, lightly beaten
(see preceding recipe)	⅓ cup chopped pistachios

Sift together the flour, sugar, and salt, and cut in the lard and butter to a coarse-meal texture. Work in the egg, egg yolk, and orange rind, and add just enough wine to hold the dough together. Your dough should be soft but not sticky. Knead for a minute or two, shape into a ball, and refrigerate for 2 hours.

Prepare the filling as directed on p. 51.

Roll out the dough to about ⅛-inch thickness, and with the help of a large plate or round dish, cut a circle about 16 inches in diameter. Using a demitasse saucer or other small dish, cut out a 4-inch circle from the center of the large circle, so that you are left with a flat ring of dough that is about 6 inches wide.

Roll it up on your rolling pin and spread it out on a greased baking sheet.

Spoon the filling onto the ring (leaving a few spoonfuls to make *cuddureddi* with the scraps of leftover pastry). Make a series of perpendicular cuts around the inside margin of the pastry ring and a few more (more widely spaced) on the outer edge, and fold the inner and outer edges up over the filling, overlapping them at the top and pinching them together with as much elegance as you can muster. With a fork poke a pattern of holes in the pastry so that the dark filling shows through.

Brush the top of the pastry ring with the beaten egg white, and sprinkle with the chopped pistachios. Bake in a preheated 350°F. oven for about 30 minutes or until delicately browned.

Sicilians who live in the Hyblaean Mountains make Christmas cookies that are filled with honey and nuts. In Vizzini, I am told, these too are known as *cuddureddi*; in Modica they are called *nucatoli*.

NUCATOLI
(Honey Cookies)

Makes 4 dozen

FILLING (must be prepared 3 days ahead)

⅔ cup honey

⅓ cup finely chopped walnuts

1 cup, more or less, durum-wheat flour (see note p. 41)

PASTRY

1 batch *cuddureddi* dough
   (see p. 50)

Heat the honey in a small saucepan. Stir in the nuts and bring to the boiling point. Remove from the heat and allow to cool.

When the honey mixture has reached room temperature, add the flour little by little, stirring it in well, until you have a firm paste. Refrigerate for 3 days.

Prepare the dough and roll it out as thin as you possibly can (at least to ¹⁄₁₆ inch). Cut into 2-by-3-inch rectangles. Using your fingers, shape a narrow roll of honey paste, about 3 inches long and no more than ¼ inch thick. Place it lengthwise along one edge of a rectangle of pastry, and roll the dough up around it as if you were rolling a cigarette (the end result should be just about the same size as a cigarette, or perhaps a little thicker). Moisten the outside edge so as to seal it. Roll the resulting "cigarette" back and forth a few times under the palm of your hand to make sure it is sealed well, otherwise it will come apart in the oven. Continue with the rest of the dough and honey paste. Twist the "cigarettes" into slight S-shapes and put on a greased cookie sheet. Bake in a preheated 350°F. oven for about 10 minutes or until the cookies begin to brown around the edges.

Honey meant more to the Greeks than simple pleasure to the palate: the cult of Aphrodite at Erice on Sicily's western coast was rich in apiary symbolism, and when Daedalus arrived safely on Sicily after his flight from Crete he is said to have wrought a marvelous honeycomb of gold to offer to the goddess.

For the Syracusans, honey may have represented some sort of vital lymph of their homeland. In speaking about the Athenaion, the great temple to Athena whose massive columns are still standing, supported by the walls of the cathedral that has been built around them, Henry Swinburne mentions the giant gold shield that decorated the frontal of the temple and caught the sunlight, its metallic gleam the first and the last glimpse that seafaring Syracusans would have of their native city. He adds:

> Every Syracusan that sailed out of the port was bound by his religion to carry honey, flowers, and ashes, which he threw into the sea, the instant he lost sight of the holy buckler: this was to insure a safe return.
>
> Henry Swinburne, *Travels in the Two Sicilies*, 1790

The golden age of Syracuse came to an end with the close of the fifth century B.C. The following centuries were marked by internal warfare and tyranny until, with the First Punic War, all of Sicily except Syracuse became a Roman province. For the next few decades Syracuse maintained both its independence and the profitable position of loyal ally to Rome, supplying grain and other foodstuffs to the Roman troops on the island. Then it foolishly switched camps and in 211 B.C. the Romans captured this last outpost as well.

Despite this long period of strife and unrest, in which the countryside was pillaged and burned and entire populations were forcibly resettled, the fertile abundance of the island continued. Agricultural production was maintained and in some periods increased notably. The Roman conquests in the eastern Mediterranean during the second century B.C. provided a steady supply of cheap slave labor. This in turn motivated the wealthy to enlarge their holdings in the interior, creating the great *latifundia*, which were to last until they were broken up during the land-reform movement a mere forty years ago.

These interminable fields of wheat, which prompted Cato to call Sicily "the Republic's granary, the nurse at whose breast the Roman people is fed," were tithed by the Senate: one-tenth of the entire wheat and barley crop (an

MOSAIC FLOOR FROM THE FOURTH-CENTURY VILLA IMPERIALE
AT CASALE, PIAZZA ARMERINA

estimated 825,000 bushels) was sent to Rome each year; a second tithe was purchased at a price set by the Senate. A tax was paid in kind on wine, olives, fruit, and vegetables; and a pasturage tax was paid in cash.

Nonetheless the Sicilians, or at least the wealthier among them, prospered under Roman rule. This was the first of the Roman provinces, and there was no preexisting bureaucracy ready to govern it, so the administration and the taxation were left in the hands of the upper-class Greek-speaking Sicilians, and the private sphere continued to be governed by Greek law. We can assume that the lifestyle also continued in the Greek manner, or at least in the local variant thereof. We are told that Damophilus of Enna, on whose estates the first of the great slave uprisings that swept the Roman provinces broke out in

MOSAIC FLOOR FROM THE FOURTH-CENTURY VILLA IMPERIALE
AT CASALE, PIAZZA ARMERINA

139 B.C., "surpassed the Persians in the sumptuousness and costliness of his feasts."

The Sicilians continued to be Greek even after the Roman Republic became, in the first century B.C., the Roman Empire: the local administration, carried out in Latin, was entrusted to the wealthier classes, who were bilingual. The Romans who owned the *latifundia* belonged for the most part to the senatorial class and did not live on the island. When they did take up residence, however, they lived well: the magnificent imperial villa at Piazza Armerina, with splendid mosaic floors in its baths and palestras and banqueting halls, suggests a style of life that could hardly be termed provincial.

With the conquest of the wheat-producing provinces in Spain and North

Africa during the early years of the Empire, Sicily lost much of its preeminence as food supplier to the empire but gained a long period of relative peace and prosperity, in which the island remained on the margin of history, little affected by the barbarian invasions that tormented other parts of Europe.

Even the transition from pagan to Christian appears to have been less bloody than it was elsewhere. Christianity was slow to arrive on the island but quick to spread. The first Christian communities date from the early third century, and in the hundred years before the Edict of Constantine rendered the new religion legal, they began to build what were to become the biggest catacombs in the Christian world and produced several martyrs, including two, Saint Lucy and Saint Agatha, who became famous beyond Sicilian shores.

Christianity was easily absorbed by an island with a long tradition of religious syncretism, and many of the old pagan rites and customs entered, either by their own persistence or by design of the clergy, into the calendar of the new church. New saints and martyrs took the place of the old gods to whom these rites had been dedicated, but the shrines, the processions, the feast days, and the ritual foods of classical Sicily remained. We have already seen a perfect example of this in *cuccìa*.

In 535 Sicily passed into the hands of the Eastern Empire of Byzantium, and the predominance of Greek tradition was once more reaffirmed in the language, in the church and monastic practices, and in the style of living. Free from the physical and cultural disruption of barbarian invasions from the north which had so drastically altered the rest of Western Europe, the island maintained a remarkable continuity with the ancient world. Invasion and change eventually did come to Sicily as well, but they came much later, and they came from the south, brought by a people who were anything but barbarian.

2

The Gardens of Paradise

Come, delight in the orange you have gathered:
  it brings happiness with its presence.
Let us welcome these rosy cheeks from off the boughs:
  let us give welcome to stars plucked from the trees.
It seems that the heavens have poured forth pure gold
  which the earth has fashioned into shining orbs.
                    Abu al Hasan Ali ibn al-Basayr
                    the Sicilian, eleventh century

The most amusing if not necessarily the most reliable account of how the next
chapter in Sicilian history began is to be found in the Byzantine imperial
chronicles, which relate how Euphemius of Messina, captain of the Greek
militia on the island, fell in love with a beautiful young girl and carried her
off from the nunnery where she had taken the veil. Her brothers appealed to
the Emperor Michael, who, despite a similar skeleton in his own imperial
closet, ordered that Euphemius be apprehended and punished. Rather than
lose his nose, the standard penalty for ravishing a nun, Euphemius fled Sicily
for Kairouan, in what is now Tunisia, and offered his services to Ziadat-Allah,
the Aghlabite Emir of North Africa, as leader of an expedition against Sicily.

It does seem out of character for Sicilians of any epoch to entrust the
reparation of their sister's honor to an emperor many leagues distant, and of
dubious morality to boot. Sources differ as to the actual motives for Euphemius's
rebellion, but whatever passions or high principles may have moved him, all
are agreed that Euphemius landed at Mazara del Vallo, on the southwestern
coast of Sicily, on June 17, 827, at the head of a Saracen army comprising
seven hundred knights and ten thousand infantry. He did not live to see his
revenge completed: it was fifty years before the Byzantine capital at Syracuse

fell to the Arabs. But by 831 Palermo was in their hands, and under their guidance it became the largest and richest city in Sicily, a primacy it was never again to relinquish.

Legend further informs us that, once the beachhead at Mazara was established, Euphemius ordered his Arab cooks to look around and see what they could find to feed the hungry troops. At the harbor of Mazara, then as now an important fishing port, they found quantities of fresh sardines, as well as wild fennel growing on the hillsides, currants drying in the vineyards, saffron and pine nuts on display in the marketplace. Tossing everything together, they came up with the Sicilian national dish.

PASTA CON LE SARDE
(Pasta and Sardines)

Serves 6

1½ pounds fresh sardines	½ cup toasted almond slivers (optional)
2 large bunches fresh wild fennel greens (about 1½ pounds)	8 anchovy fillets
1 large onion, grated or minced fine	1 teaspoon olive oil
½ cup olive oil	2 pinches saffron, soaked in 2 tablespoons warm water
½ cup pine nuts	1½ pounds bucatini or maccheroni
½ cup dried currants, plumped in hot water for 5 minutes	2 cups toasted breadcrumbs (see p. 12)

Clean the sardines in the *linguetta* style (see pp. 66–67), in this case removing the tails as well.

Trim the fennel greens and remove any tough or dried parts. Wash, and then cook them for 10 minutes in abundant salted water. Lift out with a slotted spoon (reserving the water), drain well, and chop.

Sauté the onion in ¼ cup of olive oil over a very low flame until it begins to color. Add the pine nuts, currants, almonds, the anchovies steamed in the olive oil (see pp. 11–12), and the saffron and water. Stir and simmer for a few minutes.

Reserve 4 sardines. Fry the remaining sardines in ¼ cup oil over medium heat until they are golden, turning carefully so as not to break them. Remove from the pan, and in the same oil sauté the chopped fennel and the 4 reserved sardines, mashing the latter with a wooden spoon as you stir.

Bring to a boil the water in which you cooked the fennel, add the bucatini, and cook until they are *al dente*. Drain and toss together with the onion mixture and with half of the fennel mixture. Arrange the pasta in an ovenproof dish, alternating a layer of pasta with a layer of fennel and a layer of the fried sardines, until all the ingredients have been used up. Sprinkle with some of the breadcrumbs and place in a hot oven, or simply let stand, for 5 minutes before serving. Pass the rest of the breadcrumbs on the side.

Pasta con le sarde is delicious hot and possibly even better cold the next day.

———

This is the recipe for the classic Palermo version, but there are many variants, including even a fishless variety for the very poor, wistfully known as *pasta con le sarde a mare*—"pasta with the sardines at sea."

However apocryphal the legend of its birth, *pasta con le sarde* is universally considered to be Arabic in origin. Yet its ingredients—the currants that first hung in the gardens of Alcinoüs, the fennel and pine nuts so popular in the kitchen of Apicius, the saffron that Sicily exported during the Imperial Age— are classical. The landscape of classical Sicily was also transformed in a similar fashion, and acquired at the hands of the Arabs a different and exotic beauty, quite unique in the Italian panorama.

The process of transformation was slow and painful: the conquest itself lasted more than fifty years, and the two hundred years that followed were punctuated by periodic revolts on the part of the Sicilians and infighting among the Saracen occupiers. Yet, despite all the consequent bloodshed and destruction, Sicily prospered.

In truth, it was not the Saracen army, chefs and all, that had the greatest impact on Sicily and its cuisine, but the colonists who came with them, hungry for land and armed with a highly developed agricultural technology. In particular the refined methods of irrigation that they had developed in their desert oases allowed the Saracens to introduce intensive cultivation on a scale hitherto unknown in Sicily. A new system of property-based taxation encouraged the extension of farming to lands that had previously lain fallow, and new villages were founded throughout the interior.

In contrast to the primitive extensive farming of the early Romans on the mainland, intensive Sicilian agriculture had a history of considerable sophistication, particularly evident in the famous Mediterranean *hortus*, or closed garden, which had studded the countryside around the Sicilian towns and cities since the early classical era, its fruits and vegetables protected from passing thieves and marauding flocks by neatly constructed stone walls. With the advent of irrigation and the introduction of new crops, this classical *hortus* was transformed by the Arab agriculturalists into a garden of earthly delight:

> With its rigorous enclosures, with its shining evergreen leaves, with its exquisite fruits of gold and of flame, the Mediterranean garden of oranges and lemons assumes the fascination of Paradise, and is to have an important part in the rebirth of a taste for the *bel paesaggio* in the agricultural landscape.
> Emilio Sereni, *Storia del paesaggio agrario italiano*, 1982

BASKET OF LEMONS AND FENNEL, *a detail from "The Holy Family,"*
a painting by Pietro D'Asaro, 1621

The aesthetic pleasures of the citrus fruit are not, of course, merely visual. Sicilians, for example, love a lemon—not only in lemonade or in *granita*, not merely squeezed on fish or over a salad of raw sweet fennel, but lemon plain and simple, picked from a tree, peeled with a knife, and eaten straight or with a pinch of salt. They can do this without so much as a pucker, a capacity that by now must be genetically transmitted: my daughter, who takes after her father's family, has it, whereas my son, who is a Taylor, does not.

Pirandello uses lemons (his play *Le Lumie di Sicilia* is about a gift of lemons brought north to a famous opera singer by her childhood love) to indicate the color, the perfumes, and the asperity of Sicily—perhaps because he comes from the southern coast of the island, which is barren, sun-baked, and poor. Orange is for opulence, the color of the Conca d'Oro, the valley that reaches back into the mountains behind Palermo, a golden horn of orange groves nowadays overflowing with stucco-and-terra-cotta villas.

Orange is opulence: the ineffectual, useless opulence of the past, when the gardens around Palermo were filled with what an eighteenth-century diarist describes as "common oranges, those good only for making juice or polishing copper"; and the wasteful opulence of the present, when government bull-dozers trample and crush hundreds of tons of Sicilian oranges that can find no market.

It is difficult for someone from a northern climate to become accustomed to such an overabundance of oranges. Even though they had long since lost their Victorian luxury status by the time I was a child, it was still a pleasure to know that the round bulge at the very toe of my Christmas stocking was a sweet-smelling tangerine that spoke of the sun just as the nights were longest. In my almost manic attempts to reproduce an Anglo-Saxon Christmas in Sicily, I perpetuated the tradition without a second thought, until my firstborn, at age four, decided that he was being had.

Vittorini appreciated the irony of oranges: in *Conversations in Sicily*, the returning immigrant first encounters Sicily on board the ferry, in the person of a man returning from Calabria with a basket of oranges that he has failed to sell.

> And he, the little Sicilian, remained hopefully silent for a moment, then he glanced down at his child wife, seated immobile, dark, closed, on the sack, and he became desperate, and desperately, as on board earlier, he leaned down and untied a bit of string from the basket, pulled out an orange, and desperately offered it, still leaning over on bent legs, to his wife, and after her wordless refusal, he was desperately disheartened there with the orange in his hand, and he began to peel it for himself, to eat it himself, swallowing it as if he were swallowing curses.
>
> "We eat them in salad," I said, "here."
>
> "In America?" the Sicilian asked.
>
> "No," I said, "here in Sicily."
>
> "Here in Sicily?" the Sicilian asked. "In salad with oil?"
>
> "Yes, with oil," I said, "and with a clove of garlic, and salt . . ."
>
> "And with bread?" said the Sicilian.
>
> "Sure," I answered. "With bread. I always ate them like that fifteen years ago, as a boy . . ."
>
> "Ah, you did?" said the Sicilian. "You were rich then, were you?"
>
> "More or less," I answered.
>
> And I added: "Have you never eaten a salad of oranges?"
>
> "Yes, a couple of times," said the Sicilian. "But sometimes there isn't any oil."
>
> "Right," I said. "It isn't always a good year. . . . Oil can be expensive."

A PLAINTIVE SINGSONG, *a girl selling oranges in a nineteenth-century engraving by Vuillier*

"And sometimes there isn't any bread," said the Sicilian. "If you can't sell your oranges, then there isn't any bread. And you have to eat oranges. . . . Like this, see?"

And desperately he ate his orange, his fingers wet, in the cold, with the juice of the orange, as he looked at the child wife at his feet who didn't want oranges.

Elio Vittorini, Conversazioni in Sicilia, 1941

A fancier version of this salad, served as an antipasto in some Palermo restaurants, is *insalata di arance e aringhe*, made of peeled and sliced oranges of the rather acid variety, which are known here as Portuguese oranges, and which my mother called simply "juice oranges" (so much more variety is available in American markets nowadays that I hesitate to use the names from my childhood). Navel and blood oranges, at any rate, are much too sweet for this salad, which combines the slices or chunks of sharp-flavored orange with small pieces of smoked herring that has been boned and softened in olive oil, and is dressed with more oil, salt, and black pepper. (Canned tuna, sliced scallions, and black olives make an excellent if more pedestrian alternative to the herring.)

Sicilians are very fond of this combination of orange and fish, which they also employ in *sarde a beccafico*, a dish to be found on every list of traditional Palermo specialties. The *beccafico* is a songbird that grows fat and sweet on a diet of figs, as fat and as sweet as these filleted sardines rolled about a filling of breadcrumbs, currants, and pine nuts, and baked with orange juice and bay leaves. Although they probably originated as a *tornagusto*, served cold to cleanse the palate between one major course and another, nowadays *sarde a beccafico* are most often to be found on the antipasto table, to which they make a very pretty addition, the dark gray and silver stripes of the fish skins crisscrossed by the dark green of the bay leaves, and the tails curling jauntily upward.

SARDE A BECCAFICO
(Stuffed Sardines)

Serves 6

24 fresh sardines (about 2½ pounds)	2 tablespoons minced parsley
1 cup dried breadcrumbs (see p. 12)	8 anchovy fillets
6 tablespoons olive oil	1 teaspoon olive oil
⅓ cup pine nuts	25 bay leaves
⅓ cup dried currants, plumped in hot water for 5 minutes	Juice of 1 lemon
	Juice of 1 orange
	1 tablespoon sugar

The sardines must be cleaned and prepared, either by an obliging fishmonger or by oneself, in what the Sicilians call the *linguetta* fashion. Cut off the head and the fins (but not the tail), remove the scales, slit the belly, and remove the guts. Then, holding the fish, belly upward, between the palms of your hands, run your thumb along the backbone so that the fish opens like a book, the two halves remaining joined along the dorsal ridge. Remove the backbone, breaking it off just before you get to the tail.

To prepare the filling, brown the breadcrumbs in 2 tablespoons of oil in a heavy skillet over a very low flame, stirring constantly. Remove from the fire, and add the pine nuts, currants, and parsley. Dissolve the anchovies in 1 teaspoon of oil over steam (see pp. 11–12), and add them to the breadcrumbs. Mix thoroughly and moisten with another 2 tablespoons of oil.

Open a sardine and, placing it skin side down, put a heaping teaspoon of filling on it and roll it up toward the tail. Place in a lightly oiled shallow 12-inch baking dish, so that the tail is sticking up in the air. Repeat this with the rest of the sardines, alternating them with bay leaves as if they were on a skewer, and arranging them in neat rows so that they have no room to unroll.

Sprinkle the sardines with the lemon juice, orange juice, sugar, and with 2 tablespoons of oil. Bake in a 350°F. oven for about 10 minutes. Serve cold.

Oranges and lemons and even tangerines go into another *tornagusto*, a very old Palermo recipe for artichokes in a sweet and sour sauce.

CARCIOFI AI QUATTRO SUCCHI
(Artichokes in a Citrus Sauce)

Serves 8

12 medium artichokes	4 cups water
6 onions, sliced thin	1 teaspoon salt
1 cup olive oil	¼ cup capers
1 cup orange juice	8 anchovy fillets
1 cup tangerine juice	1 teaspoon olive oil
½ cup lemon juice	2–3 tablespoons sugar
½ cup white wine vinegar	
(see note p. 20)	

Remove the tough outer leaves from the artichokes, cut off the tops of the remaining leaves, then peel the stems and bases. Cut each artichoke in half and remove the choke with the point of a sharp knife.

Place the artichoke halves and the sliced onions in a large, heavy saucepan together with 1 cup oil, the three juices, vinegar, water, and salt. Cook slowly for 30 to 40 minutes or until the artichokes are very tender but still hold their shape.

Take the artichokes from the pan, and place them in a deepish serving dish.

Add the capers (well rinsed if you have the good luck to be using salted Sicilian capers) to the sauce and cook it slowly until it is reduced and quite thick.

Dissolve the anchovies in 1 teaspoon of oil over steam (see pp. 11–12). Then add to the sauce both the anchovies and the sugar (the quantity of sugar will vary according to the strength of the vinegar you have used, and you have to go by taste). Cook for another 5 minutes until the sugar is completely dissolved, then pour over the artichokes. Serve cold.

———

Another citrus fruit of which Sicilians are very fond is the citron. This looks like an overgrown lemon, as big at times as a small melon, with a nubbled, wrinkled yellow rind. To slice it open is to discover that, between the thin yellow peel and the small center of sweet, rather insipid flesh, there is a vast expanse of white pith, which is the best part of the whole affair. Besides being candied (candied citron and citron conserves are staples in Sicilian pastry), it is also excellent eaten raw, particularly when the yellow peel is removed and the pith and flesh are cut into thin slices and mixed with slices of sweet fennel, some good oil, salt, and pepper.

A last curiosity for anyone lucky enough to have a citrus tree in the garden or greenhouse: *badduzze*, meatballs of chopped veal or beef mixed with eggs, breadcrumbs, chopped parsley and garlic, grated pecorino, and salt and pepper. The meatballs are pressed flat between two orange or lemon leaves and grilled over the coals, so that the essential oils contained in the leaves permeate the meat. (Obviously one must be very sure about the provenance of the leaves, lest it be pesticides that do the permeating.)

Northern Italians fancy themselves as having a monopoly on the consumption of rice, but in fact rice first entered Europe as a foodstuff via Arab-occupied Spain and Sicily. The Romans knew rice only as an extremely expensive commodity imported in small quantities from India for medicinal purposes, but the Saracens were so skilled in irrigation that they were able to create paddies in the area around Lentini, to the south of Catania (albeit in a climate that has since become considerably hotter and more arid), where the cultivation of rice persisted into the eighteenth century.

The rice cultivated in the Mediterranean area has always been, until this century, the fat, short-grained variety that originated in Japan, rather than the long-grained rice from India that is cultivated in the United States. The former is still being produced and is known as *riso originario*. Modern Italian cooks now prefer, for risottos and many other dishes, the twentieth-century *superfino* hybrids, of which the most famous are *arborio* and *vialone*. In the recipes that follow I have indicated which type is to be preferred when a choice is possible, but any type of Italian rice is more suited to Sicilian dishes than a long-grained American rice.

It is true that a risotto or a *riso in brodo* has no place in traditional Sicilian cooking, but Sicilians are very proud of their *arancine*—rice croquettes fried to a golden brown so that they look like little oranges, which come either *alla carne*, stuffed with meat and peas in a tomato sauce, or *al burro*, with a ham and mozzarella filling. *Arancine* are to be found at the sandwich counter of almost any bar in Sicily, not to mention (and it's a good place to make their acquaintance) in the bars of the ferryboats that ply the Straits of Messina between Sicily and the mainland. When *arancine* are good, they are very, very good, but when they are bad they are with you forever.

It takes considerable courage to enter the fray of contending *arancine* recipes: there must be almost a dozen different versions, each claiming the title of Authority. I have had success with this one:

ARANCINE
(*Little Oranges*)

Makes twelve 3-inch arancine

1½ pounds Italian rice
   (*vialone* or *originario*)
2 eggs, beaten
½ cup grated caciocavallo or
   parmesan cheese
Salt and freshly ground pepper
1 small onion, minced
1 celery rib, chopped
2 tablespoons olive oil
½ pound ground veal or beef
1 teaspoon tomato extract
   (see p. 13) or 1 tablespoon
   tomato paste

½ cup red wine
1 sage leaf
⅛ teaspoon grated nutmeg
1 cup plain tomato sauce
   (see p. 172)
1 cup blanched tiny peas,
   fresh or frozen
1 cup flour
4 eggs, beaten
2 cups dried breadcrumbs
   (see p. 12)
Vegetable oil for frying

Cook the rice in abundant boiling water, lightly salted, as you would cook pasta. When it is tender (about 15 to 20 minutes), drain it well, turn it out on a marble surface or a wide platter, and add the 2 beaten eggs, the cheese, and salt and pepper to taste. Mix well and allow to cool.

Sauté the onion and celery in the olive oil until they begin to color. Add the ground meat and brown it. Stir in the tomato extract and the wine, and simmer briefly. Add the sage leaf, nutmeg, and tomato sauce. Simmer for 20 to 30 minutes. Add the peas and simmer for 5 minutes longer, until the peas are cooked. Allow to cool.

Place the flour, the 4 beaten eggs, and the breadcrumbs in three separate plates.

When the rice and filling have cooled, place a couple of tablespoons of rice in the palm of your left hand (assuming you are right-handed), make a dent in the middle, fill the hollow with a generous teaspoonful of the meat filling, and with your right hand cover the filling with more rice, sealing the edges and molding it into a ball. No filling should show. *Arancine* can be anywhere from 1½ to 4 inches in diameter, but I find that 2½ to 3 inches is the most manageable size.

Bind the *arancina* by rolling it first in flour, then in the beaten eggs, then in the breadcrumbs, making sure that the ball is completely covered at each layer. Set the bound *arancina* to dry on a rack while you make the others. They are not particularly difficult to make once you get the knack, but to start frying before all the *arancine* have been shaped and bound really is to invite disaster.

Deep-fry the *arancine* a few at a time in abundant and very hot oil (about 375°F.) until they are rich golden brown (it is crucial that there be more than enough oil to cover them completely; otherwise they will burst). Lift out and drain on absorbent paper. Set in a warm oven to dry for 10 minutes before serving.

———

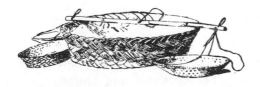

Rice is also the protagonist of *tummàla*, an elaborate casserole from eastern Sicily, which is said to derive its name from that of Mohammed Ibn Thummah, an emir of Catania during the Saracen occupation.

TUMMÀLA
(Rice Timbale)

Serves 8

1 3-pound chicken, complete with liver, gizzard, and, if possible, unlaid eggs
1 rib celery
1 onion
2 tomatoes
1 carrot
Boiling water
Salt
4 peppercorns
1 bay leaf
1 cup stale white bread-crumbs (see p. 12)
½ cup milk
½ pound ground veal or beef
¼ cup grated pecorino cheese
1 egg
2 tablespoons minced fresh parsley
2 garlic cloves, minced
Salt and freshly ground black pepper

Pinch grated nutmeg
½ pound fresh Sicilian pork sausage
3 tablespoons olive oil
1 onion, minced
¼ cup tomato extract (see p. 13) or ⅓ cup tomato paste
2 cups water
2 cups plain tomato sauce (see p. 172)
3 cups Italian rice (preferably *arborio*)
2 tablespoons dried bread-crumbs (see p. 12)
½ pound tuma or mozzarella cheese (see p. 38)
1 egg
2 egg yolks
½ cup grated pecorino cheese

Place the chicken and the vegetables in a large flameproof casserole, cover with boiling water, and add salt, peppercorns, and bay leaf. Simmer 40 minutes or until the chicken is cooked.

Meanwhile, prepare the meatballs as follows: Soften the breadcrumbs in the milk, and squeeze out any excess liquid. Add the ground meat, cheese, 1 egg, parsley, garlic, salt, pepper, and nutmeg. Blend thoroughly and shape into walnut-size meatballs. Simmer half of the meatballs in the broth with the chicken for the last 15 minutes of the cooking.

Brown the sausage in 1 tablespoon of olive oil. Remove the sausages, cut into 1-inch pieces, and in the same pan brown the remaining half of the meatballs.

Sauté the minced onion in 2 tablespoons of olive oil. Add the tomato extract, dissolving it with the water; add the tomato sauce. Simmer for 10 minutes. Add the browned sausages and the browned meatballs, and simmer for another 10 to 15 minutes.

When the chicken is cooked and cooled enough to touch, take it out of the broth, bone and skin it, and cut the meat and the giblets into bite-size pieces. Put aside, together with the boiled meatballs, also removed from the broth.

Strain the broth through a sieve (you should end up with roughly 2 quarts), add salt to taste, and bring the broth to the boiling point. Add the rice and cook until it is *al dente*. Remove the pot from the fire, correct the salt again, cover, and allow to sit until the rice absorbs all the broth.

Grease a large casserole (at least 12 inches wide and 5 inches deep) and line it with breadcrumbs. Fill the casserole in layers as follows:

A layer of rice (about one-third of the total)
The boiled meatballs and about two-thirds of the chicken
Slices of tuma cheese (using all the cheese)
Rice (another third)
The sausages and browned meatballs with ½ cup of the
    tomato sauce
Remaining rice, mixed with remaining chicken

Beat the whole egg and the yolks until fluffy. Fold in the grated cheese, and add a little salt and pepper. Pour over the top layer of the casserole. Bake in a 350°F. oven for 45 minutes or until the crust is golden brown. Serve hot with the remaining tomato and meat sauce passed on the side.

———

THE CHURCH (A FORMER MOSQUE) OF SAN GIOVANNI DEGLI EREMITI, *the twelfth-century*
Arab-Norman church in Palermo in a nineteenth-century engraving by Vuillier

Tummàla is traditionally served at Christmas, and has as many versions as
there are families that observe the tradition. All of them, however, call for
immoderate quantities of meat and cheese and eggs—a profligate celebration
of the feast day that is a recurrent note in Sicilian cooking. (One Easter specialty
from the town of Aragona, a timbale in which macaroni and pork take the

place of rice and chicken, requires more than three pounds of cheese and a total of forty eggs.)

An American writer, J. C. Grasso, attributes to this same Emir Thummah a dish in which the chicken is baked in a hollowed breadloaf instead of rice. The attribution aroused my curiosity, and a little research uncovered three very similar recipes: one in Apicius, where it is called *sala cattabia*; one that Claudia Roden has adapted from a medieval Arabic cookbook and entitled "Chicken Awsat"; and one in a contemporary Sicilian cookbook by Giuseppe Coria. Although this is not a common dish on modern Sicilian tables, it is an eloquent witness to the unity and the continuity of Mediterranean traditions that the Sicilian table embodies. I include it both because it is emblematic and because it is very good. This is my rendition of Grasso's recipe.

PASTICCIO DI MOHAMMED IBN ITMNAH (THUMMAH), EMIR OF CATANIA

Serves 8 to 10

One 4-pound chicken in parts
¼ cup olive oil
2 cups (approximately) chicken broth
Salt and freshly ground black pepper
1 large round loaf of crusty Italian bread

⅛ cup toasted almonds
⅛ cup pistachios
1 tablespoon capers
1 tablespoon chopped parsley
2 eggs, lightly beaten
Juice of 1 lemon

Brown the chicken in the oil, add 1 cup broth, salt, and pepper, and simmer until tender, adding more broth if needed. Cool the chicken, remove the skin and bones, and cut the meat into small pieces. Reserve both the meat and the broth.

Cut the bread horizontally, a little less than halfway down, so as to make a dish and lid. Hollow out the bread, combine the crumbs with the reserved broth, and press through a sieve.

Grind the almonds and pistachios, together with the capers

and parsley. Add to the bread purée together with the eggs and lemon juice. The mixture should be quite moist, so you may need to add an extra tablespoon or two of broth. Combine with the chicken meat, spoon into the empty bread crust, and replace the upper crust.

Bake 20 minutes in a 350°F. oven. Serve cold.

Note: My only reservation about this recipe has to do with the age of the bread. If you use a stale loaf, the crust is unpleasantly hard; if you use a fresh one, the dampened crumbs turn to glue. This impasse could be avoided either by drying out the fresh crumbs in a very low oven before adding the broth, or by substituting older crumbs for the fresh ones. Being a hedonist, I also prefer to use a greater quantity of almonds and pistachios (½ cup each).

Irrigated fields also permitted the introduction of new vegetables such as spinach and eggplant. Spinach appears to have taken one look at the island and headed north, since it is absent from traditional Sicilian cooking except around Syracuse and is still not always available in the markets, even in Palermo. Eggplant, on the other hand, found its fortune here, and has become as much a part of the Sicilian summer as the sun itself.

Speaking in broad terms, there are two varieties of eggplants marketed in Sicily: the so-called Tunisian eggplant, which is round rather than oval and fades from a true deep purple to lavender and then white around its stem; and the Turkish, or what the Sicilians call the *nostrano*, variety. (*Nostrano*, which is best translated as "our kind of," is an adjective used with all sorts of foods to denote a local variety.) The *nostrano* eggplant is an elongated oval of a dark brownish-purple color with a green tinge around the stem and just under the skin. Although Turkish eggplants may be specified in a few recipes, particularly those calling for small eggplants to be used as individual servings, on the whole Sicilians much prefer the Tunisian variety, which are noticeably sweeter and fresher in flavor but have a shorter season.

Any discussion of eggplants in Sicily should begin with *caponata*, whose fame has justly spread well beyond the island. *Caponata* is thought to have originated as seagoing fare, since it keeps well because of the vinegar. Virtuous

Sicilian housewives put up *caponata* for use in winter, but what seems like an enormous quantity while I am making it disappears in a matter of days in my household, without ever having a chance to show its mettle.

CAPONATA
(Sweet and Sour Eggplant)

Serves 6

2 medium-large eggplants
   (about 2½ pounds)
Salt
1½ cups olive oil
   (see note p. 39)
1 medium onion, sliced
6 ribs celery, cut into 1-inch
   lengths and blanched for
    1 minute in boiling water
1 cup pitted green olives

½ cup capers
1½ cups plain tomato sauce
   (see p. 172)
½ cup white wine vinegar
   (see note p. 20)
2 tablespoons sugar
2 tablespoons unsweetened
   cocoa (optional)
¾ cup toasted almond slivers

Wash the eggplants, cut off the stems, and cut the eggplants into ¾-inch cubes. Sprinkle with abundant salt and allow to drain for an hour. Rinse well, dry, and fry in 1 cup olive oil until golden brown on all sides. Drain on absorbent paper.

Sauté the onion in ½ cup olive oil until it begins to color. Add the blanched celery and cook a minute longer, then add the olives, capers, tomato sauce, vinegar, sugar, and the cocoa if you like. Simmer for 5 minutes.

Stir in the eggplant and simmer for 10 minutes. Correct the salt, then refrigerate for 24 hours.

Serve the *caponata*, sprinkled with the toasted almonds, either cold or at room temperature.

Note: The addition of cocoa, a very baroque, Spanish touch, renders the *caponata* richer in color and in consistency. Since my own personal preferences run to things simple, I usually leave it out.

According to one book, the chefs of the aristocracy would also serve *caponata* "sprinkled with bottarga, tuna roe, hard-boiled egg yolk, all reduced to a powder; crumbled hard-boiled egg whites, tiny octopus boiled and chopped, small shrimps, boned sardines in oil, and all the shellfish you wish." I find the idea appalling and recommend confining oneself to a liberal sprinkling of toasted almond slivers.

The range and fantasy of Sicilian eggplant recipes is quite overwhelming, but close examination shows that this vast repertoire is composed of variations on a few basic techniques. The first of these consists of frying small pieces of eggplant in oil, then simmering them or simply covering them with a sauce or dressing. *Caponata* is the most elaborate version of this. Another version, much simpler but also very good and summery, comes from Ustica, the tiny island thirty-five miles off the Palermo coast, which is thought to offer photographers some of the most beautiful underwater scenery in the Mediterranean.

MELANZANE ALL'USTICESE
(Ustica Eggplants)

Serves 6

2 large eggplants
  (2½–3 pounds)
Salt
1 cup or more olive oil
  (see note p. 39)
1 tablespoon white wine
  vinegar (see note p. 20)

1 teaspoon sugar
½ cup chopped fresh mint
  leaves
2 cloves garlic, sliced

Wash the eggplants and cut off their stems. Cut the eggplants into ½-inch slices, and then cut the slices across so that you have finger-shaped pieces. Put in a colander, sprinkle with abundant salt, and leave to drain for an hour.

Rinse the eggplant thoroughly, dry, and fry in hot olive oil until delicately browned on all sides. Drain on absorbent paper to remove the excess oil, then place in a shallow serving dish. Sprinkle while hot with vinegar, sugar, mint, and garlic. Serve cold.

———

Another technique requires small eggplants, usually of the Turkish variety. Small incisions cut into the skin of the whole eggplants are filled with garlic, mint, anchovies, or other seasonings before baking or braising in a tomato sauce. The most classic of these recipes calls for Turkish eggplants and a filling of mint, garlic, and caciocavallo cheese, as well as tomato sauce, but I find the results to have a rather murky and almost bitter taste. So I prefer a lighter version using Tunisian eggplants. The technique is the same in either case.

MELANZANE IN TEGAME
(*Braised Eggplants*)

Serves 6

6 baby eggplants (preferably the Tunisian variety)	1 medium onion, minced
Salt	½ cup olive oil
4 cloves garlic	1½ cups fresh tomatoes, peeled and chopped
1 cup fresh basil leaves	3 sprigs fresh basil
Freshly ground black pepper	

Wash the eggplants, cut off their stems, and make 5 or 6 deep incisions, starting about half an inch below the top and ending about half an inch from the bottom. Each eggplant must remain in one piece.

Soak the eggplants in salted water for a couple of hours. Chop the garlic and the basil very fine, and add a little bit of salt and some black pepper.

Rinse and drain the eggplants, and stuff a pinch of the chopped mixture into each incision. This is hard work, requiring considerable thumb power to pry open the incisions, and at the same time delicacy to avoid breaking the eggplants apart. (One Sicilian name for this dish is *milinciani ammuttunati*, which has connotations of a real heave-ho!)

Sauté the onion in the olive oil, then add the eggplants, turning them until they are brown on all sides. Add the tomatoes, a pinch of salt, and the basil sprigs. Bring to a boil, then reduce the heat and simmer, covered, for about 30 minutes, or until the eggplants are tender all the way through. Serve either hot or cold.

———

A large number of recipes require that the pulp of the eggplant be removed and treated in one way or another before being returned to the skin for a final cooking. One such recipe is called *tabacchiere* ("snuffboxes"), a name that I thought odd for a relatively humble dish, until I read that it originated in Messina, a free port where snuff was cheap enough for almost every pocket.

TABACCHIERE DI MELANZANE
(Eggplant Snuffboxes)

Serves 6

3 smallish eggplants
Salt
1 medium onion
½ cup olive oil
10 anchovy fillets
1 teaspoon olive oil
½ cup parsley
3 garlic cloves
½ cup capers

1 cup toasted breadcrumbs
  (see p. 12)
⅓ cup finely diced salami
  (optional)
2 or 3 egg whites, beaten
  until foamy
2 cups dried breadcrumbs
  (see p. 12)
Vegetable oil for frying

Wash the eggplants, remove the stems, cut in half vertically, and hollow each half, leaving ½-inch shells. Put both the shells and the pulp to soak in salted water for 2 hours. Rinse and drain. Blanch shells in boiling water for about 5 minutes and drain.

Mince or grate the onion, then sauté it in ½ cup olive oil until soft. Roughly chop the pulp of the eggplant and add it to the onion. Sauté for about 10 minutes or until soft, stirring frequently to prevent sticking.

Cook the anchovies in 1 teaspoon oil over steam until creamy (see pp. 11–12). Mince the parsley, the garlic, and the capers, then add along with the anchovies to the eggplant-and-onion mixture. Stir in the toasted breadcrumbs and salami if using it. Blend thoroughly, adding a little oil if necessary to make a fairly compact filling.

Fill the eggplant shells with the pulp-and-crumb mixture, pressing down to make it as compact as possible. Bind the stuffed shells by dipping both sides in the beaten egg whites and then in the dried breadcrumbs. Make sure they are well coated.

Fry the eggplants in ¼ inch hot oil until well browned on each side. Be sure to begin frying with the filling side down, even though this takes careful handling; otherwise escaping air bubbles will crack the crust. Turn and fry the skin side. Drain on absorbent paper and serve at room temperature.

————

Almost all Sicilian recipes require that the eggplant be fried in olive oil and, given the spongelike nature of this vegetable, quite a bit of it. Since few inhabitants of the English-speaking world can afford an unlimited supply of olive oil, and since frying has lost prestige of late, it is not a bad idea to try substituting the broiler for the frying pan.

Charcoal-grilled eggplant is a great favorite with Sicilians anyway: the eggplants should be cut into slices about ½ inch thick and sprinkled with abundant olive oil, salt, pepper, chopped garlic, and oregano, a couple of hours before being grilled over a medium fire. A variation is to grill the eggplant slices plain and spoon *ammogghiu* sauce (see p. 170) over them.

Grilled eggplant slices also work well in the most famous of all eggplant dishes, *melanzane alla parmigiana*. Accustomed to thinking of this as one of the great classics of mainland cooking, most Italians would be surprised to hear the Sicilian claim that eggplant parmesan originally had nothing to do with either the city of Parma or its famous cheese, but was first made in Sicily and with caciocavallo cheese.

Sicilians have a word, *palmigiana*, that means "shutter" and that stems from the resemblance between the overlapping louvers of a shutter and the overlapping palm fronds in a thatched roof. Someone was reminded of a shutter as he covered a pan of overlapping eggplant slices with tomato sauce and caciocavallo, hence *melanzane alla palmigiana*. Since Sicilians have a "probrem" pronouncing the *l*, confusion was sure to follow.

It is pointless for me to give the recipe for such a ubiquitous dish, but I do want to mention what for me was the ultimate experience in eggplant parmesan, eaten fifteen years ago in a restaurant near Marsala, not far from where Admiral Euphemius landed with his troops and his chefs and his taste for currants and pine nuts. It was the latter that made the difference: the tomato sauce on each layer of eggplant (it was baked in a deep dish and had about four layers) was sprinkled with currants and pine nuts, adding a sweet, distinctly Sicilian twist to a familiar flavor.

TUNA FISHING, *an eighteenth-century drawing by Houel*

The restaurant in question lay in the very heartland of Arabic cooking in Sicily, which stretches along the Trapanese coast roughly from the big fishing port of Mazara del Vallo north to Capo San Vito at the westernmost tip of the island. This area abounds in recipes that claim Arabic antecedents, most of them dealing with fish. (There used to be a small trattoria in Mazara where one could order simply *tutto pesce*—"all fish"—then sit back and let it roll in: first a small crab salad served in the shell, then a couple of raw sea urchins with lemon, then a red mullet *in umido*, then a few rings of fried squid, then a paper-thin slice of grilled swordfish, then a croquette of fried whitebait, etc., etc., until one begged for mercy. The last time my husband and I were in Mazara, we searched and searched to no avail, so I fear that this fish lovers' paradise no longer exists.)

The Arabic influence is beyond dispute in the most famous dish from the Trapani coast, *cuscus*, a Sicilian version of couscous from the Maghreb. It is served with a *zuppa di pesce* instead of the mutton stew that is most common in North Africa, and bay leaves rather than red pepper predominate.

Cuscus has long been considered a *pièce de résistance* in the Sicilian cook's repertory, at least in the western half of the island; great expertise is required to prepare the raw couscous for cooking. The initiation into this technique—known in Sicilian as *'ncocciatura*—in which two different grades of ground semolina are combined by manipulating the grains with dampened fingers so that they cling together in tiny clusters of uniform size, is difficult enough to have acquired considerable mystique. Nowadays, however, ready-to-cook (and even precooked) couscous is available in the supermarkets, and the *'ncocciatura* no longer separates the sheep from the goats.

The best *cuscus* I have ever eaten was served to me in a private house, the handiwork of a friend who was once a professional cook. Her daughter-in-law has kindly given me the recipe, and, thanks to ready-to-cook couscous, even a goat such as I can produce an excellent *cuscus*.

CUSCUS
(Sicilian Couscous)

Serves 6 to 8

THE COUSCOUS

1½ pounds ready-to-cook
   couscous
¼ cup water
¾ cup olive oil
1 large onion, minced fine
½ cup minced parsley

2 garlic cloves, minced
Salt and freshly ground
   black pepper
2 cups flour
½ cup water
10–12 whole bay leaves

THE FISH AND BROTH

3 pounds mixed fish for soup
   (the fish most commonly
   used are John Dory, which
   has flesh rather like
   flounder; grouper; gray
   mullet; scorpion fish; and
   conger eel)
1 medium onion, minced
¼ cup minced parsley

⅓ cup olive oil
3 cups plain tomato sauce
   (see p. 172)
4 cups water
2 bay leaves
Salt and freshly ground
   black pepper
3 garlic cloves, minced
   very fine

HOT SAUCE

¾ cup of the broth   1 tablespoon olive oil
Crushed dried red pepper

Place the couscous in a wide bowl, dampen it with ¼ cup of water, and sift through it with your fingers to break up the lumps. Then add ¾ cup of oil, onion, parsley, garlic, and liberal amounts of salt and pepper. Stir until thoroughly blended.

Prepare the pot in which you will steam the couscous: you will need either a special double-decker steamer or a metal colander that fits tightly into a large pot with a lid that closes it well. Fill the pot with water to 1 inch below the bottom of the steamer basket. Fit the steamer basket or the colander on top. You must now seal the two together: make a sticky dough of 2 cups of flour and about ½ cup of water, and paste a strip of this dough all the way around the edge of the pot where it joins the basket, pushing it in well and smearing the edges as if the dough were putty, so that no steam can escape.

Line the steamer basket with bay leaves and spoon the couscous gently onto them. Cover and place on the fire. The couscous must cook for 1 hour from the time that steam starts to escape from under the lid. Every so often stir the couscous gently so that the steam gets to all of it.

Wash the fish and cut it into large pieces, putting the heads and tails to one side. Sauté the onion and the parsley in the olive oil in a large pot, and when they begin to turn golden, add the tomato sauce, 4 cups of water, 2 bay leaves, salt, pepper, and the heads and tails of the fish. Bring to the boiling point, then reduce the heat and simmer for 30 minutes. Add the remaining fish to the pot and simmer slowly in the tomato broth for 10 minutes longer, or until the fish is tender and flaky.

Strain 2 cups of the broth from the fish. Spoon the couscous from the steamer into a serving bowl, and add the strained broth and the minced garlic. Stir carefully before covering with a lid, then wrap the bowl in a woolen blanket or several layers of newspaper to keep it warm. Allow the wrapped bowl to stand for 30 minutes.

Lift out the pieces of fish from the remaining broth, bone them, and place them on a serving platter. Discard the heads and tails, then strain the broth. Take ¾ cup of the broth and heat it for a few minutes with a teaspoon of crushed dried red pepper and the oil to make a very hot sauce (similar to the North African *harissa*) for those who like it.

Heat the remaining broth as is, correcting the salt, and pour it into a gravy boat. Serve the couscous, the broth, and the fish all at the same time. Pass the hot pepper sauce on the side.

———

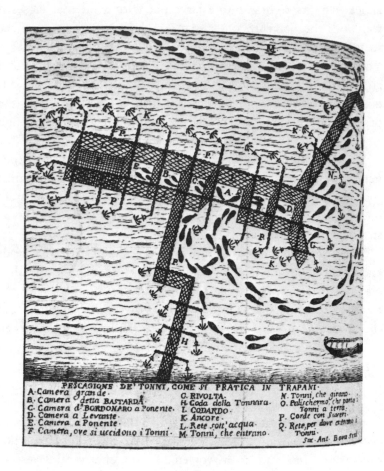

SALT FLATS, CORAL FISHING AND TUNA FISHING IN TRAPANI,
an eighteenth-century engraving by A. Bova

It was in the waters off the coast of Trapani that the Arabs first set out their elaborate traps for catching tuna, so it is no surprise that this fish plays an important role in the cooking of the area. Although tuna has had much space in the preceding chapter, I shall add one more recipe.

POLPETTE DI TONNO
(*Tuna Patties*)

Serves 6

1 pound fresh tuna or 1½ pounds fresh sardines	2 tablespoons grated pecorino cheese
2 cups stale white bread-crumbs (see p. 12)	Salt and freshly ground black pepper
½ cup milk	1 egg, beaten
2 tablespoons currants, plumped in hot water for 5 minutes	Flour
	Olive oil
2 tablespoons pine nuts	2 cups tomato sauce variation II (see p. 173)
1 tablespoon fresh parsley, chopped	

Bone and skin the fish and chop it into very small pieces.

Soak the breadcrumbs in the milk for 10 minutes or until soft. Squeeze out the excess liquid and mix the crumbs with the fish. Add the currants, pine nuts, parsley, cheese, salt, pepper, and egg. Work these ingredients together well with your hands or a slow-speed blender until they are thoroughly amalgamated, and then shape them into small patties about 2 inches in diameter. Flour the patties and brown them on both sides in a few table-spoons of olive oil. Pour the tomato sauce over the patties and simmer them for 10 to 15 minutes.

Note: Palermo cooks prepare this dish with sardines instead of tuna; and if neither fresh sardines nor fresh tuna is available, fresh mackerel fillets might do.

The roe of the tuna, known as *bottarga* when it is cured and dried, is excellent grated over freshly drained spaghetti tossed with minced parsley and olive oil. Another sauce for pasta that originated in Trapani does not require fish, but depends upon ground almonds for texture, a technique that was very common both in classical Arabic cooking and in the cuisine of the Italian Renaissance. It has long since lost its own name, thanks to its similarity to a more famous northern cousin.

PESTO TRAPANESE

Serves 6

6 garlic cloves
1 teaspoon salt
1 cup fresh basil leaves
1 cup blanched almonds,
    roughly chopped

4 ripe tomatoes, peeled
    and chopped
½ cup olive oil
Black pepper
1½ pounds bavette or spaghetti

In a mortar pound the garlic, salt, and basil into a paste; add the almonds little by little and then the tomatoes. When all the ingredients are reduced to a pulp, add the oil and the pepper. (This can be done in an electric blender, in which case the oil should be added at the beginning.)

Cook the pasta in boiling salted water, drain, and toss in a serving bowl together with the *pesto* until the latter is evenly distributed. Serve at once.

———

The Arabs did not by any means confine themselves to a mere tampering with taste, a subtle touch of lemony tartness or the textural novelty of rice. Indeed, they revolutionized the whole of European confectionery by introducing into Sicily the cultivation of sugarcane. Cane sugar differs from the sweeteners available to the classical world in that its taste is neutral, with no special character of its own, whereas both honey and *vino cotto* have distinct and at times strong flavors that leave a trace and a certain sameness in any dish of which they are an ingredient.

However lavish their embellishment of spices and pistachios and dates, the cakes and desserts described by the classical authors all sound like something one might find at the pastry counter of an organic-foods store—full of the wholesome and virtuous goodness of the granola bar or the Fig Newton. By introducing cane sugar to Sicily, the Arabs opened the door to all the possibilities and peccadilloes of European *patisserie* and introduced Sicily to the Oriental taste for the overpoweringly sweet, a characteristic that has survived until today.

There are a great number of Sicilian desserts that bear the Arab imprint, and several that even bear Arab names, of which the most famous is the *cassata siciliana*. *Cassata* comes from the Arabic *qas'ah*, a large, steep-sided terra-cotta bowl used to mold this amazing cake, made of marzipan, sponge cake, and sweetened ricotta. A proper *cassata* is spectacularly decorative: the cake, striped with marzipan colored pale green in memory of the days when one could afford to use pistachio paste, is glazed with white icing, and then crystallized wedges of oranges and pears are placed on top, spread out like the petals of a flower within curving ribbons of translucent candied squash.

CASSATA SICILIANA
(Sicilian Cassata Cake)

Makes one 9-inch cassata

ALMOND PASTE

⅓ recipe *pasta reale*
(see p. 245)

3 drops green food coloring

RICOTTA CREAM

1 pound fresh ricotta, well
drained (see note p. 18)

½–1½ cups sugar

½ cup semisweet chocolate
bits

⅓ cup diced *zuccata*
(see p. 94) or candied
citron

PAN DI SPAGNA SPONGE CAKE

5 eggs at room temperature

1¼ cups sugar

1⅓ cups cake flour or nonwaxy cornstarch (see note)

3 teaspoons baking powder

ICING

1 egg white

¾ cup sugar

1 tablespoon lemon juice

⅓ cup Marsala wine

Candied fruit (pear halves,
orange slices or wedges,
cherries, apricots, strips
of citron, or ribbons
of *zuccata*)

Prepare the almond paste according to the recipe on p. 245, and knead into the paste 3 drops of food coloring so that it becomes pale green. Put aside.

Prepare the ricotta cream according to the instructions given in the *cuccìa* recipe on p. 18. Commercial pastry shops make a very sweet cream for their *cassate*, for the simple reason that they keep longer that way. Many Sicilians do like that much sweetness, and some Sicilian recipes call for as much as 1½ cups of sugar, but as far as I am concerned, ½ cup is plenty.

Prepare the *pan di Spagna*. Separate the egg yolks from the whites, and put the yolks in a large glass or ceramic bowl set over but not in boiling water. Beat the yolks until fluffy, adding the sugar slowly and beating until the sugar dissolves.

Put the flour or starch and baking powder into a sifter, and sift them into the egg yolks, little by little, beating to incorporate them well. Beat the egg whites until soft peaks form, and fold them into the mixture.

Remove from the heat and pour into a greased and floured 9-inch round springform pan. Bake in a preheated 350°F. oven for about 30 minutes or until done (i.e., when a straw poked into the middle of the cake comes out dry).

Allow the *pan di Spagna* to cool completely before starting to assemble the *cassata*. Ideally one should be equipped with a special *cassata* mold, which is a cake pan with very sloping sides, but any round 9-inch pan or casserole will do, provided its sides aren't exactly perpendicular and that it is at least 2 inches deep. Line the pan with wax paper, using a dab of jam or of the ricotta cream to stick the paper to the pan (this is not really necessary if using a nonstick pan).

On a surface dusted with a little confectioners' sugar, roll out the almond paste to a thickness of less than ¼ inch, and cut out 8 rectangles 1½ by 2 inches.

Using a serrated bread knife, with great delicacy cut the *pan di Spagna* so that you have two layers about ¾ inch thick, and one slightly thinner layer. From this last layer cut 8 rectangles similar to those of almond paste.

Line the sides of the pan, alternating rectangles of almond paste with rectangles of *pan di Spagna* (put the cut sides of the cake outside). Trim one of the remaining layers of *pan di Spagna* so that it will fit into the bottom of the pan. Sprinkle with half of the Marsala, and spread with the ricotta cream. Sprinkle the last layer of *pan di Spagna* with the rest of the Marsala, and fit it on top of the ricotta cream, trimming if necessary so that it fits within the outer circle of paste and sponge. Cover with plastic wrap and refrigerate for a couple of hours.

Prepare the icing. Beat the egg white into soft peaks, add the sugar and the lemon juice and continue to beat at high speed for at least 5 minutes or until it becomes thick.

Remove the *cassata* from the refrigerator, take off the plastic, and turn the cake out upside down on a serving plate. Spread the icing over the cake in a very thin layer (it must be thin enough so that the contrast between the green paste and the pale yellow sponge shows through). Decorate with candied fruit and refrigerate until 20 minutes before serving.

Note: Pan di Spagna, which as its name indicates was probably brought to Sicily by the Spanish, is not meant to be that moist and flavorful thing that Americans think of as "cake." It is basically a support, whether it be for ricotta cream, as in the present case; for an egg custard, as in *zuppa imprescia* (see p. 242); or for every imaginable layer of goodness, as in "the triumph of gluttony" (see p. 251). As such, *pan di Spagna* should have as light and delicate a texture as possible, but not much character is expected of it, and moistness is usually added by soaking it with rum, Marsala, or a sweet liqueur.

This recipe for *pan di Spagna*, which comes from a cousin, is very convenient because the quantity of each ingredient is calculated per egg, so that you can scale it to your purposes (the formula is ¼ cup sugar, ⅓ cup starch, and a little more than ½ teaspoon baking powder for every egg). This cousin uses wheat starch instead of cake flour to give an even finer texture to the cake. I can find no reference to wheat starch in any American cookbook in my possession, and don't know if it is available in the United States, but according to *The Joy of Cooking* nonwaxy cornstarch can be substituted for cake flour.

———

I am of the opinion that *cassata siciliana* offers less than meets the eye, for on the inside it is unrelieved sweetness. It is also difficult to make beautifully, and since I can see no point in a sloppy *cassata*, I would suggest that all but the most dexterous leave it to the professionals and settle instead for its country cousin, known as *cassata al forno*. This is much simpler, a ricotta cream enveloped in a crust of *pasta frolla*.

CASSATA AL FORNO
(Baked Cassata)

Makes one 12-inch cassata

PASTA FROLLA CRUST

3¾ cups flour (see p. 41)
1 cup sugar
¾ cup lard

Rind of 1 lemon, grated
5 egg yolks

RICOTTA-CREAM FILLING

1¾ pounds fresh ricotta,
    well drained (see p. 18)
1½ cups sugar

½ cup semisweet chocolate
    bits
⅓ cup diced *zuccata* (see
    p. 94) or candied citron

To prepare the crust, sift together the flour and the sugar, cut in the lard, add the grated lemon rind, and work in the egg yolks. Work the dough just enough to amalgamate all the ingredients and shape them into a ball (should the dough be too dry to hold together properly, a scant teaspoon of milk or of white wine can be added). Refrigerate for at least 2 hours.

Prepare the ricotta cream according to the directions in the
cuccìa recipe on p. 18.

Knead the dough on a floured surface for about a minute and
then roll out two-thirds of it into a circle large enough to line
the bottom and sides of a 12-inch pie pan. Fill the lined pan
with the ricotta cream, roll out the remaining dough to make a
lid, and place it over the cream. Seal the edges of the pie and
decorate the top with scraps of the remaining dough. With a
fork poke some vents in the upper crust. Bake in a preheated
350°F. oven for 30 minutes or until the crust is lightly colored.
Serve cold.

Note: Pasta frolla is the basic Sicilian pastry crust, which comes
in many different degrees of sweetness and richness (see, for
example, the difference between the *cuddureddi* and *buccellato* pastries in the first chapter). I have respected these differences, which
are not haphazard but are governed by both culinary and economic
considerations—the filling that the pastry is to embrace and the
table that it is to grace—and therefore I use the term *pasta frolla*
to indicate a process rather than a specific list of ingredients.

————

Both these recipes call for *zuccata*, which in turn calls for an explanation.
Zuccata, or in Sicilian *cucuzzata*, is made from the *cucuzza*, a squash that is
proverbial for its lack of character yet much beloved by Sicilians. It is a summer
squash, long, thin, smooth of skin and pale green in color. A mythical and
frugal mother superior is said to have discovered that the *cucuzza* that had lain
neglected in the convent garden until it had grown enormously thick and as
hard as granite could by dint of week-long soaking and cooking be saved from
waste and used as a preserve.

Sometimes spiced with cinnamon or with rosewater, *zuccata* lurks at the
heart of some of Sicily's best cakes and pastries. It is somehow reminiscent of
Turkish delight, leading one to suspect that it was known to the harem long
before it hit the convent. (The techniques for preserving and candying fruit,
together with those for making sugared comfits, are in fact an Arabic legacy
that Sicily put to excellent use in later centuries.) The preserves are easy to
make, and a recipe for them follows; I confess to less success in candying whole
pieces of the squash. The recipe that called for three days of work went bad;

the one requiring ten days survived but smelled like old tennis shoes; and since no one in my family much likes candied fruit anyway, I declined to attempt the recipe that would—like the Flood—have kept me busy for forty days.

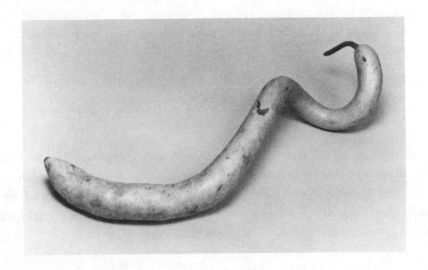

ZUCCATA
(Squash Preserves)

Makes about 2½ pounds

2 dozen fresh jasmine flowers (see note)

1 cup water

2 pounds gone-to-seed summer squash (the more tasteless the variety the better)

1½ pounds (approximately) sugar

1½ cups water

Soak the freshly picked jasmine flowers overnight in 1 cup of water. Filter the jasmine water and reserve.

Peel the squash, cut it in half lengthwise, and cut into 5-inch pieces. Cook in abundant boiling water until tender. Drain; place, seeds down, on a tray; and dry in the sun for 2 hours (longer, I should think, if your sun is less than Mediterranean in intensity).

Remove the seeds, cut into very small cubes, and weigh. Put into a heavy saucepan with an equal weight of sugar and 1½ cups of water. Cook over a low flame, stirring frequently. After the first 15 minutes, add the cup of jasmine water, and continue to cook until the preserves are thick. Pour into sterilized jars and seal.

Note: For the jasmine water you could substitute rosewater or orange water or a teaspoonful of ground cinnamon.

————

Another Sicilian dessert that is absolutely and unequivocally Oriental in origin is *gelo di melone*, a cornstarch pudding made with watermelon juice. To get the full Arabian Nights effect, this pudding should be chilled and served in individual cups, its pale rose surface sprinkled with chopped pistachios and shaved chocolate, and decorated with jasmine flowers.

GELO DI MELONE
(Watermelon Pudding)

Serves 10 to 12

1 small ripe watermelon	½ cup semisweet chocolate
½–1 cup sugar	bits
¾ cup cornstarch	½ cup candied *zuccata*
¼ teaspoon ground cinnamon	(see p. 94) or citron,
½ cup jasmine water	diced very small
(see preceding recipe) or	Chopped pistachios
⅛ teaspoon vanilla	Chocolate shavings
	Jasmine flowers

Cut the watermelon into pieces, remove the rind and the seeds, and pass it through the fine disk of a food mill.

Measure 5 cups of the resulting juice and add it little by little to a saucepan containing the sugar and starch (the quantity of the sugar you use will depend on the sweetness of your melon and the sweetness of your tooth). Stir until the starch is dissolved and any lumps have been smoothed out.

Cook over medium-low heat, stirring constantly. As soon as the *gelo* begins to boil, remove it from the heat and stir in the cinnamon and the jasmine water or the vanilla. Allow to cool.

When tepid, stir in the chocolate bits and the *zuccata*, and pour into molds. *Gelo* may be served in small dessert bowls or molded in paper cups or other small molds (or in a large mold or bowl, although individual servings are more orthodox). Whatever receptacle you choose should be moistened with cold water before filling, and once filled, chilled in the refrigerator for several hours. Serve very cold, unmolded or not, and decorated with chopped pistachios, chocolate shavings, and jasmine blossoms or other small flowers.

––––––

At the end of each October the *Fiera dei Morti* takes place, the Fair of the Dead, where vendors sell the candy and the toys that are given to Sicilian children on November 2, All Souls' Day. The streets around Palermo's Archeological Museum are crowded with stalls selling marzipan fruit and sugar statues, and barrows festooned with strings of dried figs and heaped with chestnuts, walnuts, bright red pomegranates, hazelnuts, and almonds. Still others are piled with penny candy and with enormous stacks of *torrone*, a confection similar to peanut brittle, made of almonds, hazelnuts, or sesame seeds in caramelized sugar. The vendors of *torrone* (or *cubaita*, as it is called when sesame seeds are used, a name that comes from the Arabic *qubbayt*) are equipped with gas burners on which to cook their wares, and you can watch them pour the thick syrupy mixture onto an oiled marble slab and flatten it to an even thickness with the cut side of half a lemon. As soon as it cools and begins to harden they cut it into strips, or, in the case of sesame *cubaita*, into diamond-shaped pieces. The recipe below is modern, my mother-in-law's in fact, but it is almost exactly the same as a recipe from eleventh-century Baghdad, which I mention as an etymological curiosity. According to the Orientalist Maxime Rodinson, it is by way of this diamond-shaped candy, known in Arabic as *lawzinag*, that the word "lozenge" entered the European world.

TORRONE DI MANDORLE
(Almond Brittle)

Makes about 2 pounds

1 pound shelled almonds   ½ lemon
1 pound sugar

In a heavy saucepan or skillet heat the almonds and the sugar over a very low flame, stirring constantly (it will take about 20 minutes). The sugar will color very slowly, crystallize around the almonds, and then begin to melt and turn brown. The *torrone* is ready as soon as the sugar is completely melted and a rich brown in color, but be careful as it burns easily. Turn it out onto an oiled marble surface and flatten it into a thin sheet, using the cut side of a half lemon. Allow to cool, and break into pieces, using a heavy knife and a hammer.

———

The sesame-seed version that follows requires the addition of honey as well as sugar.

CUBAITA
(Sesame-Seed Lozenges)

Makes about 2½ pounds

½ cup pistachios   1 cup honey
½ cup toasted almonds   1 cup sugar
3 cups sesame seeds   ½ lemon

Chop the nuts to a very fine grain.

Wash the sesame seeds in a large bowl of water, and discard any that remain floating on the surface. Drain.

Heat the honey and the sugar in a saucepan until the sugar dissolves and the mixture reaches the boiling point. Add the sesame and cook, stirring constantly, about 10 minutes or until the seeds become fragrant. Add the chopped nuts and continue to cook and stir until the mixture is very thick. Pour it onto an oiled surface, preferably marble, and flatten it out to a sheet about ½ inch thick, using the cut side of half a lemon to smooth it out. When partially cooled, cut into inch-wide strips, then cut again diagonally so as to form diamond-shaped pieces.

It would be logical to speak now of another Arabic innovation that spread slowly north from Sicily to the rest of Europe and thence to the United States—another Arabic accumulation of eternal merit on which the Sicilians then elaborated and of which they remain the masters. But ice cream, for it is no less than ice cream of which I speak, in all its magnificent variety of flavors and forms—*granita, gelato, cremolata, cassata, spumoni,* and so on—is such a particular mania of the Sicilians that it deserves a separate chapter, a *gran finale* all its own.

If Trapani and the other cities on the western coast are the centers of Arab-derived cooking today, during the occupation itself it was Palermo that was the economic and cultural capital. Ibn Hawqal, a merchant from Baghdad who visited the city in 977, described a flourishing commercial center crowded with palaces, markets, and more than three hundred mosques. He was somewhat less enthusiastic about local eating habits.

> Despite all these [irrigation canals], in most of the neighborhoods [of Palermo] and in the citadel itself the water is drawn from wells, and is heavy and unhealthy. They have taken to drinking it because of the lack of running water, because they are unaccustomed to thinking, and because of the great amount of onions that they eat. And in truth this food, of which they are very fond and which they eat raw, ruins their senses. There is not one man among them, of whatsoever condition, who does not eat onions every day, and does not serve them morning and evening in his house. It is this that has clouded their imagination; offended their brains; perturbed their senses; altered their intelligence; drowsed their spirits; fogged their expressions, untempered their constitutions so completely that it rarely happens that they see things straight.
>
> Mohammed Ibn Hawqal,
> *Book of the Routes and the Realms*, tenth century

THE CUBULA, *a twelfth-century Arab-Norman pavilion in the royal gardens of Palermo,*
in a nineteenth-century engraving by Bartlett

But most of the descriptions in Arabic that survive today come from a later period, from the twelfth century, after dynastic squabbles in North Africa had left Sicily relatively defenseless against the attack of Norman knights who were descending southward in search of fiefs and riches. Ibn Hamdis, the most famous of the Sicilian Arab poets, wrote in exile, having fled to Egypt after the Norman conquest of Sicily:

> I yearn for my native land, in whose dust are dissolved
>> the bones of my forefathers,
> As lost in the desert, an old and weary camel yearns,
>> among the shadows, for his home.
>>>> Ibn Hamdis, twelfth century

Other Saracens remained at the service of the Norman conquerors, who were not only extraordinarily tolerant of the Arabic culture that they found in Sicily, but highly appreciative as well. Palermo in the twelfth century continued under Norman rule to be one of the largest, richest, and most cosmopolitan cities in Europe. Arab dress became fashionable among the ladies of the court; an Arab chef cooked for the royal table of Roger II; Arabs administered the king's finances, served in the king's bodyguard, built the king's chapels and the king's palaces, and laid out the fabulous gardens and pavilions where the king took his leisure.

> Pass the mellowed golden wine and drink from morn till evening.
> Drink to the sound of lutes, and to songs worthy of the poet Mabad.
> No life can be serene, save that in the shadow of sweet Sicily,
> Under a dynasty far greater than the royal dynasty of the Caesars.
> Here are royal palaces, in which joy has lodged;
> Marvelous abodes to which God has granted perfect beauty!
>
> Abd ar-Rahman of Butera, twelfth century

In the main hall of one of these "marvelous abodes," the palace of the Zisa, a mosaic fountain pours forth water that runs through a series of canals and pools and then out into the garden. It is said that wine was served to the banqueters in small jars, which were cooled in the waters of the fountain and carried across the hall to the banqueting table by the current. Perhaps the wine was prepared according to the following recipe.

> Take one *ratl* (366 gr.) of good mustard and twenty *rub'* of juice of sweet grapes; grind the mustard into a powder; put it through a sieve and mix it with a sufficient quantity of honey. Take a new earthenware jar that has been filled with sweet water for about two days, emptied, and then left open to air for a day. Rub the inside of the jar with the paste of honey and mustard, spreading it in a very even layer, and leave it like that for a day. Then take a plentiful quantity of sweet grape juice; clarify it, and pour it very gently into the jar, filling it up to the edge of the layer of paste. The must will remain sweet, without bad taste and with neither trace nor flavor of mustard; indeed it will last at length, and will become ever more delicate and sweeter. This is prepared in Sicily.
>
> Ibn al-Awwam, *Book of Agriculture*, twelfth century

Unfortunately we have no corresponding descriptions of what the feasting kings may have eaten. Of Roger's coronation banquet we know only that it was served on "plates and goblets of gold and silver . . . with a very great and varied quantity of food and drinks," and that "everyone marveled and was

THE PALACE OF THE ZISA, *the twelfth-century Arab-Norman palace in Palermo*
in a nineteenth-century engraving by Bartlett

amazed, and even those who came from afar were moved to no little awe, because they saw so much more than that which had been rumoured."

To fill the plates of gold and silver we must look in several directions: first to our invaluable allies the visiting foreigners, whose opinions quite naturally differ according to their loyalties. The French scholar Peter of Blois, a victim of power struggles within the royal palace, had nothing good to say about Norman Sicily, diet included: "Your people err in the meagreness of their diets; for they live on so much celery and fennel that it constitutes almost all their sustenance; and this generates a humour which putrefies the body and brings it to the extremes of sickness and even death."

Hugo Falcandus, on the other hand, gives a lyric description of Palermo, to which he came in his youth and where he remained for the rest of his life, an Odysseus who never left the gardens of Alcinoüs.

There shall you admire vineyards as fecund in abundant foliage as they are magnificent in generous and joyful fruit. There shall you see gardens to be commended for the admirable variety of their fruits, and towers constructed to guard the gardens and to serve their patron's pleasure; where with the movement of a turning wheel, with which the buckets descend and rise again, you shall see the wells dry out as the nearby cisterns fill, whence the waters flow in rivulets to every place, to irrigate the gardens, to restore and nourish the cucumbers, small and short, the longer squashes, the melons which grow almost to a sphere, the pumpkins which trained on woven canes spread over a vast area.

Hugo Falcandus, Praefatio ad Petrum, circa 1290

Hugo goes on to describe all the different fruits growing in the gardens of the city: the pomegranates, the lemons and citrons and oranges—"this tree rich in signs of eternal youth which in winter neither becomes ugly and deformed from sterile age nor, assaulted by the harshness of the cold, derobes itself of its leaves, but wreathed in greenest foliage is ever a reminder of sweet spring"—and then the nuts, almonds, figs, olives, dates, and sugarcane.

Both Peter and Hugo testify to the importance of vegetables in the Sicilian diet, in contrast to continental Europe, where the Norman knights had come from and where the diet was monotonous and meat-heavy, and varied little from country to country and from class to class, at least in terms of quality, for the rich ate more or less the same things as the poor, only a great deal more of them. Although population pressures were beginning to make themselves felt, vast tracts of twelfth-century Europe were still untouched by the plow, providing plentiful pasturage and easy hunting. If the peasant could count on a rabbit for his pot, the nobleman would put away course after course of roasted meat: fowl, game, venison, mutton, and beef. A capacious stomach was in fact considered a sign of nobility and character, so much so that three centuries earlier, in 888, Guido of Spoleto lost a crown for lack of appetite. As soon as the Archbishop of Metz, preparing to host a splendid coronation banquet, learned that Guido was of parsimonious eating habits, he gave the crown to someone else, claiming that anyone who could be satisfied by a cheap and meager meal was unfit to reign over the Franks.

The medieval nobleman liked his meat heavily dowsed with spices, but the actual preparation of it was still quite crude. According to Fernand Braudel, "sophisticated cuisine, typical of all advanced civilizations, and found in China in the fifth century and in the Muslim world from the eleventh or twelfth centuries, did not appear in the West until the fifteenth century, and then in the rich city-states of Italy."

We must look then to this same Muslim tradition to which Braudel alludes, a tradition in which qualitative as well as quantitative differences in the way the various classes ate emerged very early: for the rich the exotic ingredients skillfully prepared according to the cookbooks of Damascus and Baghdad, for the poor a humble dish of lentils. This Middle Eastern tradition, which developed under the Abbassid dynasty and drew heavily on Persian cooking (in which Greek and Roman influences are also discernible), was carried by the Arabs to their states in the West, to Spain and to Sicily. Unlike the poets, the geographers, the carpenters, and the weavers from the Muslim world who served the Norman kings, the Arab cooks practiced a more ephemeral art of which no trace remains. But their presence in Palermo is a matter of record, and the tradition in which they were schooled was surely that of the East.

Finally it must be remembered that, regardless of their antecedents, these cooks and kings held court on an island that had spoken Greek for fifteen hundred years, a period in which both the agriculture and the diet had been dominated by wheat.

As early as the twelfth century, therefore, Sicilian cooking once again was drawing its ingredients and its techniques from the entire Mediterranean basin, and could boast a degree of sophistication as yet unknown on the continent. After the brief era of Norman glory, the courts of power moved north. Politically, Sicily was relegated to the margin of European history after the thirteenth century, but gastronomically it continued to export luxury to the north and at the same time to elaborate its own unique and varied culinary traditions. Developing and embroidering upon the materials and methods bequeathed by a succession of foreign conquerors, the members of each class—the feudal nobility established by the Normans, the middle-class merchants and lawyers who inherited an Arab legacy and aspired to the aristocracy, the peasants who sowed and reaped the wheat regardless of who ruled them—created the culinary tradition best suited to the requirements of their pride, their pocketbooks, and their prayers.

3

The Staff of Life...

Eu vidi picchulilli pir li porti sidiri
atorno ben da milli gridandu pan muriri;
lu patri non à figli videndu a sì piriri,
vindii infin a cavigli pir putir pani aviri.

Sichilia duglusa, plina di amancamentu,
ki eri cussì juyusa di tuttu apparamentu,
di grassa eri rifusa et tuttu furnimentu,
ora è multu affamusa, non à mancu furmentu.

I've seen them dying in the streets, the little ones, unfed,
Amidst a thousand living, who weep and beg for bread.
The father is now childless, he's seen his children dead,
He's sold all goods and chattels in order to have bread

Sicily the sorrowful, so full of want and pain,
You who were so joyful in the time of plenty's reign,
Once you were fat with flesh, with bread and fruit and wine,
But now your children starve to death, they haven't even grain.

Anonymous Sicilian poet, late fourteenth century

The 250 years following the death of Frederick II in 1250 erased many of the Arabs' agricultural achievements. Distress and devastation accompanied the passage of the Sicilian throne from Frederick's heirs to the Angevins and—after the French were thrown out by popular revolt during the rebellion in 1282 called the Sicilian Vespers—to the Spanish house of Aragon. Each royal demise or change of dynasty became the occasion for further squabbling among the feudal barons: armies swept the island, firing crops, burning forests and vineyards, and destroying villages. On their heels, in the middle of the fourteenth century, came the Black Death. Many of those who survived fled to the relative safety of the coastal towns; at least half the villages that had supported the prosperous agriculture of the interior disappeared. By 1500 Sicily's population, although growing once more, was still only around 560,000, a sad contrast to the 650,000 souls ruled by the Norman King William II at the end of the twelfth century.

For those who managed to weather the plagues and the power struggles, an age of plenty followed. The exodus from the countryside meant that many of Sicily's wheat fields and orchards reverted to pasture and woodlands. Meat, cheese, and game were plentiful; labor was scarce and therefore salaries high. A fourteenth-century assistant butcher received, in addition to his wages and his shoes, three loaves of bread a day and five and a quarter pounds of meat a week. This was beef or mutton: poultry was a dish fit for an ambassador or a viceroy, since one chicken cost as much as nine or ten pounds of the best beef. Pork, which is rarely included in the price lists of the urban markets, appears to have been consumed only in the countryside.

All this meat—an abundance even by modern standards—was well accompanied. According to contracts in public archives, the gardens within the walls of Palermo, now known as *viridaria*, supplied fifteen different vegetables and twenty different types of fruit, a variety much greater than northern Europe could offer.

The public archives are just part of a wealth of source material on medieval and Renaissance Sicily that is still being explored, and perhaps historians will soon be able to tell us more about the manner in which all this abundance of food was consumed. In the meantime, I shall indulge in a little speculation.

Although the Saracen chefs were gone from the island, together with all the rest of the Arabs, save those who had converted to Christianity and become thoroughly assimilated, a large and prosperous Jewish population remained in Sicily until 1492, when they were suddenly and dramatically expelled by Spanish royal edict. We know that these Jews wrote and spoke Arabic as well as Hebrew (many were immigrants from Moorish Spain); that they were active in commerce, especially with northern Africa; and that they constituted much of the skilled labor that carried on traditions of Arabic craftsmanship in such industries as building and the production of silk and sugar. They also appear to have been the chief consumers of what little olive oil was being produced on the island at the time.

We know, too, that in the fourteenth and fifteenth centuries Sicily was connected by prosperous trading to northern Italy. There was a flourishing

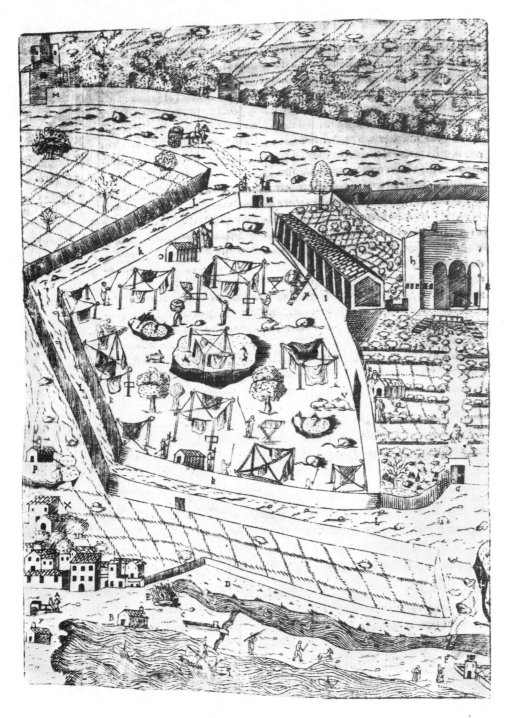

QUARANTINE IN THE TIME OF PLAGUE, *a sixteenth-century engraving*

community of merchants from the maritime republics, some of whom were successful enough to buy or marry their way into the Sicilian nobility, their success based in part on the exportation of Sicilian silk, pasta, sugar, and other luxury goods.

Given these two bridges of trade, one to the south and the other to the north, it is not too far-fetched to hypothesize Sicily as the principal link between the "court cuisine" of twelfth-century Baghdad and Damascus, and the elaborate dishes, many of them very similar to those of the Near East, that appeared on the tables of the Italian Renaissance several centuries later. It seems possible that traditions that had been imported to Palermo by the Arabs were maintained there by the Jews, and then exported to the north by Genoan and Venetian merchants.

If this is speculation, however, there is solid evidence to show that by the time the Jews were expelled from Sicily at the end of the fifteenth century, the basis for what the Sicilians call their *cucina baronale* was already established in the kitchens of the aristocracy. Here it underwent two phases of further elaboration—first under Spanish influence in the age of the baroque, and then, at the turn of the eighteenth century, when the Sicilians discovered the French cuisine. In the greatest establishments the *cucina baronale* became ever more elaborate, while in the households of the provincial nobility and the wealthy bourgeoisie it evolved along simpler lines into what today is considered traditional Sicilian cooking.

Only crumbs from these developments fell, however, to the kitchens of the peasantry. The custom of giving regular rations of meat to workers and apprentices died out after 1500. The sixteenth century brought a period of relative stability and of agricultural expansion that were paradoxically accompanied by an inexorable decline in the quality of the peasant diet.

By 1500 Sicily was part and parcel of the Kingdom of Spain, a minor jewel in the crown of Ferdinand and Isabella. The prosperity generated by the mere fact of geographical position was threatened by the new trade routes that Columbus and others were tracing across the Atlantic, and the fervently Catholic monarchs discouraged the traditional Sicilian commerce with the heathens of North Africa. Sicily's political divorce from the Italian continent isolated her from the ferment of the early Renaissance, an isolation further increased when the Spanish Inquisition established itself, with ample powers, in Palermo after 1487.

DOMESTIC FLOUR MILLS, *an eighteenth-century drawing by Houel*

When Charles I of Spain, founder of the Hapsburg dynasty, inherited both the Spanish throne and the Kingdom of Sicily in 1516, he also inherited a system of power balance between the Sicilian nobility and the foreign crown that was satisfactory enough to both parties to last until 1860, surviving the changes from Hapsburg to Savoy to Bourbon rule. In return for income and, at least in the early centuries, an abundant supply of grain to feed his troops, the king of the moment was content to leave the regulation of internal affairs in the hands of the Sicilian Parliament, an institution of Norman origin that was divided into three chambers: the baronial, the ecclesiastical, and a third composed of representatives of the cities ruled directly by the crown.

The Spanish kings financed their imperial ventures by levying duties on the export of grain and by an annual *donativo*. It was the prerogative of the baronial branch of Parliament to decide how this donation was to be collected. The barons chose to pass the burden down through the social order until it came to rest in an endless list of *gabelle*, indirect taxes on milling, baking, slaughtering, wine pressing and oil pressing, windows and hearths and so on, most of which were paid by the poor.

The nobility, whether lay or ecclesiastic, paid almost no taxes, with the exception of a fixed sum that became the accepted substitute for military service, yet it maintained almost absolute jurisdiction and rights over vast tracts of land. These, the famous *latifondi*, were rented out on an annual basis for fees fixed in advance and independent of the success of the harvest. Both renter and rentee were oriented toward immediate profit—when prices were good new land was broken, only to be left fallow when the market dropped off. There were few incentives, either cultural or economic, for the feudal land-holders to make long-term capital investments aimed at improving the land.

Meanwhile, the population began to increase rapidly, and with it the internal demand for wheat. Pastures gave way to wheat fields, the game-filled forests near the cities were cut down to fuel the sugar mills, and the supply of meat decreased just as population pressures caused salaries to shrink. Meat slowly disappeared from the peasants' diet, returning to their tables once or twice a year for the big holidays (when I arrived in Sicily in the early 1960s, most peasant families could still afford to eat meat only on Sundays), and for the next three centuries a major concern of those governing the island was that of producing bread in sufficient quantity to keep the population from either starving or rebelling.

This obligation should not have been too difficult to fulfill, for despite all the mishap and misadventure Sicily's soil remained fertile. In the thirteenth century wheat cultivated on the island gave a yield of ten bushels harvested to one sown, in contrast to a yield of four to one for the rest of Europe. Equally high yields were still fairly common in the sixteenth century, despite the persistence of very primitive means of cultivation.

But dependence on a single crop renders the farmer extremely vulnerable to atmospheric catastrophe, and there were frequently years in which the entire harvest was destroyed by drought or by locusts. The sixteenth century came to a close during a series of famines, often accompanied by pestilence, that were immensely destructive.

> In this year [1592] thirteen thousand people died in the city of Palermo. Both in the city and outside its gates you can see the dead; and the people who went to the hospitals died there immediately; and, when they were split open, their guts were found to be full of grass. Deputies were appointed, who distributed four pennies' worth of bread a head. . . . And from Calabria a ship arrived full of hens, which were sold in Palermo and taken to the hospitals. And in said hospitals twenty and thirty people died each day. And the poor prisoners, when a dog wandered into the prison, considered themselves blest to get a piece of it, and they ate it only half-cooked.
>
> F. Paruta and N. Palmerino, *Diario della città di Palermo, 1500–1613*

The economic policies with which the island was governed did little to counterbalance the havoc wrought by an ever more arid climate. In the year following the famine described above, Palermo instead celebrated at great expense the arrival in the city of a reliquary containing the head of a local virgin martyr, Santa Ninfa; a grand festival featured a triumphal arch and two enormous triumphal wagons. One wagon, built by the city government,

> was indeed a marvel, pulled by two life-sized elephants, so natural that they appeared alive, and inside these elephants there were more than 100 people, who propelled them without showing themselves. . . . For these festivities the City spent 70 thousand scudos, which it took from the Tavola. And in order to pay this debt a tax was placed upon flour, of 5 tarìs, 13 grana, and 2 picciolos every *salma*, in addition to the 9 tarìs that must be paid today. It was levied for three years; but it will never be removed; because the things that are decreed in this city for two or three years are never removed, but remain forever.
>
> Paruta and Palmerino, *Diario della città di Palermo*

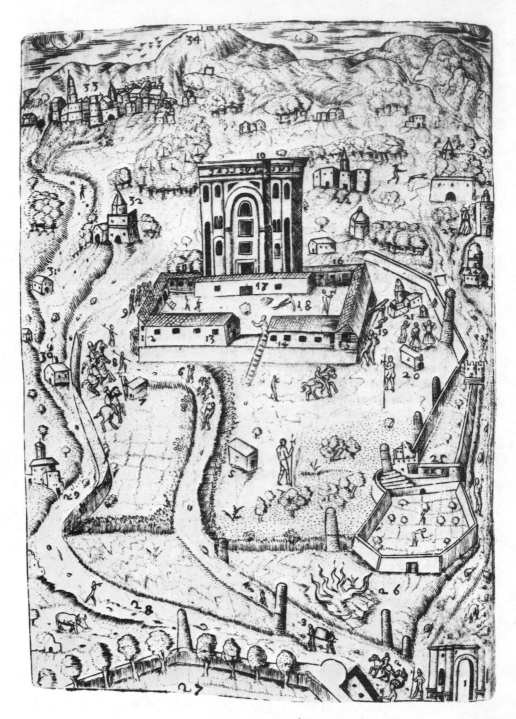

THE ZISA AS A HOSPITAL, *a sixteenth-century engraving*

Taxes on grain, which had to be transported, milled, or stored in the government silos at the ports to await export or distribution on the internal market, were among the easiest to apply and collect. For that very reason they were levied with a hand so heavy as to render Sicilian wheat steadily less competitive on the international markets. When, either because of foreign competition or a particularly abundant harvest, prices fell, the farmers refused to cultivate the fields, and famine often followed.

Various steps were taken to combat this problem, some of dubious effectiveness, as described in two diary entries for 1606:

> *22 October 1606.* A proclamation was made by order of the Marquis of Geraci and of the Royal Patrimony, that on account of the scarcity of wheat men may not wear starched cuffs and collars, under pain of a penalty of ten ounces, and that women may wear what they wish.
>
> *Saturday 18 November 1606.* A proclamation was made on behalf of the most illustrious and most excellent Lord Marquis of Geraci, that because of the scarcity of wheat no sweet biscuits or *mustazzoli* are to be made.
>
> Paruta and Palmerino, *Diario della città di Palermo*

Other measures were more drastic, as when in 1683 Palermo declared a municipal monopoly on the production and sale of bread, in order to provide both the people of Palermo and the hordes of starving peasants who flocked in from the famished countryside with a ration of bread of standard quality and weight at a subsidized price.

Not that the bread from the public bakeries was always all that it should have been.

> *September, 1774.* . . . . [A] youth called Francesco Morici, alias Saturapesci, having furnished himself not with stones but with two loaves of bread from the palace oven of the public bakery of the Piazzetta Grande, formed a band together with a few other lads, friends of his, who, armed with stones as well, were his equal in courage and in years. Together with this courageous group he set forth to the palace of the Senate to manifest his complaints . . . and grasping the bread to his breast, he made with loud voice the following declaration: "People of Palermo, put an end for once to your patience: you have suffered too long. White bread we demand, white bread."
>
> The bread was in truth in bad condition; but it seemed even blacker

seen against the white shirt of this youth. At the same time, however, it
was said that this bread had been baked of poor quality on purpose by the
very persons of the sedition themselves. But this rumor was published in
the aftermath, perhaps in defense of the viceroy, by those who are his
supporters . . . since in fact this bad bread from the aforesaid palace oven
was found to have infected all the public bakeries of the city.

F. M. Emanuele e Gaetani, Marchese di Villabianca,
Diario palermitano, 1774

A visitor from the north might well have thought that Saturapesci was
forgetting his station in life, for elsewhere in Europe white bread was the
prerogative of the rich. The rest of the population had to make do, even in
the fat years, with dark bread made of whole wheat, while in the years of
famine, which came with frequency well into the nineteenth century, the best
they could hope for was ersatz bread made of the most incredible ingredients,
such as the ones suggested by various Italian texts from the sixteenth and
seventeenth centuries:

> Water briar, acorns . . . turnips, rape, couch-grass, lupin, parsnips, wild
> radish, pine-nuts, firtree seeds, laurel berries, wild asparagus, hazelnuts,
> sorb-apples, squash, elm leaves, fava beans, the different legumes (not to
> mention mixtures of inferior grains like millet, panic grass, rye, barley,
> vetch, and sorghum) and in general all the "most innocent and flavorful"
> roots and tubers were the components of that incredible reservoir of un-
> suitable ingredients which, once boiled, dried, pounded, sieved, reduced
> to flour, and mixed together in differing proportions, could become an
> uncertain and approximate bread, vaguely similar to that made of wheat.

Piero Camporesi, *Il pane selvaggio*, 1980

In Sicily this sort of substitution was relatively rare. Lesser grains have
traditionally been cultivated only in small quantities, for ever since the classical
era most of the arable land has been dedicated to the cultivation of *Triticum
durum*, a nutritious hard winter wheat that was much sought after in the past,
since it is particularly resistant to spoilage during transport and storage, a
highly desirable quality in an era of primitive transportation. Today it is this
wheat that is considered to give the best pasta flour.

Durum wheat has a berry that is golden in color and vitreous in consistency,
so that when it is milled it shatters into the grains we know as *semola* or,

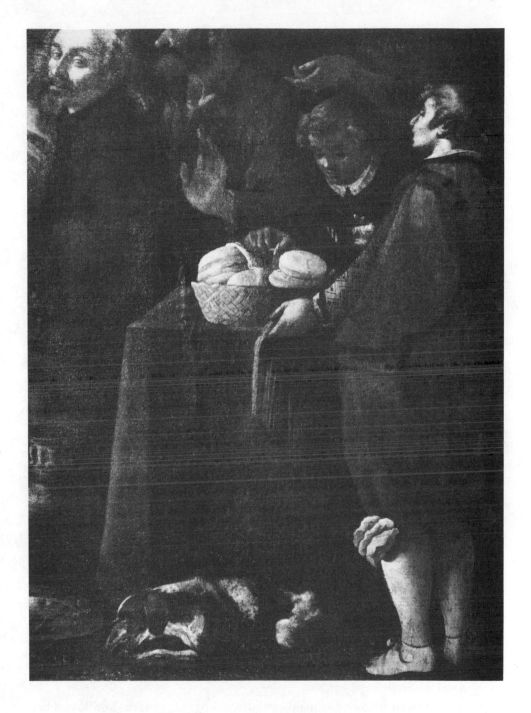

A BASKET OF BREAD, *detail from "The Last Supper," a painting by Pietro D'Asaro, 1621*

depending on the grade, as *semolina*. These tiny grains, if milled a second time, give a silky golden flour called *farina di semola rimacinata*, which makes magnificent bread.

Although the aristocracy and the upwardly mobile townspeople have always eaten white bread made of more expensive soft-wheat flour (a status symbol that makes just about as much sense to me as binding one's feet), the bread that has kept the majority of Sicilians alive across the centuries has been *pane rimacinato*, made of semolina flour, like the bread still sold in my husband's hometown of Alcamo. Baked in round two-pound loaves about ten inches in diameter and three inches high, it is coarse and springy on the inside, dark and chewy and strewn with sesame seeds on the outside, the underside tinged with ashes from a brick oven fired with almond shells.

When my husband was a child, homemade bread was still very common. His grandfather was a man of substance, and the house in Alcamo had two ovens. Upstairs in the first-floor kitchen there was the *tanura*, a beautiful big wood-burning stove built of bricks covered with majolica tiling. The oven was at eye level; on the cooking surface next to it, two or three circular holes held gleaming copper cauldrons, each with its own firebox underneath. This *tanura* served for the everyday cooking, while bread was baked in a bigger oven that stood underneath the family apartments, in a room on the ground floor that held large bins of wheat and flour, and a chicken coop as well. Next door, casks of the family vintages were stored in a wine cellar and a special, locked strongroom was filled with great earthenware jars of olive oil.

The wheat had been grown on family land, of course, and threshed and milled into flour under the watchful eye of my husband's grandfather, thus guaranteeing its quality and purity. No one wanted to eat bread of unknown origin.

My mother-in-law loved to tell me the story of what happened in July 1943, during the Allied invasion. The Simetis were out on the family farm at Bosco when an American reconnaissance plane flew over, very close to the ground, and in a show of muscle fired a round of machine-gun bullets over their heads. As soon as the plane had gone and all were pulling themselves up off the ground, my husband began to shout: "The flour! The flour! What has become of the flour!" Although he was not yet seven, he already had a firm grasp of Sicilian priorities.

Once or twice a week the maidservant would go downstairs and knead the bread in a large, sloping-sided wooden tub called a *madia*. The bread was essentially a sourdough bread, leavened by the *criscenti*, a ball of dough the size of a fist that had been carefully oiled and preserved in a covered bowl from the last baking. The bread dough was kneaded at length and then divided into fifteen pieces, shaped into round, flattish loaves, sprinkled with sesame seeds, and set to rise on long wooden boards, covered with a heavy cotton runner of crocheted rags.

It took about an hour for the bread to rise: the amount of leavening and the consequent time of rising were determined by the length of time necessary to heat the oven. This was done by building a wood fire in it, which was stoked and stirred until the bricks of the oven roof turned white from the heat. Then the fire was scraped out, the embers were shoveled into an iron canister covered with an airtight lid, where they turned to charcoal, and the ashes were put aside to use for shining the copperware.

At this point the risen loaves would be slid into the oven on a long-handled wooden paddle, and the iron door was fitted into place, to be opened in approximately an hour's time.

Those who did not have their own ovens could for a modest fee use the oven of the local bakery. A cousin remembers her family's maidservant setting off twice a week with a ten-kilo sack of flour and the *criscenti* wrapped in a clean napkin.

The large front room of the bakery had rows of *madie*, where women of the neighborhood could knead their bread. The baker charged according to the number of kilos of flour employed, and when the loaves were shaped and incised with the owner's initials, he would carry them into a smaller room behind the oven, where they were set on racks to rise. No one but the baker was allowed to enter the back room, and it was common knowledge that he had made this rule so that unobserved he could steal a small piece of dough from the bottom of each loaf. My cousin's mother told the maid to put sesame seeds on the underside as well, thus foiling the baker. When he complained about this practice, the maid would merely smile and say: "That's the way the signora likes her bread."

All this ended with the Second World War. *Tanure* and bread ovens have been dismantled in most houses, rich and poor alike. Within the towns professional bakers haven't time for homemade efforts. And middle-class families who still have ovens in their country houses use them on special occasions for making pizza or roasting lamb, much as an American family uses its barbecue. Only a few peasant women of the older generations still bake their own bread regularly, and it is becoming rarer and rarer for them to do so.

The close, proprietary relationship with the wheat itself disappeared when mechanization revolutionized Sicilian agriculture in the postwar period. The wheat is harvested and threshed by enormous combines and trucked to government or cooperative storage silos. Few mills accept anything less than a truckload of grain, and the grain itself now comes from new hybrid varieties, much more productive, but much lower in gluten. (This has so adversely affected pasta production that the Buitoni and the Barilla companies have sent agents out looking for farmers who are willing to cultivate the old strains especially for these factories.)

Nevertheless, it is still possible to find delicious *pane rimacinato* in Sicily. In general the bread here is excellent, and outside the big cities, in the smaller towns where the bakers have continued to use wood ovens, it can be fabulous. That is how I would describe the bread that I buy at the Panificio San Francisco in Alcamo. The Lombardo brothers who own this bakery have a fancy new electric oven with an electric leavening chamber, but they also have an enormous brick oven, which they fire with almond shells. This choice of fuel, dictated by questions of comfort (the almond-shell fire needs less tending than one of wood, and can be stirred easily by a long-handled shovel, thus allowing the bakers to stand further back from the hot flames), has the happy side effect of imparting a special flavor to the bread.

The Lombardos make their *pane rimacinato* in the old way, using the *criscenti*, but add a small amount of fresh yeast to speed the rising process, since they have so many batches of bread to bake each day. The big round loaves are baked in the brick oven. Smaller ones of various shapes are baked in the electric oven, and although malt is added to give them color and steam is injected into the oven to improve the crust, the end result is very different.

The *pane rimacinato* I buy during the winter when we are in Palermo comes from the electric oven of the bakery on the ground floor of our apartment building. I eat it with pleasure, although it is much less coarse in texture than the Alcamo bread and, to my mind, less interesting. But in compensation the bakery will deliver it still hot from the oven to my door twice a day (heaven forbid that at supper one should eat bread that was baked before noon!).

The result of such coddling is that I do not know how to make bread. In more than twenty-five years in Sicily I have learned how to make wine and to cure olives, and have acquired a myriad other unlikely skills. But, with a wealth of wonderful bread at arm's reach, I have never felt the urge to conquer the mysteries of kneading and leavening. To be absolutely honest, there has been a downright refusal on my part: I vetoed my husband and children's suggestion that the restoration of the farm should extend to rebuilding the oven that had caved in during the earthquake. I knew that in the happy scenes of pizza making that they were imagining, they had failed to notice that something was lacking: our available family includes none of the sisters, aunts, mothers, and in-laws who, elsewhere in Sicily, take turns at the kneading.

For the purposes of this book, I have done considerable research on how Sicilian bread is made. Most of the people to whom I have talked, however, learned to make bread as fairly small children, either at their mother's side or as their father's apprentice. They are not people accustomed to pondering questions of cause and effect, nor are they particularly articulate in describing what they know how to do from habit or experience: the dough at any given stage should be "not too much and not too little," or else it should be *come Dio comanda*—"as God orders." I have neither a direct line to the Almighty nor knowledge of my own with which to supplement such vague directions, and my experiments have given only mediocre results.

I comfort myself with thoughts on the ineffableness of baking, inspired by the story I was told about a family in Alcamo, bakers for four generations, who moved to Pallavicino, some thirty miles away, and opened a bakery there. They brought their equipment with them, they continued to use the same flour, they tried and tried, they even went so far as to transport canisters of water from their old taps, but they were never able to produce bread in Pallavicino that was as good as the bread they had made in Alcamo.

The recipe that follows will make an adequate *pane rimacinato* dough for use in making *impanata* and other recipes in this chapter. It will also provide an initial *criscenti* for any accomplished bakers who would like to experiment for themselves. It should be made with semolina flour ground so fine as to be silky to the touch, if you can find it, or with what is known in the United States as durum-wheat flour.

PASTA DI PANE RIMACINATO
(Sicilian Bread Dough)

5 teaspoons active dry yeast granules or scant 2 ounces fresh brewer's yeast	7½ cups semolina or durum-wheat flour
2½ cups lukewarm water	Salt (about 2 teaspoons)
	¼ cup olive oil

Dissolve the yeast in 1 cup of the water and let it stand for 15 minutes, until a foam develops.

Put the flour in a large mixing bowl and make a well in it. Pour the dissolved yeast into the well, then stir it into the flour with your fingers, running them around the edge of the well until all the flour is gathered in. Then rub the dampened flour between the palms of your hands until you achieve a uniform consistency throughout.

Add the remaining water, little by little, rubbing and stirring until you have a dough that holds together. Turn it out onto a floured board or tabletop and knead it for 3 to 4 minutes. Punch it soundly a few times with your fists to develop the gluten, then shape it into a ball, place it in a large oiled bowl, cover the bowl, and set the dough to rise for an hour. In Sicily a woolen blanket is usually placed over the bowl in wintertime, but in centrally heated American kitchens this is probably not necessary.

When the dough has almost doubled in size and its surface has begun to crack, turn it out onto a floured board or tabletop. If you want to make *criscenti* with which to make more bread on another day, this is the moment to do so. Take some of the dough, roll it into little balls about the size of golf balls, oil the surface of each ball well, and place them in an airtight jar. Refrigerated, these balls will keep for about a week. Each one, when kneaded at room temperature with ¾ cup of flour and a little water and left to rise overnight (here too you must oil the surface, otherwise a crust will form), will give the yeast for 2 pounds of flour. If you know what you are doing you need only one ball of dough for all subsequent bread, because that in turn will provide enough yeast for the next *criscenti*, but the first time around it's probably a good idea to make several, just in case.

Knead the remaining dough for a minute, then flatten it out with your fists. Sprinkle it with some salt and one-third of the olive oil. Fold the dough over upon itself, knead it until the oil is absorbed, and then punch it until it is flattened out again. Repeat twice more, tasting in between to gauge whether more salt is needed. The dough is now ready for use in the recipes beginning on page 123.

———

A diet based on *pane rimacinato* is open to as much variety as one's resources, both in finance and in fantasy, permit. First of all, there is the question of *companatico*—a wonderful word that means "accompaniment to bread" and that can indicate whatever the landowner is required by contract to provide for his workers along with their loaves of bread, or whatever a mother can find to keep her children happy:

> The more fortunate ones, like me, could eat, when we were children, bread and cheese, bread and apples, or jujubes with their faded purple-pink colors, olives in oil, or roasted on the coals. Or soak our bread in honeyed *vino cotto*, or in the juice of black mulberries, come to Sicily from the southern shores of the Caucasus, from Persia and from Greece. At other times we ate bread to which our mothers would add thin slices of more

bread, telling us "You can pretend that the thinner bread is the thigh of
a pheasant, a stewed hen's ventricle or *biscotti regina*."

Giuseppe Bonaviri, L'incominciamento, 1983

Bread all by itself is known as *schiettu* ("nubile"), whereas married to a *companatico* it becomes *maritatu*, and there is a proverb describing the Palermitani as *Pani schiettu e Cassaro*, loosely translated as "Plain bread and Broadway," which pokes fun at the Palermitani's love of conspicuous consumption, and their willingness to forgo *companatico* in favor of finery in which to stroll up and down the main street.

A field worker in the past would at best have onions or olives as a *companatico*. (My son once announced that his friend Antonio was on *pane e olive*; it turned out that Antonio was eating well but lacked a girlfriend.) Whatever the worker might bring from home to eat today, whether a tomato salad, a dish of *caponata*, or some meatballs in tomato sauce, it is still essentially a *companatico*, with lots of juice to be mopped up.

Sicilians have also found a great many ways to vary and embellish their bread before they put it in the oven. Just the mixing and kneading varies enough from place to place to give each town's bread a distinctive character, and minor changes in the ingredients can radically alter the finished product. Poppy seed is used in place of sesame in some towns, and my cleaning woman says that when she was a young girl her neighbors used to knead elderberry flowers into their dough, an oddly Renaissance touch in a tiny mountain town.

On Saturday nights the bakeries in Alcamo sell *muffolette*, soft, flat rolls made of *pane rimacinato* dough that has been kneaded with more water than used for regular bread, and is flavored with fennel seeds. The purist takes them home still hot, splits them open, toasts them lightly on the fire, and then fills them with fresh ricotta, anchovies, oregano, and olive oil. In my family we are enthusiastic purists, but we also buy a few extra for Sunday breakfast.

More variety comes from using bread dough for purposes other than making bread. Eastern Sicily in particular has a confusing abundance of such dishes—some baked and some fried, some sealed between two crusts in a pie pan, some rolled over on themselves like a strudel or folded into a half-moon like a *calzone*, all subject to a variety of fillings. The same name denotes different techniques from one town to another, so that the *impanata* of Messina differs in appearance from that of Syracuse or that of Modica. I am including three archetypal recipes with alternative fillings for each: outer form may be paired to inner grace as fancy dictates.

When I want to make one of these, I simply buy *pane in pasta*—unbaked bread dough—from the bakery downstairs. Those who lack this commodity can use dough prepared according to the recipe on p. 120, or even experiment with whatever is available in the way of frozen pizza and bread doughs.

IMPANATA
(Bread Pie)

Makes 2 nine-inch pies

⅔ recipe *pane rimacinato* dough, about 2 pounds (see p. 120)

The *impanata* is simply a pie in which bread dough has been rolled out to a thickness of about ¼ inch and used to form the two crusts. Oil one 12-inch pie pan or two 9-inch pans. Line with a sheet of bread dough, add the filling, and cover with another sheet of dough. Seal the edges and poke vents in the upper crust with a fork. Bake in a 400° F oven for 30 minutes. If you are serving the *impanata* as a first course, this recipe will serve 12, as a main course 6 to 8.

FILLING I   Combine:

1½ pounds raw Swiss chard, washed, drained, and chopped
8 dried tomatoes, cut into small pieces

Crushed red pepper to taste
Salt to taste
¼ cup olive oil

FILLING II   Combine:

1½ pounds cauliflower or broccoli, cut into flowerets and cooked *al dente* in boiling salted water
¼ pound raw fresh Sicilian sausage, crumbled, or ¼ pound ground pork plus ¼ teaspoon fennel seeds

¼ pound tuma, primosale, or mozzarella cheese, diced
Salt and freshly ground black pepper to taste
¼ cup oil

FILLING III   Combine:

2 pounds spinach, washed,
  steamed, and chopped
1 pound fresh ricotta
Salt and freshly ground black
  pepper

½ cup grated caciocavallo or
  parmesan cheese

SCACCIE
(Stuffed Bread Rolls)

Serves 6

⅔ recipe *pane rimacinato* dough,
  about 2 pounds (see p. 120)

Scaccie are disks of bread dough that are spread with a filling and
rolled up more or less like a strudel. You can make small *scaccie*
as individual servings, or large ones to serve in slices. This recipe
will make 6 *scaccie* about 9 inches long, sufficient for 6 people
as a main dish.

Divide the dough into 6 equal parts and stretch or roll each
piece into a disk no more than ¼ inch thick. Spread the filling
over the disk and roll it up, sealing the ends and the seam
carefully. Bake on a greased cookie sheet in a 400°F. oven for
about 30 minutes.

FILLING I

4 eggplants, cut into slices
  and fried until brown in
  olive oil
6 ripe tomatoes, peeled,
  drained, and chopped
½ cup chopped fresh basil
  leaves

½ cup grated caciocavallo or
  parmesan cheese
3 tablespoons olive oil
Salt and freshly ground black
  pepper

FILLING II

1½ pounds fresh ricotta
6 scallions, sliced
½ cup grated caciocavallo or
   parmesan cheese

2 eggs
Salt and freshly ground
   black pepper

PITUNI
(Fried Turnovers)

Makes 18 to 20 turnovers

FILLING I

3 heads escarole, washed and
   chopped into small pieces
¼ pound diced tuma,
   primosale, or mozzarella
   cheese

10–12 anchovy fillets,
   cut in pieces
½ cup olive oil
Salt and freshly ground
   black pepper

FILLING II

6 onions, sliced very fine
   and fried until soft in
½ cup olive oil

½ cup capers

⅔ recipe *pane rimacinato*
   dough, about 2 pounds
   (see p. 120)

Vegetable oil or lard
   for deep frying

Combine all ingredients of the filling you choose.

Divide the dough into small pieces (about 18–20) and flatten them out into disks about 5 inches across and ¼ inch thick. Place 2 heaping tablespoons of filling on each disk, moisten the edges, fold over into a half-moon and seal carefully. Deep fry in abundant and very hot oil until golden brown.

At the other end of the island, in the province of Trapani, bread dough is used to make a sort of pizza liberally sprinkled with oregano: hence its name, which means "oreganata."

RIANATA
(Oregano Pizza)

Makes 2 twelve-inch pizzas

⅔ recipe *pane rimacinato* dough, about 2 pounds (see p. 120)

1 large red onion, cut in very thin slices

4 large ripe tomatoes, peeled, seeded, and chopped

½ pound fresh caciocavallo, primosale, or mozzarella cheese, diced

10 anchovy fillets, cut in small pieces (optional)

½ cup olive oil

4 tablespoons dried oregano

Salt and freshly ground black pepper

Oil two 12- or 13-inch pizza pans. Divide the dough in half, and spread one-half out over each of the pans, stretching it with your fingers.

Cover the dough with a layer of onion slices, then sprinkle with the tomatoes, cheese, anchovies, olive oil, and oregano, in that order. Top with a pinch of salt and a little black pepper. Bake in a 450°F. oven for 20 to 30 minutes.

———

Palermo seems never to have developed as many ways of using bread dough, probably because the municipal monopoly on baking meant that for several centuries it was illegal to bake bread at home. It does have, however, something called *sfincione*, a springy, rather oily sort of pizza made with soft-wheat flour, which is baked in large rectangular pans and cut into squares.

SFINCIONE
(Palermo Pizza)

Makes 2 thick 9-inch pizzas

DOUGH

2 ounces compressed yeast or
  6 teaspoons dry granules
2½ cups (approximately)
  warm water

5½ cups flour (see p. 41)
3 tablespoons olive oil
Liberal pinch of salt

TOPPING

1 large onion
1 cup water
½ cup olive oil
1½ cups plain tomato sauce
  (see p. 172)
Salt and freshly ground
  black pepper
8 anchovy fillets, cut in pieces

¼ pound caciocavallo,
  primosale, or mozzarella
  cheese, diced
1 cup toasted breadcrumbs
  (see p. 12)
2 tablespoons dried oregano
2 tablespoons olive oil

Dissolve the yeast in ½ cup warm water. Stir in about ¾ cup of the flour, blend well, and form a ball. Allow to rise for about 30 minutes.

Chop the onion into small pieces, simmer it in 1 cup of water until soft, then drain. Sauté the onion in olive oil until golden. Add the tomato sauce and simmer for 10 minutes. Season with salt and pepper.

Put the remaining flour in a heap on a pastry board. Place the risen dough in the middle and work the flour and the salt into it, adding as much of the remaining 2 cups of water as is needed to make a dough that is soft and elastic. Knead it until it no longer sticks to the working surface. Then add 3 tablespoons of olive oil and work the dough until the oil has been completely absorbed.

Oil liberally two 9-inch cake pans. Divide the dough in two, and put half in each pan, spreading it out with your fingers so that it covers the bottom in an even layer (unlike a pizza, this should not be thicker at the rim). Distribute the pieces of anchovies and of cheese over the dough, sticking them down in as far as they will go. Spread the tomato and onion sauce evenly over the dough. Mix the breadcrumbs and oregano together, and sprinkle them in an even layer over the sauce. Cover the pans and leave them to rise for 2 hours.

Bake for 30 minutes in a 425°F. oven. Sprinkle the *sfincione* with 2 tablespoons of olive oil before serving.

———

Perhaps the most significant recipe for bread is really not a recipe at all but a proverb, the first Sicilian proverb I learned when I came here. It moved me greatly even though I could not then appreciate how quintessential it was.

S'avissi pignateddu,	If I had a saucepan,
acqua e sali,	water and salt,
facissi pani cottu	I'd make bread stew
—avennu pani.	. . . if I had bread.

The truth is that however nutritious and flavorful and varied a diet based on *pane rimacinato* might potentially be, even this became steadily less available to the Sicilian peasantry during the seventeenth and eighteenth centuries. The repeated if ineffectual promulgation of sumptuary laws and the abundant splendor of Sicilian baroque architecture are two different witnesses to the considerable wealth that was still being produced on the island, but this wealth circulated in the hands of a very few and was rarely reinvested in agricultural improvements. The condition of the people in the countryside grew steadily worse, and if numerous writers wrote with pious approval of the abstemious eating habits of the peasants and their abhorrence of meat, there were others who recognized hunger when they saw it.

The farmer's wife bakes her bread each Saturday, but alas! two thirds of that bread goes every Monday before dawn into her husband's knapsack; a third part, and in this is included the bran (we call it *ranza*), remains for the family's consumption, and often the family has more mouths than it needs. The husband during the day eats only bread, accompanied by, although not always, half an onion or three or four olives; and when even such a meager accompaniment is lacking, he sprinkles his bread with a pinch of ginger, which he carries with him in a holder made from a cane; his evening meal is a soup of fava beans, which have had their shells trimmed and in dialect are called *pizzicati*. His wife and children, for whom bread is often an object of luxury, ease their hunger in the winter with carobs, in spring with wild greens, in the autumn with the fruit of the prickly pear.

Serafino Amabile Guastella,
L'antica carnevale nella Contea di Modica, 1887

PRICKLY PEARS, *a nineteenth-century engraving by Vuillier*

Guastella is describing scenes from his boyhood in the early nineteenth century, but parliamentary inquiries carried out at the beginning of the twentieth century revealed little or no improvement, at least in the conditions of the salaried day laborers, who in 1871 represented more than 60 percent of those employed in agriculture.

HARVEST FESTIVAL, *an eighteenth-century drawing by Houel*

If hunger is one—and possibly the best—reason for looking upon bread as the staff of life, the Sicilian peasant was also heir to a centuries-old iconography of bread, an awe and veneration for this basic foodstuff that is lost to contemporary America. Even today the Sicilian feels closer to the ancients in this regard than he would to the diet-conscious U.S. housewife who "tries not to keep bread in the house."

For the Greeks, in fact, the cultivation of grain and the baking of bread were the distinctive marks of civilized man: "men who eat bread" is the conventional formula with which Homer distinguishes the Greeks and their likes from giants and lotus eaters and other exotic and barbaric races. All activities involving the production and processing of wheat were circumscribed by an intricate net of invocations, taboos, rituals, and festivities, many of which have survived to the present century, albeit in a more or less Christianized version. The first ears of ripened wheat, which are still offered to the Madonna in many towns of the Sicilian interior, were once placed on the altars of Demeter, and it is hard to tell just where on the religious continuum one should place the eighteenth-century harvest festival witnessed by Houel:

> In the countryside surrounding this town [Catania], the peasants celebrate the wheat harvest with a sort of orgy, a popular festival of thanksgiving for the good harvest they have gathered. Young people dancing in a circle open the procession; they are followed by a man riding on an ass and beating a drum; five or six men similarly mounted parade after him carrying long poles decorated from top to bottom with sheaves of wheat; in their midst another man, also mounted, carries a large banner which floats majestically in the breeze. A young woman, dressed in white and seated on an ass, comes next; she is surrounded by men on foot who carry bunches of wheat on their heads and in their arms, and who seem to be paying her homage. An entire crowd of country people follow this procession, playing on different musical instruments.
>
> The most educated people in Catania have assured me that this is a very old custom, of which the origins are unknown; but they do not doubt that it is a remnant of the ancient festivals dedicated to Ceres, and that the young woman represents this goddess, to whom the harvests thought to have been obtained through her good will are offered.
>
> Jean Houel, *Voyage pittoresque*, 1785

The Greeks were not the only people in the ancient world to venerate bread. Ever since the Egyptians first stumbled upon the mystery of leavening, some four millennia before the birth of Christ, bread has played an important part in the religious traditions of the Near East, and this liturgy of bread was easily absorbed by the followers of Moses, of Christ, and of Mohammed. Documents in the Palermo archives speak of Muslim Sicilians who take oaths *tacto pane ad legem Mukumet*—touching bread according to Mohammedan law. And bread was, of course, central to the celebration of the Jewish Passover and the Christian Eucharist.

In Sicily the symbolic value of bread was not confined to the churches. At home, the women who kneaded and baked bread paused at each step to recite special prayers and invocations, such as this one from southeastern Sicily, to be uttered just as the last loaf is placed in the oven.

Pattri, Figghiu e Spirdussantu	Father, Son, and Holy Ghost
pozza crìsciri n'àuttru tantu;	may the bread double in size;
Santa Rrosulia,	Santa Rosalia,
iancu e rrussu comu a-ttia;	white and red just like you;
nné-gghiàriu nné-passatu	neither acid nor grown stale,
comu Mmaria senza piccatu;	just like Mary without sin;
crisci pani ô furnu	may the bread grow in the oven,
comu Ggesuzzu crisciu nta lu munnu.	just as little Jesus grew in this world.

Antonino Uccello, *Pani e dolci di Sicilia*, 1976

Once baked, bread must be treated with the greatest respect: in the past the task of slicing the bread was the prerogative of the head of the household, who would trace the sign of the cross over the loaf before touching the knife to it, and would take care never to place it upside down on the table. Probably few Sicilians still believe that if they let a breadcrumb fall on the floor they will be punished in the hereafter by having to gather it up with their eyelashes. And few families today would do as my husband's family did when he was small: kiss a piece of bread that had fallen on the floor before throwing it away (not into the garbage, of course, but to the chickens). Nonetheless to waste bread is still considered very, very wrong.

This pious frugality no doubt helps to explain the importance of bread-crumbs in Sicilian cooking. Breadcrumbs were commonly used to thicken sauces in both Roman and Renaissance recipes, and this may be where the Sicilian habit of sprinkling them over pasta originated, but elsewhere their function is economical. An addition of breadcrumbs serves to stretch out more expensive ingredients such as meat or eggs: when our tenant farmer's wife prepares meatballs for the harvest crew, she mixes the ground meat with almost twice its quantity in breadcrumbs. Another harvest favorite is *frittatine*, eggs beaten up with breadcrumbs, parsley, and cheese, fried in little omelets about two inches in diameter, and then simmered like meatballs in tomato sauce. The memory of such economy remains in the different kinds of *involtini* that are to be found on almost every restaurant menu in Sicily, in which slices of meat or fish or even eggplant are wrapped around a breadcrumb stuffing.

Piety can be expressed not only in the use of bread but also in its shaping. The forms of *pane rimacinato*—the rings and braids and curves into which Sicilian bakers, be they housewives or professionals, fashion the dough—are legion. Most perpetuate ancient traditions, like the flower-shaped *rosetta* or the braided *mafalda* or the ring-shaped *cucciddatu*, which an English traveler to nineteenth-century Catania found "hanging in bunches upon forked sticks on the outside of almost every cottage door." All these can be traced back through the centuries in the descriptions of Theocritus, in the ashes of Pompeii, and in the carvings on the Adelphia sarcophagus in the Archeological Museum at Syracuse.

Bread dough is also fashioned for the amusement of children into dolls and animals: roosters or birds or fish for the fun of it, and spectacles for Saint Lucy (the patron of eyesight), grasshoppers for Saint Biagio, and twin children for the feast of Saints Cosimus and Damian. And, to celebrate pure creative verve, into the intricate Nativity scenes, scaly crocodiles, or three-foot motorcycles complete in every detail that are displayed by the Palermo Bakers' Confraternity at their annual exhibit.

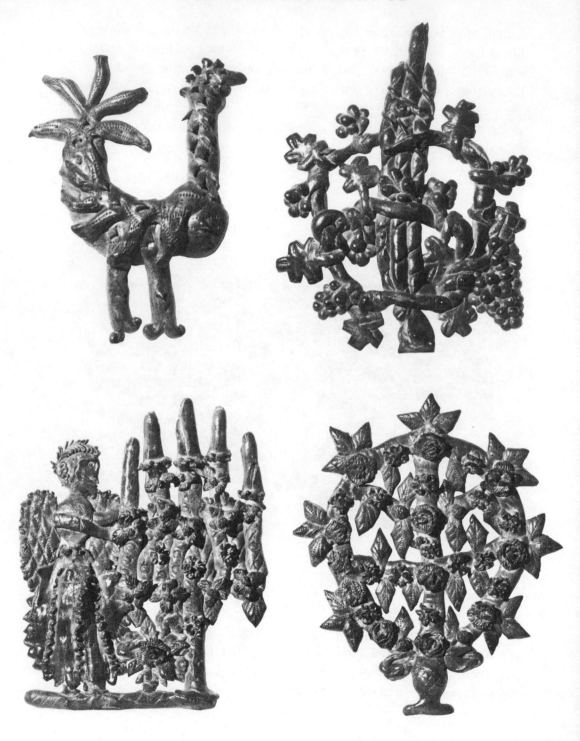

Of all the various saints, Catholic, pagan, or postmodern, to whom these edible votive offerings are dedicated, the most important is Saint Joseph. He is celebrated on March 19 with a ritual banquet known as the *altare di San Giuseppe*. Like the bread around which it revolves, the shape and the liturgy of this ritual vary greatly from town to town. In some places it is a votive offering from the whole community, but more frequently the banquet is offered by a single family whose prayers the saint has answered—a thanksgiving for an illness cured or a disaster averted.

In the mountain towns east of Palermo, the banquet is a fairly simple meal prepared in enormous quantity and served to all and anyone, friend or stranger, who passes by. At the one I attended in Làscari we ate in four shifts of at least sixty people each, including all the members of the town band. Elsewhere it is traditional to prepare a very elaborate meal for the benefit of three poverty-stricken townspeople dressed up for the occasion as the Holy Family. In Alcamo, for example, a professional Saint Joseph, an old man known as a *San Giusepparo*, who knows the rites and prayers, chooses a young girl and a little boy of his family or acquaintance to play Mary and the Christ Child. Costumed and crowned with flowers, the "saints" wander up and down the street, knocking on doors from which they are turned away, until they arrive at the house of the family that has prepared the altar. This door is flung wide and with cheers and music the saints are welcomed in.

There is also considerable variation in the dishes that are served at Saint Joseph's altar, but these always include legumes and bread. The former may appear, as at Làscari, in the simple guise of *pasta con fagioli*. Or they may go almost unremarked amidst the ten or fifteen different first courses of a banquet at Alcamo or Salemi. Elsewhere legumes play a protagonist's role: in the interior and to the south the main dish of the day is often a special soup, made of all different kinds of legumes mixed together, the leavings of the past year's harvest. These soups are reminiscent of the Roman *tisanum* described in Chapter One, and like *cuccìa* and other ritual dishes bear witness to the conservative power of religious tradition.

I have never managed to stray far enough from home on Saint Joseph's Day to taste any of these soups in their proper setting, and my expectations as I approached the recipes in the Sicilian cookbooks were anthropological rather than gastronomic. The rest of the family shared my skepticism when I brought one to the table, but we were very pleasantly surprised. This is a soul-satisfying soup, and to a hungry wanderer on a raw March day it would indeed seem like a gift from heaven. The ingredients would change, of course, from place to place and from year to year, depending on what the fields and the cupboard had to offer, so don't feel that you can't try the soup because you lack one or two ingredients from the list.

MACCU DI SAN GIUSEPPE
(Saint Joseph's Soup)

Serves 6 to 8

½ pound dried shelled fava
  beans
¼ pound dried Borlotti or
  kidney beans
¼ pound dried chickpeas
½ pound dried chestnuts or
  ¾ pound fresh, shelled
¼ pound dried split peas
¼ pound dried lentils
2 dried tomatoes, cut into
  small pieces

1 onion, sliced
1 teaspoon fennel seeds
3 ribs celery
3 sprigs fresh wild fennel
1 large bunch fresh
  borage shoots
½ pound fresh spinach or
  Swiss chard
Salt and freshly ground
  black pepper
¼ cup olive oil

Soak the fava beans, Borlotti or kidney beans, chickpeas, and chestnuts overnight in abundant water (if using fresh chestnuts, you don't need to soak them). Add the split peas and the lentils for the last hour or two of soaking.

Drain and place in a large earthenware pot with 9 to 10 cups of water. Bring to a boil and simmer for about 3 hours or until all the legumes are tender.

After the first hour and a half, add the tomatoes, onion, and fennel seeds. Chop the celery and other greens into fairly small pieces, and add them to the soup. Salt to taste. About 5 minutes before removing from the heat, correct the salt and add pepper and olive oil.

Note: Pino Correnti suggests accompanying the soup with croutons fried in olive oil, and although these are not an orthodox presence at the altar of San Giuseppe, they are a good idea.

———

Legumes also appeared most unexpectedly at the end of the banquet in Làscari, when baskets of fried turnovers called *cassateddi* were passed about, and turned out to be filled not with the usual sweet ricotta but with chickpeas, boiled and mashed with sugar and spices.

CASSATEDDI DI CECI
(Sweet Chickpea Turnovers)

Makes about 3 dozen

PASTRY

3¾ cups flour	½ cup white wine
⅓ cup sugar	(approximately)
Pinch of salt	½ cup lard

FILLING

2 cups puréed boiled chickpeas (cooked without salt)	¼ cup almonds, toasted and chopped
¼ cup honey	1 teaspoon ground cinnamon
¼ cup sugar	¼ cup semisweet chocolate bits
¼ cup pine nuts, toasted and chopped	¼ cup diced *zuccata* (see p. 94) or candied citron

Vegetable oil for frying	Sugar
Cinnamon	

Sift together the flour, sugar, and salt onto a marble or wooden surface. Make a well, and add the wine slowly, using just as much as it takes to keep the dough together. Cut the lard into small pieces and knead it piece by piece into the dough. Knead for at least 15 minutes, working the dough out into a long strip and then folding it back on itself so as to incorporate as much air as possible, until you have a very smooth and elastic dough that is shiny but not greasy to the touch. Cover the dough and let it stand for at least 1 hour.

Mix together all the ingredients for the filling, and blend well.

Roll out the dough to a very thin sheet, and cut out 3-inch disks. On each disk place a scant tablespoon of filling. Fold the disk over into a half-moon and, moistening the edges with a little water, seal them carefully.

Fry the turnovers in abundant and very hot (about 375°F.) vegetable oil (at least 3 inches deep) until they are delicately browned. Drain on absorbent paper and serve while still warm, sprinkled with ground cinnamon and superfine sugar, or granulated sugar that has been ground to a fine texture in a mortar.

Note: Some people prefer to make *cassateddi* dough using ⅓ cup white wine and ⅓ cup *vino cotto*, and eliminating the sugar.

————

At Làscari we were given bread with our meal as well as legumes; it was special bread only in that, as ritual required, it had been baked at home. At the altars over which San Giuseppe presides "in person," bread assumes much greater significance. One of the more common loaves is the ring-shaped *cucciddatu*. In the past the *cucciddati* that were baked for San Giuseppe were enormous, weighing as much as twenty-five pounds and requiring that some of the bricks around the oven door be removed before they could be put in to bake. The saints would carry the *cucciddati* home at the end of the ceremony, slung over their shoulders like coils of rope. But today the poor are no longer so poor as to welcome twenty-five pounds of stale bread, and the *cucciddati* have shrunken noticeably.

In the towns west of Palermo the altars themselves, spectacularly decorated with intricate forms of bread, become the center of attention: the women of these towns work together for weeks to prepare the altars, in a marathon of collective creativity in which they obviously and rightfully take great pride.

In Salemi, a small town in the Belice Valley, the altar is placed within a most extraordinary bower, constructed of poles covered with myrtle branches, decorated with oranges and lemons, and hung with hundreds of little breads, each one lovingly fashioned into a flower, a beast, a saint; roses, daisies, and fava beans in their pods; butterflies, birds, and fish; even Saint Joseph himself, the bread of his monk's habit colored dark brown by cocoa added to the dough.

The amount of bread baked varies according to the possibilities of the family: a modest altar would require 350 to 400 pounds of durum-wheat flour, and more than a week's work on the part of eight or ten women, but a really fancy altar could employ as much as 900 pounds of flour.

The bread dough is prepared with a *criscenti*, the same way as normal bread, except that the amount of water is slightly reduced. The dough must be kneaded, with the help of one's feet when the quantities are big enough, just as *Dio comanda*, so that it has a very fine grain and no large bubbles, which would distort the shapes. It is then shaped into the basic forms and "put to bed" under tablecloths and woolen blankets.

After this single rising, the details—the flower petals and tiny birds, the decorative cuts and curlicues—are added, the surface is brushed with egg beaten up with a few drops of lemon juice, and the bread is ready to be put in the oven to bake.

Once they have finished with the bread, the women set to cooking the banquet. One family told me with understandable pride that they had prepared sixty-two different dishes. Of each of these the children representing the Holy Family would eat barely a mouthful, and they would distribute the rest to the people who came to see the altar.

Unlike in Salemi, in Alcamo there is no bread on the canopy itself, which in older and simpler times was contrived out of the best fringed silk bedspread. Nowadays it is possible to rent an entire stage set with receding arches, angels clinging to rococo columns, and a banner reading, "Long Live Jesus, Mary, and Joseph!"

Here the bread is fashioned into about twenty large forms, each with precise symbolic significance, and into a series of smaller, merely decorative pieces, all of which are displayed on a seven-tiered reredos behind the altar. At the top is the monstrance with the Host, an angel bearing a candlestick on either side. On the second step stands the "Name of Mary," an elaborate *M* decorated with flowers and angels, which is flanked by branches heavy with fruit and flowers. The third level belongs to the eagle, insignia of Alcamo, a noble beast sitting at Mary's feet. Below him there is a bower of roses through which Saint Joseph leads the Christ Child, and then the *Calata degli angeli* (the "Descent of the Angels"), a tower of roses surmounted by a cross, with three angels descending on each side. (The preparations and the symbolism were explained to me by an elderly woman in Alcamo who had been a great specialist in the preparation of Saint Joseph's bread. Inspecting with critical eye the photographs I had brought with me, she remarked that she herself used to get *eight* angels onto *her calata*.)

The tradition of preparing the Saint Joseph's altar appears to enjoy great vitality and an encouraging ability to incorporate modern elements. The fresh pineapples decorating the altars, the Coca-Cola served to the saints along with the wine, and the pop hits that alternate with Sicilian tarantellas on the record player or the hired accordion are innovations that may be anathema to the purists, but to the ethnologically open-minded they spell good health.

The tenacity of this tradition in the face of all the distractions offered by the advent of consumerism in Sicily bears witness to how profoundly significant it is to the people here, significant in ways of which they are only dimly aware, but which speak of centuries of bitter experience. The altar of Saint Joseph is most commonly read as a rite in propitiation of the saint for the new harvest, and the banquet as an orgy in which the last remnants of the old harvest are consumed just before the new crop of fava beans ripens and the new wheat quickens into seed, an overabundance of eating to invoke a commensurate generosity on the part of the saint.

Yet the banquet of Saint Joseph is also a ritualization of famine relief. It comes during Lent, a period of liturgical fasting that coincides with and gives religious significance to the fasting imposed by nature, the period when the provisions of the summer are exhausted, and when, in years past,

> crowds of poor people, hungry and undernourished, who wandered through the countryside in search of food, gave a disquieting and threatening air to the agrarian and to the human landscape. . . . Saint Joseph's Day, which falls in the middle of Lent, was the festivity in which the search for and the offering of food could take place in a ritualized, controlled and regulated form.
>
> V. Teti, "Carni e maccarruni assai," 1985

I belong to that very small percentage of humanity that has the great good fortune never to have known real hunger. Had I continued to live in America, I might still consider bread as one more element in the category of foods that are delicious yet potentially dangerous and not really necessary, like chocolate or jam or gravy. Sicily has taught me otherwise.

> He never asked, it's true, but I gave him a loaf of bread which I had taken out of the oven not an hour before, and I put oil and salt and oregano on it, and he sniffed the air and the smell of the bread, and said, "Bless the Lord!"
>
> Elio Vittorini, *Conversazioni in Sicilia*, 1941

A BEGGAR, *a nineteenth-century engraving by Vuillier*

4

...And the Stuff of Dreams

In a month's time (if the winds are not against you) you will arrive on the affluent island of Sicily, where you will eat some of those macaroni that have taken their name from the [Greek word] "beatify": they are usually cooked together with fat capons and fresh cheeses dripping butter and milk on all sides, and then, using a wide and liberal hand, sprinkled with sugar and cinnamon of the finest that can be found. Oh dear, how my mouth waters just remembering them.

Ortensio Landi, Secretary to Lucrezia Gonzaga, sixteenth century

However grateful we may be for our daily bread, it is only human to desire something more: a Sunday roast, a birthday cake, or a Christmas pudding to satisfy a particular hunger or to celebrate a special occasion. The higher our income, the more frequently such occasions occur, so much so that the ability to transform the extraordinary into the ordinary—to eat meat every day, for instance—becomes a symbol of newly augmented economic and social status.

Sicilians are no exception to this rule. If now they seem to make much of the possibility or even the appearance of eating meat, it is because for centuries meat was so rare and limited to so few. In fact, it has had comparatively little hold upon the popular imagination. To celebrate his feast day, to confirm his status, and to satisfy his soul, what the Sicilian really craved was a nice big plate of pasta!

Historians have as yet been unable to pinpoint the moment in Italian history when *pasta asciutta* as we think of it—the heaping dish of spaghetti or fettuccine crowned with sauce and cheese—was born. There is good reason to believe, however, that it all began in Arab Sicily. Noodles known as *rishta* were eaten in ancient Persia and are mentioned in the cookbooks of medieval Islam. In Italy, the earliest mention of pasta's being produced on a commercial scale comes from a survey of Sicily written by an Arabic geographer at the request of the Norman King Roger II.

> To the west of Termini lies the town of Trabia, a most pleasing site, rich in perennial waters and in mills, with a fertile plain and vast farms, where they manufacture vermicelli in such great quantity as to supply both the towns of Calabria and those of the Muslim and the Christian territories as well, to where large shipments are sent.
>
> Al-Idrisi, *The Book of Roger*, 1150

The geographer called the vermicelli *itriya*, an Arabic word that has survived as *tria* in Sicilian dialect until the present and which was exported north along with the pasta by twelfth-century Genoese merchants. A cookbook from thirteenth-century Bologna gives instructions on how to prepare *tria genovese* for invalids (cook them in salted almond milk).

As pasta took hold in the kitchens of Italy, the cooks continued to acknowledge its southern origins: a famous cookbook from Renaissance Florence gives a recipe for "Sicilian Soup."

> Knead well sifted white flour together with egg whites and rosewater, or plain water. Then roll into a sheet and cut into strips as thin as straws, which you will cut crosswise into short pieces. With a light hand run them through with a wire, so that when you draw the wire out, the single pieces will remain hollow on the inside. Dry them in the sun and they will last even for two or three years, especially if they have been made during the August moon. Cook them in a fat broth, pour them into the plates and add grated cheese, fresh butter and sweet spices. This dish requires two hours' cooking.
>
> Bartolomeo Platina, *Il piacere onesto e la buona salute*, 1474

Platina was translating into fine humanist Latin a series of recipes that had been collected and published in Italian a few years earlier by a professional chef known as Maestro Martino da Como. I wonder how much macaroni either of them ever made in the manner they describe: the thought of trying to push a wire up a damp noodle is daunting, no matter how "light" one's hand. In Sicily today homemade macaroni (which in most households are made only on special occasions) are shaped with the help of special straws called *busi*: a small piece of dough is placed on the straw and then rolled out on the table under the palms of both hands, as children roll out long snakes of clay, so that as

MACARONI FACTORY, *engraving taken from a nineteenth-century photograph*

it thins out the dough wraps itself about the straw. When the straw is drawn out from one end, it leaves a more or less tubular length of pasta, somewhat like a very wide bucatino, which is commonly known as *maccarruna di zitu*.

There are, of course, many other forms of pasta made in Sicilian homes, or at least there used to be. A partial list compiled in the nineteenth century includes:

ciazzìsi	gnucchitti	filatieddi
ciazzisuotti	lasagni	gnuòcculi
maccarruna a lu 'usu	taccuna	pastarattedda
maccarrunedda ri zita	pizzulatieddi	virmicieddi
scivulietti	ncucciatieddi	alica, etc.
cavatieddi	melinfanti	

Serafino Amabile Guastella, *L'antica carnevale nella Contea di Modica*, 1887

The sound of these names intrigues me, and I wish I had some idea of which one might correspond to Goethe's description—much more persuasive than Platina's—of domestic macaroni making.

> Since there are no inns in Girgenti, a family kindly made room for us in their own house and gave us a raised alcove in a large chamber. A green curtain separated us and our baggage from the members of the household, who were manufacturing macaroni of the finest, whitest and smallest kind, which fetches the highest price. The dough is first molded into the shape of a pencil as long as a finger; the girls then twist this once with their fingertips into a spiral shape like a snail's. We sat down beside the pretty children and got them to explain the whole process to us. The flour is made from the best and hardest wheat, known as *grano forte*. The work calls for much greater manual dexterity than macaroni made by machinery or in forms. The macaroni they served us was excellent, but they apologized for it, saying that there was a much superior kind, but they hadn't enough in the house for even a single dish. This kind, they told us, was only made in Girgenti and, what is more, only by their own family. No other macaroni, in their opinion, can compare with it in whiteness and softness.
>
> J. W. von Goethe, *Italian Journey* (1786–88)

To return to Platina and the Renaissance, it is important to note that his recipe calls for "sweet spices." In his next recipe, entitled simply "Vermicelli," he is more specific: in addition to spices, he orders, "when they are cooked, remember to sprinkle them with sugar."

In the medieval and Renaissance periods, in fact, sugar was sold by the *speziale*, the seller of spices, who was also an herbalist and apothecary, with one foot in the kitchen and the other in the sickroom. It was very expensive, to be used sparingly like other imported spices, but it appears in almost every dish, from the beginning of the meal to the end, just as honey or *vino cotto* appears in so many of Apicius's recipes.

This antique taste for sweet spices in pasta has survived to the present in a few Sicilian preparations. One of these is *sciabbò*, which is eaten at Christmastime in Enna, at the very heart or, as Cicero called it, the umbilicus of Sicily. This is a pasta dish made with lasagne ricce, wide flat noodles with a ruffled edge. According to Pino Correnti the name *sciabbò* alludes to the ruffles, being a Sicilianization of the French *jabot*. In any case, the sweet spices here are cinnamon and sugar, with a later Spanish addition of bitter chocolate.

SCIABBÒ
(Christmas Noodles)

Serves 6

1 medium onion, minced
¼ cup olive oil
¾ pound pork meat,
    diced small
2 tablespoons tomato
    extract (see p. 13) or
    3 tablespoons tomato
    paste
½ cup red wine

2 cups plain tomato sauce
    (see p. 172)
2 cups water
Salt
½ teaspoon ground cinnamon
1 tablespoon sugar
1 tablespoon unsweetened
    cocoa
1½ pounds lasagne ricce

Sauté the onion in the olive oil until soft. Add the pork and cook, stirring, until browned. Add the tomato extract and the wine, stirring to dissolve the extract completely, then add the tomato sauce and the water. Bring to a boil, reduce the heat, and simmer for about 40 minutes or until the meat is tender and the sauce thick. Correct the salt (the extract is salty and it may not be necessary to add any more). Stir in the cinnamon, sugar, and cocoa.

Cook the pasta in abundant salted water until it is *al dente*, drain well, and toss with the sauce. You may wish to serve grated cheese on the side, although I think *sciabbò* is better without it.

Cinnamon and cloves, this time without the sugar, are the hallmark of a pasta dish that was invented by the friars of the Monastery of San Francesco di Paola in Palermo. These monks were vowed to perpetual abstinence from meat, and thus looked elsewhere to give variety to their diet.

PASTA ALLA PAOLINA
(Pasta Paolina Style)

Serves 6

15 or 16 anchovy fillets	⅛ teaspoon ground cloves
2 tablespoons olive oil	Salt
2 cups tomato sauce, variation	1½ pounds spaghetti
I or II (see pp. 172–173)	1 cup toasted breadcrumbs
¼ teaspoon cinnamon	(see p. 12)

Dissolve the anchovy fillets in the olive oil over steam (see pp. 11–12), and then add the sauce and the spices and cook for 10 minutes. Correct for salt.

Cook the spaghetti in abundant boiling salted water until they are *al dente*. Drain, toss with the sauce, and serve accompanied by the toasted breadcrumbs.

A MONK, *a nineteenth-century engraving by Vuillier*

The Renaissance households in which pasta was served liberally doused with expensive "sweet spices" were wealthy establishments: the poorer households weren't serving pasta at all. In the price-control lists of fourteenth- and fifteenth-century Palermo, in fact, pasta cost three times as much as bread, and was therefore a dish confined to the aristocracy and to the richest of the middle class. In 1415 a delegation of eight Palermitani representing the city government traveled to Catania, where the viceroy was holding court. To the joy of scholars in later ages, they were on an expense account. Their careful records show that, in the course of a month's journey, they purchased macaroni only once (and since their travels lasted from January 15 to February 14, it is possible that they bought their macaroni to celebrate the last day of Carnival).

The idea that pasta is an expensive dish, one that you would serve to an honored guest, renders all the more appealing a lovely story about a Sicilian hermit, the Blessed William of Scicli. Sometime toward the end of the fourteenth century the local seigneur invited the Blessed William to dine, ostensibly to do him honor, but in fact to do him wrong: the *maccarones* that he ordered his servants to prepare were filled with mud. But lo! the miracle, offered in evidence at William's beatification trial two centuries later: when the Blessed William sat down at the table and blessed the food, the filling of mud was transformed into fresh ricotta.

Be it miraculous or be it more mundane, pasta remained a very special dish throughout the seventeenth century, a dish to dream about. The possibility of eating endless amounts of pasta was synonymous with utopia for the Italian peasant, a utopia known as Cuccagna, a miraculous land of plenty that started as a popular myth and entered into courtly literature as early as the fourteenth century (and in its English form, "Cockaigne," into a twentieth-century cookbook—to designate the authors' favorite recipes in *The Joy of Cooking*!).

> [There is] a district called Bengodi where vines are fastened to the stakes with sausages, and a goose can be had for a penny, with a duckling thrown in for good measure. A wonderful mountain was also to be found in that country, he told him, all made of Parmesan cheese, and inhabited by folk who spent all their time making macaroni and ravioli, which they boiled in capon broth and then spilled out pell-mell, so that whoever was the nimblest obtained the largest share.
>
> Giovanni Boccaccio, *The Decameron*, 1353

Italian scholars such as Piero Camporesi and Vito Teti have traced the evolution of the Cuccagna myth from its earliest form, in which the mountains of macaroni heaped up for the taking are a culinary symbol of more far-reaching aspirations, a dream of equality that is social and economic as well as dietary. With the famines and the economic crises that struck the whole of the Italian peninsula during the seventeenth century, the social implications were lost in the desperate scramble for mere survival, and the word *cuccagna* came to mean, in Sicily at least, a distribution of food to the poor on the occasion of some particular feast, a part of the governing policy of the "three F's"—*feste, forche, e farina*—festivals, gallows, and bread flour—with which the masses were kept under control. There are some rather appalling descriptions of such *cuccagne* in the diaries of the Marchese of Villabianca. One of these took place

> for the happy occasion of the royal festivities celebrated in Naples in May of 1768 for the marriage of the King our Lord Ferdinand with the Majesty of Maria Carolina of Lorraine. . . .
>
> The *cuccagna* was sacked by the people on the day of the 13th of June, at the twenty-third hour, in the piazza of the Royal Palace, and was formed in the guise of a flowering garden with obelisks of cypress—that is, pyramids to the number of sixteen, three shipmasts, encircled, and two great fountains of wine in front of them. And all of this was enriched with comestibles, such as veal, beef and mutton, live pigs and even live sheep, live goats, castrated kids and he-goats, numerous suckling pigs, hams, *caciocavallo* and other cheeses, salt cod, bread, turkeys, fowl, game, and ordinary roosters, hens and capons; and above the crest of each mast were placed prizes, albeit small ones, of silver coins, silk handkerchiefs, shoes, stockings, and others that I was unable to identify.
>
> It is to be noted that the sheep and the greater part of the other animals hanging on the pyramids died before the hour 23 because they were unable to survive hanging there in the rays of the sun.
>
> The wine was three barrels' worth, mixed with six barrels of water, and it was distributed in the fountains from the hour 23 on. And at this hour, the troops of infantry and cavalry which had guarded the *cuccagna* moved away from it, allowing the plebs to assault it, as in fact it did from all sides, with such a fury that it was entirely sacked and nothing remained that had not been torn to pieces. Three columns of half-naked porters were the festive contestants, who in the action raised such horrendous cries to the heavens, in chorus with those of the spectators, that they led one to believe that a question of arms was in course rather than a celebration.

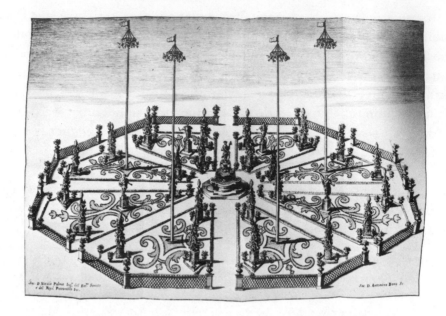

A CUCCAGNA HONORING A ROYAL BIRTH, 1748, *an engraving by* A. Bova

And this in itself was a motive for rejoicing, that in the midst of the shouting *Long live the King!* should ring out. The pillaging troops included porters, sailors, charcoal makers, and rustics, especially from the surrounding towns. . . . Numerous troops could be seen in front of the Royal Palace, standing at attention, in order to prevent any sinister incidents, which by the grace of God did not come to pass, since everything took place felicitously and without the least mishap.

In half an hour the entire *cuccagna* had disappeared from sight, and all the goods had been taken away by the people. The woodwork, the cypresses, the vases, and all that was there was carried off; and had it been possible they would have carried off the very ground itself.

Marchese di Villabianca, *Diario palermitano*, 1768

Shortly after this the locus of the Land of Cuccagna began to shift, as rumors started filtering down to Sicily about a country where the streets were paved with gold. A century later the southern peasant's dream of utopia centered on the price of a steamship ticket that would carry him across the ocean to the New World.

Even in the late nineteenth century, after the Land of Cuccagna had taken concrete though distant form, pasta every day remained something to dream about when all one had to fill an empty stomach was bread and onions. For the ne'er-do-well son of the Malavoglia family, in Verga's *I Malavoglia*, it was the hallmark of the idle rich:

> We'll do what the others do. . . . We won't do anything, that's what we'll do! . . . We'll go to live in the city, and not do anything, and eat pasta and meat every day.
>
> Giovanni Verga, *I Malavoglia*, 1881

For the majority of Sicilians, such culinary dreams came true only on very special occasions. One of these was New Year's Day.

> *Cu mancia a Capu d'annu maccarruni,*
> *Tuttu l'annu a ruzzuluni.*
>
> He who eats macaroni on New Year's Day
> For the whole of the year keeps trouble away.

In many parts of the island, tradition required that the New Year's Day pasta be store-bought, not made at home (perhaps in the hope that to start the year by spending money would augur an influx of cash in the following months), and that it be of the ruffled variety known as lasagne ricce. In Palermo these are still served with a dark red *ragù* and lots of fresh ricotta, and the Palermitani are very graphic about the appearance that this bestows.

LASAGNE CACATE
(Lasagne à la Merde)

Serves 6

½ pound lean veal in one piece
½ pound pork in one piece
¼ cup lard
1 medium onion, minced
2 tablespoons tomato extract (see p. 13) or 3 tablespoons tomato paste
1 cup red wine
2 cups plain tomato sauce (see p. 172)

2 cups water
1 bay leaf
Salt and freshly ground black pepper
1½ pounds lasagne ricce
1 pound fresh ricotta (see p. 18)
1½ cups grated salted ricotta or caciocavallo cheese

To make the *ragù*, sauté both pieces of meat in the lard in a heavy casserole until browned on all sides. Remove from the pan and in the same fat sauté the onion over very low heat until it begins to color. Add the tomato extract and the wine, stirring until the extract dissolves. Add the sauce, the water, and the bay leaf. Return the meat to the pan and simmer for an hour, or until the meat is well cooked and tender. Remove the bay leaf. Dice the meat and return it to the sauce. Correct the salt and add a sprinkling of pepper.

Cook the pasta in abundant boiling salted water. Put the fresh ricotta in a large bowl and soften it by stirring in a ladle of the water in which the pasta is cooking.

Drain the pasta when it is *al dente* and toss it together with the ricotta. Serve by the plateful, topping each plate with a ladle of the *ragù* and a liberal sprinkling of grated cheese.

If washed down with abundant wine, *lasagne cacate* sets you up for twelve months:

> *Lasagni cacati e vinu a cannata*
> *Bon sangu fannu pri tutta l'annata.*
>
> Lasagne *à la merde* and wine by the pitcher
> Make good blood for the whole of the year.

Although not everyone in the nineteenth century could afford pasta at New Year's, no sacrifice was too great to ensure that pasta was served at one's wedding breakfast. Here too a certain type of pasta was obligatory: *maccarruna di zitu* (*zitu* means fiancé in Sicilian), once more served with a *ragù* of pork meat cooked in tomato sauce and, in some towns, *'ncaciata*—with pieces of cheese incorporated. It is not necessary to get married in order to enjoy *pasta 'ncaciata*, much to the satisfaction of my children, who love it. I usually make the very simple version I learned from my mother-in-law. It merely requires that I sprinkle little cubes of primosale or caciocavallo over pasta with a pork-and-tomato sauce, then return it to the saucepan and heat it for a few minutes until the cheese begins to melt. A wedding breakfast would call for this fancier version.

PASTA 'NCACIATA
(*Cheesed Pasta*)

Serves 8

4 cups pork and veal *ragù*
  (see preceding recipe)
2 large eggplants
Salt
1 cup olive oil
  (see note p. 39)
1½ pounds rigatoni, penne
  rigate, or other fluted pasta

¼ cup dried breadcrumbs
  (see p. 12)
½ pound tuma, primosale,
  or mozzarella cheese, sliced
3 hard-boiled eggs, sliced
1½ cups grated pecorino
  cheese

Prepare the *ragù* as directed on p. 154.

Wash the eggplants, remove the stems, and cut the eggplants into thin (¼-inch) slices. Sprinkle with abundant salt, and allow to drain in a colander for an hour or so. Rinse well, pat dry, then fry in the olive oil until tender and browned on each side. Drain on absorbent paper.

Cook the pasta in abundant boiling salted water and drain when barely arrived at the *al dente* stage. Mix together with the *ragù*.

Grease a large, deep ovenproof casserole, line it with bread-crumbs, and then line the bottom and sides with the eggplant slices, overlapping them so as to make a pretty pattern. Fill the casserole layer by layer as follows: pasta, slices of cheese, pasta, slices of egg, pasta, slices of cheese, pasta. Sprinkle ½ cup of the grated cheese over the top and bake it in a 375°F. oven for 15 to 20 minutes.

Remove the casserole from the oven. Allow it to stand for 10 minutes, and then turn it out upside down onto a platter. Cut in wedges and serve, passing the remaining grated cheese on the side.

Note: The classic version requires a layer of diced salami as well, but since my family feel strongly that salami loses its charm when hot, I always omit it from cooked dishes. You may wish to do otherwise.

––––––––

Finances permitting, one could proceed to further courses at one's wedding breakfast, but all the pioneer ethnologists of the nineteenth century report that it was the pasta that made the party, and Carlo Levi bears witness to this tradition's having survived the Second World War.

I had climbed up to the villa, marvelous in its architecture and in the gardens high above the town in front of the sea, where the wedding banquet of one of the maidservants was going on, with a flight of doves from the wedding cake, and dancing, and a dinner consisting, as was the custom, in one sole course of *pasta al forno* with a meat sauce, followed immediately by Jordan almonds, cakes, almond crisps, beignets, colored desserts, mac-aroons, chocolate rolls, ladyfingers, Swiss pastries, and by an endless quan-tity of spumoni and cassatas, of ice-cream molds in chocolate and mocha, filled with hazelnut, with cream and strawberry. The duchess ruled the party with good-natured authority.

Carlo Levi, *Le parole sono pietre*, 1951

The most important moment of all, as far as culinary celebrations were concerned, came in February, at Carnival. Rooted in traditions that dated from the classical period and that had been incorporated into the Christian calendar, this festival was a moment of total indulgence and licentiousness, a liberation from the normal social order, and a time for games and disguises: tourneys and pageants for the aristocracy, mock battles (oranges were the most common ammunition in Palermo) and street shows for the populace. No less important than the merrymaking was the gastronomic side of Carnival, the splurge of eating before the rigors of Lent set in.

It requires great effort and imagination for anyone living in the Western world today to understand what Carnival meant in the past, before the infinite variety and quantity of food now available throughout the year altered the quality of the feast day. In the past the poverty of everyday fare and the rigorous observance, whether by choice or by necessity, of Lenten fasting made the feasting of the days preceding Ash Wednesday a veritable celebration. Some of the traditional dishes—pancakes in England or egg noodles in Sicily—were designed to use up all the fresh eggs; whatever the hens produced during Lent would be hard-boiled and then decorated for Easter. But chickens and eggs were in any case something of a luxury in Sicily, where most of the peasants lived in the towns and could at most keep a pair of hens in an upside-down basket on the sidewalk in front of the door, and under the bed at night. Pork had become the most commonly consumed meat, especially in certain areas: a Frenchman visiting in 1784 complained that "Almost all the ragouts of the Syracusans are composed of pork meat, an indigestible food, which can do no other than whip up the blood, heat it and render it into a state of orgasm and continual effervescence."

That was just what was wanted at Carnival, of course, and families who were lucky enough to raise a pig each year would slaughter it shortly before Carnival began. Nothing was wasted: the *cotenna*, or skin, was scraped free of its bristles and added in small pieces to the *ragù* or rolled up with slices of egg and mortadella and cooked in tomato sauce. The blood was boiled in a sausage, either with garlic, parsley, salt, and pepper, or in a sweet version flavored with sugar, raisins, chopped almonds, and pieces of *zuccata*. (A similar treat—"goat stomachs, ready on the fire / to stuff with blood and fat, good supper pudding," is the only dish described in any detail in *The Odyssey*.)

Those parts of the pig that could be salted or cured were put away for the rest of the year. What remained was either eaten immediately or given away

DRUMMERS, *a nineteenth-century engraving by Vuillier*

as a present. Shrove Tuesday was the day of exchanging gifts of food, and Guastella describes how, at the beginning of the nineteenth century, this custom would transform the streets of Chiaramonte Gulfi, a small and very pretty town in southeastern Sicily.

> That last day of Carnival resembled a food fair. In every street, every alleyway and courtyard, the roofs and the windows were festooned with baskets in which all possible varieties of homemade macaroni were stretched out to dry in the sun. Strings of kids and lambs, their entrails dripping, crossed paths with strings of freshly butchered rabbits and hares; capons met up with partridges; the flask of Zibibbo wine destined for the notary public passed the big bottle of white *'nzolia* being presented to the family confessor; often part of a pork liver would encounter another piece from the same beast and appear to exchange a word or two: "Where are *you* going?"—"To the carpenter's."—"And *I* to the family cobbler." The serving maids scurried from this house to that, burdened with wheat flour or cheese, with ricotta or meat . . . and even the family's dependents reciprocated with gifts: the swineherd brought truffles, and the warden brought game, the cowherd field cardoons, blanched and swollen from months of careful tending, the day laborer an enormous bunch of wild asparagus, the dairymaid her eggs and pullets.
>
> Serafino Amabile Guastella,
> *L'antica carnevale nella Contea di Modica,* 1887

The fat of the slaughtered pig was rendered into lard, which would keep for months. A few large pieces went into a special soup, which was prepared on the last Thursday of Carnival, *jiovi du lu larduloro.* I have found no recipe for this, but only a description of something very similar to Saint Joseph's soup (page 136).

> The last Thursday before Lent was called *di lu lardaloru* in honor of a minestrone, which it was customary to prepare on that day. . . . The principal ingredient was large pieces of lard, to which were added as many different dried legumes and fresh vegetables as possible; and since the different kinds of legumes and of vegetables require different amounts of cooking, the culinary art of the peasant housewife lay in choosing the proper moment for adding to the pot now one, now another of these ingredients. . . . The minestrone has the virtue of a magnet: it draws to its bosom the quarreling members of the family: the sons- and daughters-

in-law, the children themselves, since it would be considered a most scandalous gesture to refuse the father's invitation, especially on Shrove Thursday, when this minestrone spreads its beneficent influence.

Guastella, L'antica carnevale

The biggest Carnival feast of all came on Shrove Tuesday, *martedì grasso,* when pasta presided, a mountain of *maccarruna di zitu* worthy of the Land of Cuccagna, and crowned once again with the tomato and pork *ragù* so beloved of the Sicilians. This *ragù* has many versions, each family's choice determined by the dictates of its pocketbook. The poorest, for whom this represented the only meal of the year in which meat would grace their table, might have only bits and pieces of sausage and *cotenna* floating in their sauce. Not that that is such a bad lot: Sicilian sausage is excellent, fresh pork chosen under the vigilant gaze of the purchaser and chopped with a knife rather than ground, then spiced with salt, black pepper, and wild fennel seeds. If it is to be simmered in a *ragù* it is usually quite thick—more than an inch in diameter—and is tied into links. Sausage destined for the frying pan or, better still, for the coals, is narrower and without links; a meter's length is cooked in a flat coil secured with skewers.

The richer the family, the more meat would go into the *ragù* pot, until the acme of the economic scale was reached in the following recipe.

RAGÙ SICILIANO DELLE FESTE
(Sicilian Feast Day Ragout)

Serves 12 to 14

1 *farsumagru*, uncooked
  (see p. 211)
1 cup stale white bread-
  crumbs (see p. 12)
½ cup milk
1 pound ground beef
1 egg
¼ cup grated pecorino or
  caciocavallo cheese
2 cloves garlic, minced fine
1 tablespoon minced parsley
Salt and freshly ground
  black pepper
12 fresh Sicilian pork
  sausage links
6 tablespoons olive oil
2 pounds potatoes, peeled
  and cut in large pieces

1 large onion, minced
2 tablespoons tomato extract
  (see p. 13) or 3 tablespoons
  tomato paste
2 cups red wine
2 cups plain tomato sauce
  (see p. 172)
1 pound ripe tomatoes,
  peeled and chopped
2 bay leaves
1 small marrow bone
1 cup blanched baby peas
3–3½ pounds maccheroni
  (a hollow spaghetti slightly
  larger than bucatini)

Prepare the *farsumagru* as the recipe directs.

Soak the breadcrumbs in the milk for 10 minutes. Squeeze out the excess liquid, then blend thoroughly with the ground meat, egg, cheese, garlic, parsley, and a little salt and pepper. Shape into small patties.

Poke holes in the sausage links with a fork to let the excess fat escape, then brown them in 2 tablespoons olive oil. Remove the sausages from the pan, and in the fat brown the potatoes on all sides. Remove the potatoes and brown first the *farsumagru*, turning to color it on all sides, and then the beef patties.

In a very large flameproof casserole, sauté the onion in 4 tablespoons olive oil until soft. Add the tomato extract, dissolving it in the wine, tomato sauce, tomatoes, and the bay leaves. Place the *farsumagru* in the middle of the casserole and fit the sausages, marrow bone, and meat patties around it. Cover pan and simmer over low heat for 60 minutes.

Add the potatoes (at this point the sausages and the patties will be cooked, and if you have problems of space you can take them out and put the potatoes in their place) and cook for another 20 to 30 minutes or until the potatoes are tender. Add the peas for the last 10 minutes. Correct the salt and add some black pepper.

Meanwhile cook the pasta in abundant boiling salted water until *al dente*. Drain, place in a large bowl, and ladle some of the sauce from the *ragù* over it. Serve at once.

Remove the *farsumagru*, let it cool for 20 minutes while you are eating your pasta, cut off all the string binding it, and place it on a platter. Slice it, arranging it so that the filling shows in all its glory, surround it with a row of sausages, a row of patties, and a row of potatoes. Spoon the remaining sauce over all.

This really is a magnificent dish, and not the least of its virtues is that you won't want to look at meat again until Easter! It took fourteen of us to polish it off, and it was serious eating!

———

WINE FLASK, *an eighteenth-century majolica flask from Caltagirone*

Those who had large pieces of meat or a *farsumagru* in their *ragù* would fish them out and carve them up for the second course, to be followed by slices of blood sausage and wedges of raw sweet fennel to cut the grease and cleanse the mouth. Those who had none were happy nonetheless, for everyone, rich or poor, washed his pasta down with lots of wine, told a great many ribald jokes, and greeted with loud groans and cries of delight the arrival of dessert.

Carnival was and still is celebrated with a wide variety of sweets. By the end of January marzipan pigs wearing bowler hats or dunce caps appear in the windows of Palermo's pastry shops, and the bakeries display trays filled with sugar-dusted ribbons of fried dough and pyramids of tiny round fritters dripping with honey or caramelized sugar. These are called *pignoccata*, from *pigna* or pine cone, which they vaguely resemble and which is one of Western civilization's most ancient fertility symbols.

PIGNOCCATA

Makes 12 to 15

3 cups flour (see note p. 41)
Pinch of salt
4 large eggs
Vegetable oil for frying
1 cup honey

½ cup sugar
2 tablespoons grated orange
  rind (optional)
1 teaspoon ground cinnamon

Mix the flour and salt in a bowl or on a pastry board. Add the eggs one by one, mixing well and kneading until the dough has a uniform consistency. Let it stand for 30 minutes.

Take the dough, one small piece at a time, and roll it between the palms of your hands into thin pencil-like strips. With a sharp knife cut the strips into ¼-inch pieces. Each piece should be about the size of a pea.

Fry the bits of dough in vegetable oil 1 inch deep. It is essential that the oil be warm (about 200°F.) but *not* hot when you put the bits of dough in to fry, and that you fry them slowly over medium heat, otherwise they will not puff up as they should.

When the balls of dough reach a rich golden color, lift them

from the oil, put them on absorbent paper to drain, and remove
the pan from the fire to cool the oil down again before adding
the next batch of dough.

Heat the honey, sugar, and orange rind to the boiling point,
and cook for about 1 minute, until it becomes syrupy. Remove
from the fire, add the balls of fried dough, stir to coat them well,
and with the help of a large spoon, arrange them in small heaps
on a sheet of waxed paper or aluminum foil. Sprinkle with cinnamon and allow to cool.

Note: Messina has its own version of *pignoccata*, made at Christmastime. The little balls, made of a more elaborate dough, are
baked rather than fried, and then heaped into one large pyramid,
which is then iced, with chocolate on one side and a white sugar
glaze on the other.

———

But the king of Carnival is the *cannolo*, which in its plural form, cannoli,
is now a part of the American language.

> *Beddi cannola di carnalivari,*
> *megghiu vuccuni a lu munnu non c'è.*
> *Sù biniditti spisi li dinari,*
> *ogni cannola è scettru di re!*

> Lovely cannoli of Carnival weekend,
> no better morsel exists in the world!
> Blessèd the money spent for to buy them,
> every cannolo's the scepter of a king!

To be good, cannoli have to be very fresh (the best coffeehouses and bars
in Palermo offer *cannoli espresso*—filled while you wait), so if you are a cannoli
fan and you can get good ricotta, it is worth the effort to make them at home.
Actually it takes experience rather than effort to knead the cannoli dough just
long enough so that the bubbles that the wine produces in the crust are small;
if big bubbles form, the cannoli will unroll as they fry. If you know any expert
cannoli makers, you can avail yourself of their experience; otherwise you will

have to acquire your own by trial and error. You will also have to acquire cannoli tubes, either the ready-made metal ones, or 5-inch pieces of cane. Using a pasta machine helps in the kneading and rolling out of the dough.

CANNOLI

Makes 20 small cannoli

CRUST

2 cups flour (see note p. 41)
2 tablespoons sugar
Pinch of salt
⅛ teaspoon baking soda
½ teaspoon cinnamon
1 tablespoon unsweetened cocoa (optional)

1 egg yolk
½ cup Marsala wine (approximately)
2 tablespoons lard
Vegetable oil or lard for frying

FILLING

1 recipe ricotta cream (see p. 18)

Candied orange peel

Heap on a pastry board the flour, sugar, salt, baking soda, cinnamon, and, if you want the crust to be dark brown, the cocoa. Work in the egg yolk and the Marsala, using just enough wine to pull the dough together. Cut the lard into pieces and knead it piece by piece into the dough. Continue to knead for about 15 minutes or until you have a smooth, elastic dough similar to tagliatelle dough.

Roll the dough out into a very thin sheet, as near to paper-thin as you can get it. Cut out 4-inch circles, and wrap each circle around a greased cannoli tube, moistening the edges where they overlap and pressing them to seal well.

Fry the cannoli, still on their tubes, two at a time in 2 inches of hot oil or lard, allowing them to color slowly. Drain on absorbent paper, and when the cannoli have cooled, slide them off the tubes with care.

Fill the completely cooled cannoli with the ricotta cream, using a small spatula or a coffee spoon, and decorate at each end with a sliver of candied orange peel. Serve immediately.

———

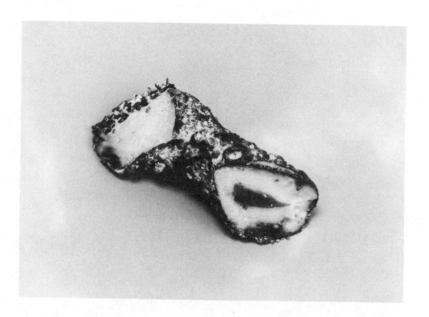

A really fancy Carnival feast would have a *testa di turco*—a "Turk's head"—as well as individual cannoli. A *testa di turco* looks more like a Turk's hat, or better still the flat-brimmed helmet with a round crown that Genghis Khan might have worn. In the good cause of literary research, I set out for my favorite pastry store to buy one for the family this past Carnival. There it was in the window, the helmet, almost two feet in diameter and fashioned entirely of cannoli dough fried to a dark brown. The crown had been filled to overflowing with sweet ricotta cream, which had run down the sides and collected in little pools on the brim. The brim itself was heaped with tiny cannoli, their ricotta filling tinted in pastel shades of pink, blue, and yellow. Little sugar pastilles in the same colors, resembling paper confetti, were sprinkled over everything. It was the quintessence of the Carnival spirit, so excessive, so vulgar, and so overpoweringly gooey that it was more than I could stomach. So I went home and made my own admittedly inhibited idea of a Carnival treat.

CASSATEDDI DI RICOTTA
(Ricotta Turnovers)

Makes 3 dozen

PASTRY

3¾ cups flour (see note p. 41)   1 cup white wine
¼ cup sugar   ½ cup lard
¼ cup unsweetened cocoa

FILLING

1½ pounds ricotta, well   ½ cup semisweet chocolate
  drained (see note p. 18)   bits or grated rind
1 cup sugar   of 1 lemon

Vegetable oil for frying   1 teaspoon ground cinnamon
½ cup superfine sugar,
  or granulated sugar
  ground fine

Sift together the flour, sugar, and cocoa onto a marble or wooden surface. Make a well and add the wine slowly, using just as much as it takes to make a fairly compact dough. Cut the lard into small pieces and knead it piece by piece into the dough. Knead for at least 15 minutes, working the dough out into a long strip and then folding it back on itself so as to incorporate as much air as possible, until the dough is very smooth and elastic, and shiny but not greasy to the touch. Put the dough into a bowl, cover with a towel or a lid, and let it stand for at least 1 hour.

Sieve the ricotta. Beat in the sugar, and stir in the chocolate bits or, if you prefer something less sweet, the lemon rind.

Roll out the dough to a very thin sheet, and cut out 3-inch disks. On each disk place a scant tablespoon of ricotta. Fold the disks over into half-moons and, moistening the edges with a little water, seal them carefully.

Fry the turnovers in abundant and very hot (about 375°F.) vegetable oil (at least 3 inches deep) until they are delicately browned. Drain on absorbent paper and serve while still warm, sprinkled with ground cinnamon and granulated sugar that has been ground to a fine texture in a mortar.

Guastella's descriptions of the Carnival of his childhood were published toward the end of the nineteenth century, when folk traditions and popular eating habits suddenly became of literary and scientific interest. Little detail is available from earlier periods to enable us to date the steps by which pasta and other celebratory foods traveled from the Land of Cuccagna to daily life. From the end of the eighteenth century, however, foreign visitors to Sicily bear witness to the fact that pasta was widely accessible, even in small towns and villages, to those whose pockets were well lined.

In the letters written home by young Englishmen who extended their Grand Tour to Sicily, "All we could find was a dish of macaroni" is a frequent lament (despite the fact that macaroni were all the rage in London's coffee-houses, and had become synonymous with anything elegant, which explains Yankee Doodle's odd behavior). One such meal is described in detail:

> We halted to dine at the village of Scaletta, at the same cottage where I
> was so much entertained on my journey to Riposto; and I had no sooner

reached the door, than I was warmly greeted by little Antonino, who came running to welcome me on the strength of our late acquaintance. Inside the house, the hens, chickens, and turkeys appeared more numerous than ever; and the dogs and slim tabbies beset me the moment I entered. When seated, the good woman turned out a rotolo of maccaroni into a large dish, which I expected was intended for me; but to my surprise and astonishment, the whole family surrounded it instantly, and began to demolish it with wooden forks, cramming as much into their mouths at first as possible, and then dexterously pushing in the depending filaments with their fingers. This is the true Sicilian mode of eating maccaroni, though certainly not the most polite. After the family meal was over, there was a second dinner prepared for me, which my hostess served on a trencher, and, without any ceremony, or even consulting my taste on the subject, she poured over it some tomata, or red pepper sauce, fried in oil, and then scattered the salt over my plate with her fingers.

George French Angas,
A Ramble through Malta and Sicily in the Autumn of 1841

Mr. French Angas's confusion about the sauce is quite understandable, since the use of tomatoes was still quite a novelty when he was traveling. Tomatoes had been imported to Europe by the Spanish in the sixteenth century, but European cooks were slow to discover the versatility of this strangely acid fruit from the New World. Thus spaghetti with tomato sauce is a young variation on a very old theme. One scholarly book claims that it was not common fare in Naples before 1830, and this can probably be applied to Sicily as well. In any case, it was in the early nineteenth century that the tomato claimed its place in Sicilian cooking, becoming a genial addition to some old classics, such as *caponata*, and giving birth to some new ones, such as *pasta con le melanzane*.

Tomato plants are set out in March in Sicily, and harvesting begins in July. The first ones to ripen are the sweetest and the best for making sauce, especially those known, around Alcamo at least, as *siccaniu*—that is, grown dry, on unirrigated land. My amazement is renewed each year at these plants, which if it has been a particularly dry spring receive at best a few ladlefuls of water in June, yet produce intensely flavored tomatoes dripping copious amounts of juice.

Many Sicilian pasta dishes are therefore summer fare, requiring the heady flavors of sun-ripened tomatoes and fresh basil. I have made many a last-minute summer lunch with "carter's pasta."

PASTA ALLA CARRETTIERA
(*Carter's Pasta*)

Serves 6

6 ripe tomatoes	Salt
(about 1½ pounds)	⅓–½ cup olive oil
4 or 5 garlic cloves	1½ pounds spaghetti
1 cup fresh basil leaves	1 cup grated salted ricotta
A few flakes of crushed	or pecorino cheese
red pepper	

Peel and chop the tomatoes, being careful to conserve their juice.

Chop very fine or—better still—pound in a mortar the garlic, basil, red pepper, and a pinch of salt. Add the oil to the mortar little by little. When you have reduced these to a fairly smooth paste (it needn't be as creamy as a pesto), pour it into the tomatoes and mix well.

Cook the spaghetti in boiling salted water until *al dente*, drain, and place in a serving bowl. Sprinkle with ½ cup of the grated cheese, mix well, add the tomatoes and mix again. Serve accompanied by additional cheese.

————

I assume this recipe is attributed to the cart drivers because of its simplicity, the idea being that they could whip it up at the side of the cart track while their pasta was cooking over the campfire. Good as it is made in this fashion, it is even better if you make the sauce a few hours beforehand, so that the flavors have time to amalgamate.

If you add a little more oil to this sauce you have *ammogghiu*, presiding muse of every Sicilian cookout, to spoon over grilled meat and fish, or onto slices of grilled eggplant, or simply to spread on *bruschette*, slices of day-old Sicilian bread toasted on the coals.

The bulk of the tomato crop is, however, conserved for the winter, either as *'strattu*, or halved, salted, and dried in the sun on woven cane mats and

A CART DRIVER FROM CATANIA, *a nineteenth-century engraving by Vuillier*

then preserved in olive oil (these, I believe, have recently become a fashionable antipasto in America), or boiled into sauce. Every rural household in Sicily and many an urban one as well is equipped with outsized copper cauldrons and colanders, with gargantuan ladles and slotted spoons for sauce making. This elaborate and exhausting ritual takes place each summer and produces crate after crate of beer and soda-pop bottles filled with tomato sauce to keep the family going through the winter.

Although there are various methods, each espoused with passion by its adherents, the greater part of this sauce is merely a purée of tomatoes that have been briefly boiled, drained thoroughly, and then passed through a food mill, with no seasoning other than that furnished by a sprig of fresh basil tucked into each bottle before it is filled. The sauce is either bottled and then sterilized by boiling, to be kept for future months when it will taste of summer even on the most wintry day, or it is consumed immediately. This plain tomato sauce can if necessary be replaced by commercially canned tomato purée: either one needs only a little tinkering, as in the variations below, to be ready for pasta.

SALSA DI POMODORO
(Tomato Sauce)

Makes approximately 4 cups

4 pounds fresh very ripe tomatoes

Wash the tomatoes and remove the stems, which if cooked would make the sauce bitter. Place the tomatoes in a saucepan with just enough water to barely cover the bottom of the pan, cover, and bring to a boil over a medium-low flame. Simmer for 5 minutes, then drain well and cool slightly before passing through a food mill. Discard skins and seeds.

VARIATION I

1 medium onion	The tomato purée
4 sprigs parsley	Salt
¼ cup olive oil	Sugar (optional)

Mince the onion and the parsley, and sauté in the oil. When the onion begins to turn golden, add the tomato purée. Simmer for 15 to 20 minutes, salt to taste, and if the sauce seems too acid, add a pinch of sugar.

VARIATION II

The tomato purée	½ cup olive oil
2 or 3 garlic cloves	Salt
2 sprigs sweet basil	

Simmer the purée together with the garlic cloves (pressed or whole, according to preference), the basil, and the oil for about 15 to 20 minutes or until creamy. Salt to taste.

———

Among the many manipulations to which this basic sauce is subject, there is one that reaps great success in my household.

PASTA CAPRICCIOSA
(Pasta with Capers and Mint)

Serves 6

½ cup capers, rinsed	½ cup cream
3 or 4 garlic cloves	1¼ pounds rigatoni, cooked
¾ cup fresh mint leaves	and drained
2 cups plain tomato sauce,	Grated parmesan cheese
variation 1 (see p. 172)	

Place the capers, garlic, and mint leaves together on a board or in a chopping bowl and chop them fine. Add to the heated tomato sauce.

Simmer for 5 minutes, then add the cream. Simmer without boiling, stirring constantly, for 1 minute, until well assimilated.

Pour over pasta and serve with grated parmesan.

In the heat of summer I often forgo the cream, and find the result to be every bit as good.

———

However warm a welcome the Sicilians may have given to the tomato, they have by no means forsaken their old ways of eating pasta, especially those that combine pasta with green vegetables. Sicilians consume enormous quantities of greens, such as mustard, Swiss chard, escarole, and borage, both cultivated and wild, simply boiled in salted water and dressed with crude olive oil. Very often they will chop the greens before boiling them, and add pasta to cook in the same water—very simple, very unassuming, and very good. Anyone with a large patch of borage in an herb garden might try cooking about a pound of fresh borage sprigs, picked before the plant blossoms and becomes tough, in boiling water until they are tender, then adding 1½ pounds of spaghetti broken into short lengths, and a sprinkle of olive oil at the end.

Sautéed zucchini and other tender summer squashes are also mixed with pasta, with excellent results.

PASTA CON ZUCCHINI FRITTI
(Pasta with Fried Zucchini)

Serves 6

1½ pounds zucchini	Freshly ground black pepper
Salt	1½ pounds penne rigate,
⅓ cup olive oil or more	or pennette
2 garlic cloves, minced	1 cup salted ricotta or
2 tablespoons minced parsley	parmesan, grated
leaves	

Wash the zucchini, cut off ½ inch from each end, and slice very thin. Sprinkle with a little salt and sauté in ⅓ cup olive oil in a heavy skillet, covered, until tender. Stir frequently but with care, so as to avoid breaking the slices. When the zucchini are tender and just beginning to color, add the minced garlic, parsley, and some pepper. Mix well, and cook for 1 minute longer.

Cook the pasta in boiling salted water until *al dente*. Reserve ½ cup of the cooking water, then drain the pasta. Toss with the zucchini; if it seems too dry add a little of the reserved liquid and a few tablespoons of olive oil. Pass the cheese on the side.

A SICILIAN CART, *a nineteenth-century engraving by Vuillier*

Cauliflower makes a delicious if surprising companion to pasta. Sicilian cauliflowers, a treat to the eye as well as to the palate, are usually a bright pea green in color, although white ones and even dark purple ones do exist. Twenty years ago, when I first used to drive along the road that leads down from the mountains behind Monreale into Palermo, I would pass in the early morning a string of gaily painted Sicilian carts stacked high with bright green cauliflowers, each with its flower facing outward and carefully arranged in a pyramid stable enough to survive the lurching of the high-wheeled carts as they trundled down the curving mountain road, bells jingling, pompoms bobbing, and mirrors flashing on the donkeys' harnesses. Today the carts have been replaced by Vespa pickups, and although the carters often honor tradition and have their Vespas expensively painted to look like the old carts, and although the pyramids of vegetables are still constructed with care, the effect is hardly the same.

All by itself, cauliflower can be fried in batter, in pieces or even whole, or cooked "all in the pot."

BROCCOLO A TUTTO DENTRO
(Cauliflower All in the Pot)

Serves 6

1 large cauliflower	8 anchovy fillets, cut in
5–6 tablespoons olive oil	small pieces
1 cup pitted black olives	½ cup red wine
⅓ pound fresh caciocavallo	Salt and freshly ground
cheese, diced	black pepper

Wash the cauliflower and divide it into flowerets. Drain well.

Sprinkle the bottom of a heavy, deep saucepan with the olive oil, and cover with a layer of cauliflower. Cover this with a third of the olives, a third of the cheese, and a third of the anchovies. Repeat until the four ingredients are "all in the pot." Cover tightly and cook over a very low flame for 10 minutes. Add the wine, then replace the cover and continue cooking for 10 to 20 minutes longer. When the cauliflower is tender, add some black pepper and correct the salt. Serve immediately.

Note: It is important to use a very fresh, young cauliflower for this recipe. In Sicily it should be attempted only with winter cauliflowers, since in the Sicilian climate, "after Easter, sermons and cauliflowers lose their flavor."

It is, incidentally, easy to be misled by the Palermo habit of calling cauliflower *broccolo*, whereas its dark-green cousin, known elsewhere as "broccoli," here is known as *sparaceddi*.

Cauliflower reaches its greatest glory when served with pasta. I was amused to discover a recipe in Apicius that calls for cauliflower "covered with boiled spelt [a variety of wheat] and pine nuts and sprinkled with raisins," followed by a note in which the translator declares that "the Apician formula with cereal and raisins added is too exotic for our modern taste." Were Mr. Vehling still alive I would invite him to Palermo to try this classic:

PASTA CON I BROCCOLI ARRIMINATI
(Pasta Stirred Up with Cauliflower)

Serves 6

1 medium-size cauliflower (about 2 pounds)
1 medium onion, minced fine or grated
⅓ cup olive oil
6 anchovy fillets dissolved over steam in 1 tablespoon olive oil (see pp. 11–12)
⅓ cup pine nuts
⅓ cup dried currants, soaked in hot water for 5 minutes
1 pinch saffron dissolved in 2 tablespoons warm water
1½ pounds bucatini
1 cup toasted breadcrumbs (see p. 12)

Wash the cauliflower and divide into flowerets. Cook in a large pot of boiling salted water until just tender. Lift the cauliflower out with a slotted spoon, reserving the water.

Sauté the onion in the oil until soft. Add the anchovies, pine nuts, currants, and saffron with water. Simmer and stir for a minute or two, then add the cauliflower and simmer, stirring constantly, over a low flame for 10 minutes, or until the cauliflower is so soft that it disintegrates into a cream.

Cook the pasta in the same pot and water in which you cooked the cauliflower, adding a little more salt if necessary. When the pasta has reached the *al dente* stage, add a ladleful of the cooking water to the cauliflower, then drain the pasta thoroughly. Combine the pasta and the cauliflower in a large serving bowl, mixing well. Sprinkle with some of the breadcrumbs, and allow the pasta to stand for 10 minutes before serving. Pass the remaining breadcrumbs on the side.

Note: This recipe calls for the vegetable to be boiled in abundant water, enough to then cook the pasta in. Although this may sound like heresy, the fact is that Sicilian cauliflower is so intense in flavor that mere steaming tends to turn it sour, so the boiling water is a good idea.

———

A SMALL VIEW OF ETNA TAKEN FROM THE HOUSE OF THE AUGUSTINE FRIARS
AT TAORMINA, *an eighteenth-century engraving*

The meal of macaroni described by French Angas is of interest not only because it introduces us to tomatoes but also inasmuch as it shows how far down the social scale pasta as a daily fare had reached. The village where he stopped to dine is near Taormina, on the road leading both to Catania and to Mount Etna, the ascent of which was an absolute must for anyone's tour of Sicily. Little Antonino's family, so well equipped with macaroni and fowl, was clearly making a good thing out of its location, and although their manners remained plebeian, their income and their diet were inching toward middle class. Yet, even for those who had succeeded in planting both feet firmly in the bourgeoisie, the apotheosis of good eating was still a carnivalesque mountain of pasta and *ragù*. That this esteem was no longer shared by the aristocracy is made clear in the memoirs of the most famous Sicilian aristocrat of them all, the novelist-prince Giuseppe Tomasi di Lampedusa.

> Wives, daughters, sisters stayed at home, both because women in the country (1905–14) did not pay visits, and also because their husbands, fathers, and brothers did not want them around. My mother and father would go and visit them once a season, and with one, famous for her gastronomic arts, they would even sometimes take luncheon; sometimes, after a complex system of signals and warnings, she would send over by a small boy, who came galloping across the piazza under the broiling sun, an immense tureen full of macaroni done with barley in the Sicilian mode with chopped meat, eggplant, and basil, which was, I remember, truly a dish fit for rustic and primigenial gods. The boy had precise orders to set this on the dining room table when we were already sitting down, and before leaving, he would say, " '*A signura raccumannu: u cascavaddu*" ("The Signora recommends: caciocavallo cheese"), an injunction perhaps sage but never obeyed.
>
> Giuseppe di Lampedusa, *Two Stories and a Memory*, 1962

What is described here (the barley, incidentally, is a mistake: Archibald Colquhoun's translations of Lampedusa are splendid, but he was understandably stymied by "*maccheroni di zito*") belongs to the category of *piatti vastasi*. *Vastasu* is a Sicilian word meaning "vulgar," often used with just the same undertone of affectionate disdain that the author of *The Leopard* employs to describe the bourgeois signora's offering: however delicious, it was a case of gastronomic slumming.

According to what his poet cousin, the late Baron Lucio Piccolo, declared in a newspaper interview, Lampedusa "adored French cooking, above all the timbales, and when he went to Paris, together with the authors whose works we were to discover, he brought home the most elaborate recipes, and colored envelopes containing essences with unlikely names." Such tastes reflected the traditions of a class as well as the whims or eccentricities of an individual, and even if Lampedusa does not confer his own tastes upon the protagonist of *The Leopard*, what graces Prince Fabrizio's table is a different kettle of macaroni.

> The Prince was too experienced to offer Sicilian guests, in a town of the interior, a dinner beginning with soup, and he infringed the rules of *haute*

cuisine all the more readily as he disliked it himself. But rumors of the barbaric foreign usage of serving insipid liquid as first course had reached the major citizens of Donnafugata too insistently for them not to quiver with a slight residue of alarm at the start of a solemn dinner like this. So when three lackeys in green, gold, and powder entered, each holding a great silver dish containing a towering mound of macaroni, only four of the twenty at table avoided showing their pleased surprise: the Prince and Princess from foreknowledge, Angelica from affectation, and Concetta from lack of appetite. All the others, including Tancredi, showed their relief in varying ways, from the fluty and ecstatic grunts of the notary to the sharp squeak of Francesco Paolo. But a threatening circular stare from the host soon stifled these improper demonstrations.

Good manners apart, though, the appearance of those monumental dishes of macaroni was worthy of the quivers of admiration they evoked. The burnished gold of the crusts, the fragrance of sugar and cinnamon they exuded, were but preludes to the delights released from the interior when the knife broke the crust; first came a smoke laden with aromas, then chicken livers, hard-boiled eggs, sliced ham, chicken, and truffles in masses of piping-hot, glistening macaroni, to which the meat juice gave an exquisite hue of suède.

Giuseppe di Lampedusa, The Leopard, 1960

This delightfully sensual description has provoked a good deal of discussion among Sicilian chefs. Anna Pomar's book gives a simplified version.

TIMBALLO DI MACCHERONI BIANCO
(*White Macaroni Timbale*)

Serves 8 to 10

PASTA FROLLA PASTRY (see note p. 94)

3¾ cups flour (see note p. 41)
2 tablespoons sugar
Pinch of salt
½ cup sweet butter

⅓ cup lard
1 whole egg plus 1 yolk
½ cup white wine

FILLING

2 ounces dried porcini
   mushrooms
2 cups hot water
¾ pound chicken livers,
   giblets, and, where
   available, unlaid eggs
   (these are the hard-boiled
   eggs Lampedusa refers to)
½ onion, chopped
⅓ cup olive oil

2 tablespoons plain tomato
   sauce (see p. 172)
½ cup white wine
Salt and freshly ground
   black pepper
½ cup butter
1 pound maccheroni or sedani
   (see note)
½ cup grated parmesan
¼ pound cooked ham, diced

1 egg white

Put the mushrooms for the filling to soak in the hot water for 2 hours.

Prepare the *pasta frolla* by sifting together the flour, sugar, and salt, cutting in the butter and the lard until you achieve the texture of a coarse meal. Stir in the egg and egg yolk (the leftover white will serve to glaze the pasta) and then add just enough wine to bring the dough together. Work the dough for a minute, shape into a ball, and refrigerate for at least an hour.

Wash the livers and other chicken giblets well and cut them into smallish pieces. Sauté the onion in the olive oil until soft, stir in the tomato sauce, turn up the heat, and add the livers and giblets. Brown them on all sides, stirring constantly, and then add the wine. When the wine is well reduced, add the mushrooms and the water they have been soaking in, and salt and pepper to taste. Bring to the boiling point, then turn down the heat and simmer for 30 minutes. Add ¼ cup of butter, stirring and cooking until it has melted.

Cook the pasta in abundant boiling salted water until just barely at the *al dente* stage. Drain well, put in a large bowl, and add the remaining ¼ cup of butter, the chicken-giblet-and-mushroom sauce, the grated cheese, and the diced ham. Mix well and correct the seasoning.

Divide the pastry into two pieces, one slightly larger than the other. Roll out the large piece to a circle wide enough to line a large (12-inch), deep casserole or pie dish. Fill the lined dish with the pasta mixture, then roll out the remaining dough and place it as a lid over the pasta. Seal the edges, decorate the upper crust with scraps of pastry, poke vents in the lid with a fork, and brush it with beaten egg white. Bake in a moderate oven for 30 to 40 minutes.

Note: This recipe calls for maccheroni, but I think its author has in mind fresh homemade macaroni, which are rather limp. Commercially prepared and dried maccheroni are much more rigid, and when you attempt to cut and serve this timbale they whip about in a splatter of sauce that would surely provoke much more than a "threatening circular stare" from Prince Fabrizio were he present. In the interests of elegance I would suggest using either fresh pasta or a shorter, more docile form of dried pasta, such as sedani or penne.

—————

But Lampedusa's *timballo* is perhaps the *summa* of an ancient tradition rather than the product of a single recipe. It is curiously reminiscent of the *patina apiciana* from classical Rome, in which layers of *laganum*, an early version of lasagna, alternate with layers of chicken, fish, or songbirds. The sugar and the cinnamon recall the timbales and the *torta* described in fourteenth-century Tuscan cookbooks; the ham and truffles sound a note of nineteenth-century France. Its presence on a princely table in the middle of the nineteenth century, albeit as a provincial alternative to consommé, speaks volumes about the evolution of the Sicilian "baronial cuisine."

5

Princes, Priests, and Not So Humble Friars

The rage to excel in the size of fish for their grand entertainments yet exists, and I have seen the late Prince of Butera, than whom nobody better understood good cheer, place a whole tunny, garnished round like a mullet, like a Leviathan, in the centre of his festive board.

W. H. Smyth, *Memoir descriptive of the resources, inhabitants, and hydrography of Sicily and its Islands . . .* , 1820

A whole tuna on the table is an odd form of oneupmanship, but given the inflation of aristocratic titles that took place in Sicily between the sixteenth and the eighteenth centuries, any means of asserting one's rank was worth a try. At the end of the fifteenth century the feudal aristocracy in Sicily was composed of fifty-three families, each well armored with hereditary tax exemptions. The easiest way for the Spanish kings to tap this pool of wealth was through the creation and sale of new titles: in the seventeenth century alone 102 principalities were created. By the end of the eighteenth century, within a population of 1,500,000 Sicily counted 142 princes, 95 dukes, 788 marquises, 59 counts, and a walloping 1,274 barons. In the most powerful and wealthiest families the same person often held several titles, which made rank all the more difficult to determine. It was not uncommon for the streets of Palermo to remain blocked for hours by the encounter of two carriages, their aristocratic occupants each claiming precedence over the other. In such a contest, the show of wealth was a powerful weapon.

Sicilian historical debate has been concerned for many years with finding a culprit for the island's economic and political stagnation. In the past the Sicilians quite naturally preferred to attribute the responsibility to the avariciousness of foreign despots, while the English historian Denis Mack Smith has placed the blame squarely on the shoulders of the local aristocracy. More recent studies have done much to examine the role of the middle class. This book is not the right place, nor am I the right person, to enter into such a debate. For present purposes, it is enough to sketch very rapidly the evolution of the Sicilian aristocracy after 1500.

An influx of Spanish nobility on the one hand and a proliferation of merchants, jurists, and civil administrators wealthy enough to purchase titles and estates on the other, swelled the ranks of the aristocracy in the course of the sixteenth century. At the same time increased population pressure and a consequent increase in the price of grain meant an enormous growth in feudal revenues, while urban salaries lagged, thus keeping the cost of construction and the prices of luxury goods down. It was here, in this sixteenth-century margin for expenditure, that the aristocratic tradition of lavish spending and extravagant living developed—a tradition that, once rooted, remained, even when feudal income diminished and the great patrimonies became riddled by debt.

The impression one has of the sixteenth and seventeenth centuries is that of an introverted and rather static court life, protected by the rigorous filtering of the Spanish Inquisition from the ferments of the North and governed in its pastimes and its expenditures by the elaborate and formal tastes of the Spanish court, with its predilection for tourneys, masques, and tableaus.

Each royal wedding or birth was the occasion for decorating the façades of the most important public buildings and private palaces, and for erecting theatres, jousting fields, and elaborate fireworks displays. Each death found the city swathed in black and silver: the local notables, when they died, were displayed on immense catafalques; distant royalty were mourned *in absentia* by interminable processions of black-robed aristocrats and ecclesiastics.

The diarists and chroniclers of this period are the despair of the food historian: "they dined" . . . "copious refreshments were served" . . . "pages bearing silver basins of diverse sweets and confections." To these chroniclers, the sweets merit an inventory, but the rest of the menu is unworthy of note.

One can only postulate that the Sicilian table saw the same elaborate Renaissance cookery that reigned elsewhere in sixteenth- and seventeenth-century Europe, expressive of local tastes and ingredients but now as slow to change as it had once been quick to innovate. There were some novelties: it was in this period and through the agency of the Spanish that chocolate crept

I QUATTRO CANTI, *a view of the center of baroque Palermo*
in an eighteenth-century engraving by Bova

into the Sicilian cupboard, where it first found shelf space next to the "sweet spices" that were sprinkled over everything from soup to nuts. In most classic Sicilian pastries, such as cannoli or *cassata*, in fact, chocolate is added on in bits and shavings to the ricotta or the *biancomangiare* filling, a modern afterthought rather than a basic and original ingredient. Other recipes, as we have seen, call for chocolate to be grated into a meat pasty or into a sauce for pasta.

Another recipe with chocolate is for a sauce to be served with boiled potatoes or steamed artichokes. "Saint Bernard's Sauce" is said to have originated in the monastery of that name, while one old version of the recipe specifies that the breadcrumbs required for its concoction be "toasted to a San Francesco di Paola color"—the dark brown, that is, of a friar's habit.

A small bowl of this sauce is sitting in the back of my refrigerator, a mournful monument to a whole afternoon of grinding almonds, sugar, breadcrumbs, and anchovies in a mortar and then steaming them in a double boiler together with bitter chocolate and vinegar. "Interesting" was the kindest comment anyone could offer, but I have yet to gather the courage to dump such an investment of energy into the garbage. However weird and unappealing this combination of tastes may seem to most of us today, it was highly prized by the baroque palate, and continued to maintain its place on the Sicilian table well into the nineteenth century, long after it had passed out of fashion elsewhere in Europe. King Ferdinand's granddaughter Maria Carolina, Duchess of Berry, who passed much of her childhood in Sicily, remained faithful to her early love of *caponata* as she knew it, spread with a thick layer of Saint Bernard's sauce, then heaped with baby octopus and slices of swordfish, and garnished with shrimp, asparagus, stuffed olives, and *"uova nere"*—slices of hard-boiled eggs that had been shelled and pickled in red wine vinegar until their whites turned black.

The Spanish are also given credit for the Sicilian love of the *frittata*, which is the endlessly versatile Italian cousin of the Spanish *tortilla*, the French omelet, and the Arabic *eggah*—not to mention Apicius's *alia patina de asparagus*. Sicilians today are very fond of just this same sort of *frittata*, preferably using very young and very tender shoots of the *asparagus tenuifolius* that grows wild in the hills, or the slightly less bitter shoots of an ornamental shrub with the Latin name *Ruscus hypoglossum*.

FRITTATA DI ASPARAGI
(*Asparagus Omelet*)

Serves 4 to 6

1 pound tender wild asparagus shoots or cultivated asparagus	8 eggs
	¼ cup grated parmesan or caciocavallo cheese
¼ cup olive oil	Salt
Freshly ground black pepper	

Remove any tough parts of the asparagus, then wash and cook them in abundant salted boiling water for 5 to 10 minutes or until tender.

Drain thoroughly and put in a heavy skillet or omelet pan with the oil and a sprinkling of pepper. Cook over a low flame until the asparagus have absorbed most of the oil.

Break the eggs into a small bowl. Add the cheese and some salt, beat lightly with a fork, and pour over the asparagus. Cook slowly, lifting the edge of the *frittata* with a fork and tilting the pan so that the liquid part of the eggs runs down under the solidified part, until almost completely set.

Cover the skillet with a lid or an upside-down platter, and holding this firmly in place with one hand, turn the pan over so that the *frittata* is resting upside-down on the platter. Slide it back into the pan and cook for a minute or two until the underside is browned. Slide the *frittata* onto the platter once more, cut into wedges, and serve either hot or at room temperature.

Note: Sautéed zucchini, string beans, peas, onions, slices of boiled potato or of fried eggplant—almost any vegetable in Sicily can find its way into a *frittata*. The technique is always the same, and is most accommodating to small quantities of leftovers. This resourceful dish also travels well, large and pie-shaped in a well-equipped picnic basket, or as a small, one-egg *frittata* tucked inside a sandwich in a box lunch.

———

The Spanish domination of Sicily came to an abrupt end in 1713, at the close of the War of the Spanish Succession, when the Treaty of Utrecht assigned Sicily to the rule of Vittorio Amedeo, Duke of Savoy. Seven years and another war later, the Sicilian crown passed once again to a Hapsburg emperor, Charles VI of Austria, until the Spanish reconquered the island in 1734 and joined it to the Kingdom of Naples under the rule of Charles III. The reign of the Bourbons had begun, and although the Sicilian nobility offered equal resistance to all attempts at reform, whether they came from Savoy officials or Austrian viceroys, this last change in crown heralded the beginning of much more far-reaching changes. The connection with Naples opened Sicily to stronger currents of Italian influence; the presence of Lord Nelson and the British fleet during the Napoleonic Wars created a fashion for things English; and especially after the Treaty of Vienna Sicilian aristocrats discovered the pleasures of Paris.

In Sicily, despite ferment and contrast, the *ancien régime* was slow to fade:

> A few moments before a great lady of Noto passed us, who seemed very truly an admirer of ancient etiquette and the pomp of feudal times. For three ages ago, a rich and grave baron could not have visited his vassals with more lacqueys and servants, more trappings bedizened with silver and gold, more liveries embroidered, more housings displayed, more mules, and more trunks with covers, surmounted with shields and escutcheons of the family with all their quarterings, than did this good lady delight in exhibiting. And . . . reflecting upon this motley masquerade, we agreed, that as every season has its fruit, and every age its "form and pressure," the times and the taste of the nineteenth century require another sort of *régime* than that of pride and parade.
>
> Thomas Wright Vaughan, *A View to the Present State of Sicily*, 1811

Entertainments, although they gradually became less stylized and more intimate in character, remained lavish: a case in point is the ball given by the Prince della Cattolica.

> Immense salons, their walls covered from top to bottom with mirrors, were masked by trees that had been uprooted whole from the earth and were festooned with fruit. The spaces between the foliage and the mirrors gave the idea of another world existing on the other side of the passage: the illusion was complete. We danced English quadrilles along trellised aisles from which ripe bunches of exquisite grapes dangled, and French country dances in tree-ringed squares disposed about a pool in which a

PALAZZO CATTOLICA, *a nineteenth-century engraving by Vuillier*

graceful jet of water gushed and played. At the very back, in the last salon, a delightful little hill rose up, this too covered with trees, and in the middle a path leading to its summit, bordered on each side by a great abundance of sweets and cakes of every variety. The guests could see no servants, but at the foot of the hill there was a row of thirty or forty little taps, and signs indicating different drinks and every conceivable refreshment, such as hot punch, cold punch, cream, tea, coffee, Bordeaux wines: and underneath were the glasses, which, once lifted, caused the flow to cease. The sound of music was very clear, but just as there was no sign of servants so also were the musicians hidden, concealed in grottoes covered with foliage. Only at suppertime could we see that there were servants present.

Michele Palmieri de Miccichè, *Pensées et Souvenirs*, 1830

The author of this description was the younger son of a noble Palermo family who took part in the separatist revolt of 1820 and was exiled to Paris for many years, where he became well versed both in the economic and political ideas of the time and in its sophisticated social mores. The memoirs that he published in Paris poke gentle fun at the world of his youth. We shall have occasion to consult them again.

The high point in Palermo social life came in 1798, when Napoleon's army invaded Naples, forcing King Ferdinand and his court to take refuge in Sicily. The presence of royalty inebriated the aristocratic families, who redecorated their palaces, refurbished their wardrobes, and squandered large fortunes in a race to offer the most lavish hospitality possible.

It was only natural that the new fashions in thought, in dress, and in furnishings—Queen Maria Carolina was particularly fond of *chinoiserie*, and the charming Chinese Pavilion on the outskirts of Palermo was built for her pleasure—that all these foreigners brought with them should reach to the dining room as well as to the drawing room. Austrian by birth and sophisticated in taste, the queen did not share Ferdinand's rustic passions for hunting and for agricultural pursuits, but she no doubt approved of his scheme for the construction of a Crown dairy in Partinico, thanks to which Palermo, according to English travelers, was the only city on the island where butter was available. Exile no doubt seemed slightly less bitter when there was "a little bit of butter for the royal slice of bread."

Royal breakfast requirements aside, the establishment of a Crown dairy marked the introduction of new gastronomic tastes that had matured in north-

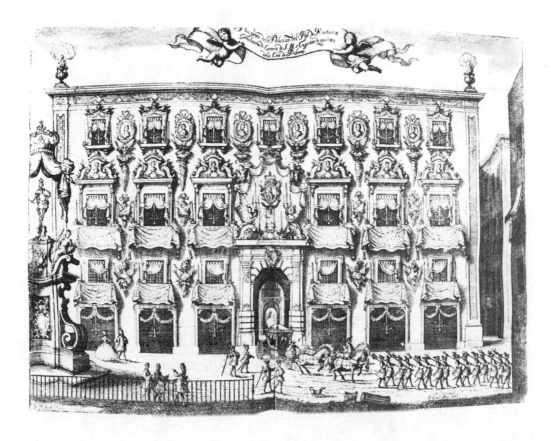

PALAZZO RAMACCA DURING THE CORONATION CELEBRATIONS, 1736,
an engraving by A. Bova

ern Europe during the eighteenth century, where the vinegar-rich sweet and sour condiments so dear to medieval and Renaissance cooks had been abandoned in favor of the butter- and cream-based sauces of the French *haute cuisine*.

Butter came upon a scene in which other animal fats vied with olive oil for preeminence. The island's oil production had suffered a severe setback during the Saracen era, for the Sicilian Arabs preferred to import oil from the vast olive plantations of the Maghreb, and many of the Sicilian groves that in classical times had produced oil for export were uprooted to make way for citrus trees and other irrigated cultures. Lard had thus become the principal fat for cooking purposes, and it was not until the eighteenth century that there was a significant increase in the cultivation and production of olives, and oil gained an important place on the table of all classes, as Patrick Brydone noted:

> The Sicilian cookery is a mixture of the French and Spanish, and the olio still preserves its rank and dignity in the centre of the table, surrounded by a numerous train of fricassees, fricandeaus, ragouts, and pot de loups, like a grave Spanish don amidst a number of little smart marquisses.
>
> Patrick Brydone, *A Tour Through Sicily and Malta*, 1773

Brydone's words show that French cooking had already begun to infiltrate the Sicilian kitchen in the eighteenth century. But Henry Swinburne, traveling in 1790, testifies that progress was slow: "A most splendid entertainment was served up. I found the Sicilian cookery entirely different from that of France or England: sugar and spices were predominant in almost every dish."

Eight years later the court arrived from Naples, and the tastes of the aristocracy began to change rapidly. Turning their backs on the traditional *cucina baronale*, the Sicilian aristocrats sent to Paris for their chefs. Originally Frenchmen and later Sicilians or Neapolitans who had served an apprenticeship in the culinary capital of the world, these chefs merited the title of *monzù*, a corruption of *monsieur*. This most-coveted appellation was reserved for the *cuochi di casata*, the chefs who served in the baronial households, while the cooks who worked for the middle class, no matter how rich or distinguished their employers might be, were known as *cuochi di paglietta*—"the cooks of the shysters"—and were not permitted to mingle socially with their superiors.

If the title of *monzù* conferred prestige—the chef of the Paterno family in Catania went to the market accompanied by two lesser mortals who carried home in ample baskets the wares that he dubbed worthy, indicating this head of lettuce, that cut of swordfish with a flourish of his silver-pommeled walking stick—so did the employment of a *monzù*. The best chefs were much sought after, and Denti di Pirajno actually received one as a wedding present (and sent him back as soon as the first month's grocery bills arrived!).

In the beginning the French chefs appear to have imported the *haute cuisine* of the nineteenth century pot and *potage*, with very few concessions to local tradition, as a description of princely hospitality in 1841 demonstrates:

> The Prince Partanna retires to a shady arbour, where he has a private consultation with his French cook: and the result of their combined taste and skill, about four o'clock, is truly astonishing. We form a rather numerous party at dinner, and sit down more than twenty in number. I am the only plebeian guest among them. The Sicilian nobility is one of the oldest in Europe, and six princes, with a proportionate number of dukes and marquises, are present at the table. It is useless to give you a bill of fare, as it would be nearly the same as any other well dressed French dinner; the only custom which seems to me to present any national peculiarity is that of invariably eating iced melon immediately after the soup. After dinner we repair to the saloon, where coffee is served, and soon after iced lemonade and iced water; tea and cakes follow, and a slight supper of rusks, butter, sandwiches, and liqueurs terminates our "eating cares."
>
> Arthur John Strutt, *A Pedestrian Tour in Calabria and Sicily*, 1841

Nor is there anything particularly Sicilian in the buffet described in the ball scene of *The Leopard*, unless it is the way in which intimations of mortality have penetrated even to the dinner table.

> Beneath the candelabra, beneath the five tiers bearing toward the distant ceiling pyramids of homemade cakes that were never touched, spread the monotonous opulence of buffets at big balls: coralline lobsters boiled alive, waxy *chaud-froids* of veal, steely-tinted fish immersed in sauce, turkeys

gilded by the oven's heat, rosy *foie gras* under gelatin armor, boned wood-
cock reclining on amber toast decorated with their own chopped insides,
and a dozen other cruel colored delights. At the end of the table two
monumental silver tureens held clear soup the color of burnt amber. To
prepare this supper the cooks must have sweated away in the vast kitchens
from the night before.

                              Giuseppe di Lampedusa, *The Leopard*, 1960

But by the end of the nineteenth century orthodox French dishes seemed
to be slipping from favor as the *monzù* turned their attention to reelaborating
traditional Sicilian dishes. One might argue that this was a reaction to the
rule of the Savoy monarchs to which Sicily passed once again with the expedition
of Garibaldi and the unification of Italy. This Piedmontese dynasty was as
foreign in temperament and outlook to the islanders as the Bourbons of Naples
had been familiar, and the changes in menu may have reflected a return to
Sicilian tradition in the face of the "enemy."

In any case, the acme of this period in Sicilian cooking corresponds to the
last great flowering of Sicily—the Belle Époque in which the immense mercantile fortunes of the Florio family and of the Anglo-Sicilian Whitakers min-
gled with those of the aristocracy, and transformed the outskirts of Palermo
with theatres, opera houses, Art Nouveau villas and hotels. Franca Florio,
whom Gabriele D'Annunzio called the *beltà divina*, was reputed to be one of
the most beautiful women in Europe (and to own one of the longest and most
beautiful pearl necklaces). Palermo social life was judged to be the gayest and
the most opulent, Sicily's climate the most delightful. It was a last enchanted
moment in Sicilian history, and it is lovingly and delightfully described by
Fulco di Verdura in his memoirs, originally published in England under the
title *A Sicilian Childhood: The Happy Summer Days*.

Kings and kaisers visited, and the hospitality offered them was no less
lavish than that which had been offered Ferdinand and Maria Carolina a century
earlier—a rare occasion for the *monzù* to show their skills. Many of the masterpieces, however, survived in the memory of the people who ate them rather
than in the notes of their creators, in descriptions well flavored with a yearning
for long-lost delights, but vague about the actual ingredients.

One dish often cited in this manner is *pasta alla cardinale*, which blends
elements of French cuisine—*sauce velouté* and *mousse de jambon*—with shrimp
from Sicilian waters and *'u strattu* from Sicilian villages. It was all bound
together with cream and with what was considered by many to be the hallmark

of the *monzù*'s art, *essenza di cipolla*: minced onion cooked so slowly and for so long that it was reduced to a quintessence.

Pasta alla cardinale strikes me as expensive rather than interesting. I am much more attracted by what the *monzù* accomplished when they worked more strictly within the limits of local traditions. One of the areas in which they made their greatest contribution was in the *pasticcio*, the filled pie or pastry beloved by Sicilians throughout the millennia.

The "Leopardesque" timbale of macaroni (*gattopardesco* has entered the Italian language, serving to describe anything that reflects the opulent tastes of the Sicilian aristocracy) has already introduced us to this theme. Another example is a recipe from Messina in which the humble bread dough that envelopes the traditional *impanata* becomes a delicate crust of *pasta frolla* fragrant with grated orange peel and filled with swordfish. Of the various baronial dishes that I have tried, this one is perhaps the most restrained and at the same time the most enjoyable.

IMPANATA DI PESCESPADA
(Swordfish Pie)

Serves 8

PASTA FROLLA PASTRY (see note p. 94)

3¾ cups flour (see note p. 41)
2 tablespoons sugar
Pinch of salt
⅔ cup lard

¼ cup sweet butter
Grated rind of 1 orange
2 eggs
½–1 cup white wine

FILLING

3 medium zucchini
½ cup olive oil plus
  2 tablespoons
1 onion, grated or minced
  fine
1 cup celery cut in ½-inch
  slices, blanched
½ cup pitted green olives
⅓ cup capers

⅓ cup sultana raisins,
  plumped in warm water
  and drained
⅓ cup pine nuts
1 cup plain tomato sauce
  (see p. 172) or 1½ cups
  fresh tomatoes, peeled
  and chopped
2 pounds swordfish, skinned,
  boned, and diced

Sift together flour, sugar, and salt. Cut the lard and butter into small pieces and cut them into the flour, working them in until you have the texture of a coarse meal. Add the orange rind, and stir in 1 whole egg and 1 yolk (reserve the extra white). Add the wine little by little, using just as much as is necessary to bring the pastry together. Knead briefly, shape in a ball, and refrigerate for at least an hour.

Wash the zucchini and cut them into ⅛-inch slices. Sauté them in 2 tablespoons of olive oil until delicately browned on each side. Put aside.

Sauté the onion in ½ cup oil over a very low flame until it is soft. Add the celery, olives, capers, raisins, and pine nuts. Sauté for 3 minutes longer, stirring occasionally, then add the tomato sauce and simmer for about 5 minutes. Add the swordfish and simmer for another 8 to 10 minutes.

Grease a deep 12-inch pie dish. Knead the dough for a few minutes, then divide it into two parts, one of them slightly larger than the other. Roll out the larger piece into a circle wide enough to line the bottom and sides of the dish. Fill the lined dish with a layer of swordfish, a layer of zucchini, and then another layer of swordfish. Roll out the remaining pastry, place it over the pie, and seal the edges. Make vents in the upper crust with a fork and decorate it with scraps of pastry. Beat the reserved egg white until foamy and brush it over the top of the pie.

Bake in a 350°F. oven approximately 60 minutes or until the crust is a pale golden brown.

————

A similar dish, filled with chicken rather than fish, has a much more imposing and quite irresistible name—*pasticcio di sostanza*, "pie of substance." In his book on Sicilian food, Denti di Pirajno gives a recipe that he has copied from some earlier source, fascinating in its archaic language and frustrating in its imprecision. What follows is my attempt at reconstruction.

PASTICCIO DI SOSTANZA
(A Pie of Substance)

Serves 6 to 8

BRISÉE PASTRY CRUST

3 cups flour
  (see note p. 41)
Liberal pinch of salt

1 cup less 2 tablespoons sweet
  butter at room temperature
½ cup water

FILLING

1 frying chicken, cut into
  pieces
3 tablespoons olive oil
1 medium onion, minced
2 tablespoons minced parsley
4 ripe tomatoes, peeled
  and chopped
1 bay leaf
Salt and freshly ground
  black pepper
½ pound chicken giblets
  (livers, hearts, gizzards,
  and unlaid eggs)

1 tablespoon butter
½ pound fresh Sicilian
  sausage, crumbled, or
  chopped pork meat
¼ cup red wine
1½ cups plain tomato sauce
  (see p. 172)
Sugar
Ground cloves
Ground cinnamon
1 egg yolk, beaten

Prepare the crust: Heap the flour and salt on a pastry board, and rub the soft butter into it with your fingers, using a light, chafing motion. When the butter is completely absorbed and there are no more lumps, make a well in the flour and add about ½ cup water, stirring it in with your index finger. The resulting dough should be soft but not sticky. Form into a ball and refrigerate for at least 2 hours.

In a large flameproof casserole brown the chicken in 2 table-spoons of the olive oil. Remove the chicken, and in the same oil sauté the onion until soft. Add the parsley, tomatoes, bay leaf, salt, and pepper. Return the chicken to the pot and simmer, covered, for 30 minutes or until cooked. Uncover for the last 10 minutes to reduce the sauce. When cool, skin and bone the chicken and cut the meat into small pieces. Remove the bay leaf from the sauce and return the meat to the sauce.

Cut the chicken giblets, except the livers, into small pieces and sauté in the butter until browned. After about 10 minutes add the livers, also cut up into small pieces, and continue cooking for another 2 or 3 minutes.

Brown the sausage in the remaining tablespoon of oil. Add the wine, reduce, and add 1 cup tomato sauce, salt, and pepper. Simmer for 20 minutes.

Divide the pastry into two parts, one of them slightly larger. Roll out the larger piece into a circle wide enough to line a deep 9-inch pie dish. Fill the pastry with a layer of chicken meat and its sauce, a layer of sausage, and a layer of giblets. Repeat a second time with the remaining ingredients. (Ideally the last layer should consist of unlaid eggs, a delicacy very dear to the Sicilian aris-tocracy, but difficult to come by in these days of modern chicken farming.) Sprinkle each layer with a pinch of sugar, a pinch of cloves, and a pinch of cinnamon, and pour ½ cup of plain tomato sauce over the top.

Roll out the remaining pastry and cover the pie. Seal the edges and cut a vent in the center. Make a small cone of paper and insert it in the vent so that the escaping steam will be directed away from the crust and won't make it soggy. Brush the crust with beaten egg yolk and bake in a hot oven for 30 minutes.

———

An equally buttery crust is to be found in an almond tart that a cousin of my husband's makes, setting it apart from the classic Sicilian almond pastries such as *bocconetti* (p. 255) and *biscotti ricci* (p. 253), and leading one to suspect the hand of a *monzù*. I know nothing of its history, but I like it.

CROSTATA DI MANDORLE
(Almond Tart)

Makes one 12-inch tart

PASTA FROLLA PASTRY (see note p. 94)

2¼ cups flour (see note p. 41) ¾ cup sweet butter
Small pinch salt 1 egg

¾ cup apricot jam 2 cups finely ground
2 egg yolks   blanched almonds
⅔ cup sugar 2 egg whites

Prepare the pastry: Sift together the flour and salt. Cut in the butter until a coarse-meal texture is reached, then stir in the egg. Work the pastry just enough to combine the ingredients, then shape into a ball and refrigerate for 2 hours.

Preheat oven to 350°F.

Roll out the dough into a circle large enough to line a 12-inch fluted tart pan. Transfer the pastry to the pan as best you can. It is almost impossible not to tear the pastry en route, but this dough patches as easily as it breaks. Press the edge of the dough into the flutes.

Spread the jam in an even layer over the pastry.

Beat the egg yolks until fluffy and lemon-colored. Beat in the sugar little by little and then the ground almonds. Beat the egg whites until soft peaks form, fold them into the almond mixture, and blend carefully. Cover the jam with spoonfuls of the almond mixture, and smooth into an even layer with the help of a fork dipped in cold water. Use the fork to make a decorative pattern of parallel lines on the surface.

Bake for about 30 minutes or until delicately browned.

Another family of dishes dear to the *monzù* were those involving *scuma*—"foam"—a very fine pasta, even finer than *capellini d'angelo*, which has long been a delicacy in eastern Sicily. The simplest way of serving *scuma* is as *pasta fritta*, cooked for an instant in boiling water before being wound on a fork, dipped into beaten eggs and breadcrumbs, and then fried in boiling lard. The swirls of pasta, crisp on the outside and soft within, served hot and accompanied by a bowl of heated honey diluted with orange-blossom water, are of uncertain classification: one book includes them in the *pasta asciutta* section, one among the desserts, and still another suggests adding grated cheese to the egg while maintaining the honey.

A closely related recipe has the wonderful name of *pasta a vento barba di San Benedetto*—roughly translatable as "Pasta Saint Benedict's Beard Blowing in the Wind." This product of Catania's baronial kitchens was a sheet of fresh egg pasta folded in an accordion fashion, cut crosswise in very thin strips, and fried directly. The wavy threads of crisp pasta were then heaped into a tall pyramid, dowsed with orange-blossom honey, and sprinkled with chopped pistachios and tiny pieces of *zuccata*.

In the hands of the *monzù*, *scuma* twists first in one direction, then in another. The fine strands of pasta, boiled briefly and then dressed with butter and parmesan, could be woven around a filling of chicken giblets and lamb sweetbreads cooked with peas in a wine sauce, then breaded and fried into a sophisticated version of *arancine*. Or they could be wrapped around metal baba tins and weighted to keep their shape when fried into crisp baskets. They could then be filled with creamed mushrooms, chicken in béchamel, or even, in the hands of the *monzù* employed by the aunt of a friend of mine, with artichoke hearts and sea-urchin roe.

If these elaborations of the *scuma* tradition betray influences from the North, other *monzù* returned to the roots. Not long ago, the late Giovanni Messina, chef to the Conte Tasca, reworked a seventeenth-century recipe from the Tasca archives for a family wedding: he served medallions of chicken in baskets woven of pasta and decorated with fresh flowers dipped in wax. His favorite pupil and successor, Mario Lo Menzo, has perpetuated this skill, and performed the same feat recently for the wedding of the count's granddaughter.

It is rare, however, to find the sons and pupils of the great *monzù* still at work in Sicily today in the service of private employers. For the most part they have abandoned the legendary dishes, since few private households can afford the exorbitant investment of time and money that was required for their production. In a newspaper interview, Messina claimed with pride that he needed twenty-two pounds of liver to produce a pound of his special pâté. Another example of such conspicuously extravagant meat consumption is the veal *glace* that was a common ingredient in the recipes of the *monzù*. It was probably this that, in the timbale brought to Prince Fabrizio's table, gave the macaroni its "exquisite hue of suède." Today it is the by-product of what is considered to be a proper and even an "important" second course.

CARNE AGLASSATA
(Glazed Pot Roast)

Serves 8 to 10

3 pounds veal in one piece
  (see below)
1 sprig rosemary
⅓ cup olive oil
1 cup white wine
5 pounds white onions,
  sliced

2 beef bouillon cubes
Freshly ground black pepper
Warm water to cover
1 pound green peas, shelled
  (optional)
1 pound carrots, peeled and
  sliced (optional)

The proper meat for *carne aglassata* is veal, not baby veal but the young steer known as *vitellone*, and more precisely the *lacerto* (known in northern Italy as the *girello*), which is a long, cylindrical muscle from the rump. Any cut suitable for pot roast would do, I should think, but it should not have an outer layer of fat. Ask your butcher to tie it up like a pot roast, and stick a sprig of fresh rosemary under the twine.

In a large, heavy saucepan, preferably of an oval shape such as is used for poaching fish, heat the oil and brown the meat, turning to color it on all sides. Add the wine and, when that has partially evaporated, the onions, the bouillon cubes, a little pepper, and enough warm water so that the meat is almost covered. Simmer, covered, for 2½ to 3 hours, turning the meat occasionally.

Some people prefer to put in less water at the beginning, and to keep a small pot of water on top of the lid of the big pan, thus having water at exactly the same temperature as the meat to add from time to time as needed.

Add the peas and the carrots, if you want them, for the last 45 minutes of cooking.

Allow the meat to cool and then refrigerate for 24 hours so that it can be easily sliced into very thin slices. You may serve it either cold or hot. In the latter case run a skewer through the meat to keep the slices neatly together while reheating them in the gravy. The gravy is served as is, or, for those who haven't added peas and carrots and who want a smoother texture, it can be puréed in a blender.

Note: Canned beef or veal stock is not available in Italy, and not being fond of *bollito* as the northerners are, a Sicilian cook would not have homemade stock on hand. The recipe would no doubt be improved if one were to substitute stock for the water and bouillon cubes. But however you make it, the most you will get, in my opinion, is a glorified pot roast that is quite undeserving of all the hullabaloo Sicilians make about it!

––––––

The gravy from this dish, known as '*a glassa*, can be found served on pasta even in a simple Palermo waterfront trattoria. In the kitchens ruled by the *monzù*, however, enormous quantities of veal were reduced to tasteless pulp simply to provide a sufficient quantity of *glace*.

It is too early to give a fair evaluation of the role of the *monzù* in the history of Sicilian cooking. Almost everything that has been published on Sicilian food is quite recent, and was written by elderly aristocrats who grew up in Palermo's heyday, nourished by the masterpieces and the myths of the *monzù*. They began writing in the wake of the publication of *The Leopard*, when once again the world at large discovered the opulence and the beauty of aristocratic Sicily. These were moments to be proud of, in sharp and welcome contrast to the economic and moral squalor that has obscured the island during much of the rest of this century, causing Sicily to be identified with poverty and Mafia.

It is quite possible, although in suggesting this I shall surely give offense to many, that when the nostalgic glow fades and further historical research is published, less importance will be attributed to the *monzù*, whose fires were fanned by the transient winds of fashion, and more paid to the ancient *cucina*

A PROCESSION OF PRIESTS, *a nineteenth-century engraving by Vuillier*

baronale, which had inspired them, and which was perpetuated with greater rigor in the more conservative kitchens of Sicily's monasteries and convents.

> I learned with surprise that in this town [Giuliana], where there are barely three thousand five hundred souls, there are nineteen churches, two convents of nuns, and one abbey of Benedictine monks, lodged in an old castle which they have appropriated, and which they have converted into a magnificent monastery. This number is not yet sufficient, and while I was there, they were busy building another church. It is in these monasteries and these chapels that are locked up all the riches of the country, that is to say, the little wealth that is produced; everywhere one sees nothing but the deepest misery, the most frightful filth, the most debilitated health, which are the necessary consequence of the extreme indigence.
>
> Jean Houel, *Voyage pittoresque en Sicile*, 1785

The situation in Giuliana that Houel observed with surprise was by no means unusual. Sicily was absolutely littered with religious institutions. They were not all of them the treasure houses that Houel imagined, since there were many, especially in the provinces, where the vow of poverty was observed willy-nilly and where "the well-loved refectory bell rang only *pro forma*."

It should also be remembered that within the walls of these institutions there were many men and women who had joined the order in answer to an authentic vocation, and many who in all good faith saw no discrepancy between the intent of their monastic life and the style of it.

Having said this, however, one can then proceed to say that the monasteries and the convents of Sicily represented a pillar of the aristocratic economy. By 1500 the barons had established their right to dispose of their feudal holdings as they wished, and from that point on their main preoccupation was to keep their patrimony in one piece by establishing a strict system of primogeniture. By means of a testament known as a *vinculum*, the eldest son was designated as universal heir and denied the right to sell or divide the property. The remaining sons were guaranteed a life income, the *vita milizia*, equal to one third or one half of the income that would have been theirs if all the property had been divided equally, and they were seldom allowed to marry. Sent at an early age to be educated in the monasteries and the Jesuit colleges, a few of them later left to be admitted to the upper ranks of the royal administration, but many of them remained.

Apart from the income derived from its cut of the *vita milizia* of its members, a well-placed monastery was usually endowed with a large feudal patrimony of its own, both in land and in tithes and taxes, which had been granted at the moment of its founding or subsequently acquired through the pious bequests of the faithful. Such orders enjoyed an enormous and tax-free income, much of which was employed in the building of sumptuously decorated churches, such as San Domenico or San Giuseppe dei Teatini in Palermo. These monasteries themselves were hardly spartan, as anyone can testify who has stayed at the San Domenico in Taormina, formerly a Dominican monastery but now Sicily's most luxurious hotel.

A good portion of the income went into the kitchen. The younger sons of Sicily's aristocratic families may have been denied the pleasures of marriage and fatherhood (legitimate, at least), but it seems unlikely that they ate much worse than their elder brothers. The Convent of San Domenico in Palermo, in order to celebrate the election in 1796 of a new provincial, offered Palermo notables a dinner composed of twenty-four main dishes, sixty-four *intramezzi* and *tornagusti*, as well as the *postpasto* and the ices. This was an exceptional occasion, of course, the Epiphany menu served to the young aristocrats who were being educated at the Abbey of San Michele Arcangelo in Troina was somewhat simpler:

MENU FOR EPIPHANY

Antipasto del monastero and *biancomangiare*
Pasta di sostanza
Timbales
Roast chicken
Pork chops
Farsumagru
Game (hares, rabbits, woodcocks)
Stuffed chanterelle mushrooms
Sfinci
Schiumone
Pastries
Cordials
Coffee

COLLEGIO DEI NOBILI IN TRAPANI, *an eighteenth-century engraving by Bova*

This menu is interesting both because it is fairly modern—dating from around the year 1800—and because it comes from an institution that was way up in the mountains and probably did not count among its pupils the scions of the great noble families of Catania and Palermo, but rather the sons of a lesser, more provincial aristocracy. The food served would have been that of the eighteenth-century *cucina baronale*, still relatively unaltered by the fashions from France.

There is no way of knowing what the "antipasto of the monastery" might have been, but blancmange has been a favorite in Sicily for centuries. Puddings made from rice flour and other starches are very popular throughout the Middle East, and it is not unlikely that *biancomangiare* arrived in Sicily with the Arabs. Although nowadays it is most frequently used as a filling in pastries, it can stand on its own as a separate dish, and as such was very popular in the Renaissance. The version served to the young students at San Michele probably differed very little from the fifteenth-century version for which Platina gives a recipe:

BLANCMANGE ALLA CATALANA

For ten people, dissolve pounded almonds in a fat veal or chicken broth, pass them through a sieve and pour into a pan with two ounces of rice flour. Cook for half an hour over a slow flame, stirring continuously so they don't stick to the pan. Then add half a pound of sugar and the breast of a capon boiled and pounded in the mortar. When everything is cooked, add rosewater and put immediately in serving plates, with a sprinkling of sweet powdered spices. This is a very nutritious dish, but slow to digest and it weighs the body down. It is good for the liver, but it is astringent and therefore not to be advised for those who suffer from colics.

Bartolomeo Platina, *Il piacere onesto e la buona salute*, 1474

There was also a Lenten version made with fish broth rather than chicken stock, but neither of these has survived—perhaps understandably. The modern blancmange is purely sweet, and in the area of Ragusa it is still made with almond milk.

Almond milk, which makes a delicious drink and an even more delicious *granita*, can be made by putting ground and pounded almonds in a muslin bag and soaking them in cold water for an hour, then wringing them out and dipping them in over and over again until all the essence of the nuts has been squeezed out into the water in beautiful cloudy white swirls. It is sort of like making a Tintoretto sky. In Italy condensed syrups and pastes for making *latte di mandorle* are available in the supermarkets (Saba brand is excellent), or one can make it at home by using ½ pound blanched almonds, 5 cups of water, and then adding 1 cup of sugar. The almonds should be as fresh as possible, and ideally should include 10 percent bitter almonds. I was startled to read in Carol Field's book on Italian baking that bitter almonds are outlawed in the United States because they are toxic. Despite having read dozens of detective stories in which a faint odor of bitter almonds hung about the corpse's lips, I had never paused to think what potential mayhem was growing outside my kitchen door.

BIANCOMANGIARE DI MANDORLE
(Almond Blancmange)

Serves 6 to 8

5 cups sweetened almond
  milk

¾ cup cornstarch
1 small strip of lemon peel

Prepare as for a normal milk *biancomangiare* (see p. 18). When it has thickened, pour into individual molds or cups moistened with water. Giuseppe Coria suggests serving the *biancomangiare* unmolded onto a fresh lemon leaf, dusted with ground cinnamon, and garnished with a jasmine blossom—an entrancing suggestion and well worth following where possible.

————

THE MONASTERY OF SANTA MARIA DI GESU, PALERMO, *an engraving by P. Dewint, 1823*

Elsewhere in Sicily *biancomangiare* is made with cow's milk and used in preparing sweets such as *cuccìa* or *pasticciotto*, or as a nursery and sickroom food. For my husband and my brother-in-law it seems to offer the same sort of mindless comfort that Campbell's chicken noodle used to offer me.

According to the historian who has studied the monastery archives, the next course on the Epiphany menu would be a timbale of cauliflower and sausage meat that still goes by the name of *pasta di sostanza* in present-day Troina. Timbales and roast meat are generic but self-explanatory; *farsumagru*, on the other hand, requires an explanation.

Farsumagru is a large meat roll with an interesting history of upward social mobility. It originated as a humble and economical dish: a thin slice of meat, when rolled around a stuffing of breadcrumbs, can be stretched out to feed many more people than the meat alone would satisfy. The early version is still a great favorite.

INVOLTINI SICILIANI
(Sicilian Skewered Meat Rolls)

Serves 6

1 medium-small onion,
  minced
2 tablespoons oil
1 cup stale white bread-
  crumbs (see p. 12)
¼ cup pine nuts
¼ cup currants, plumped in
  hot water for 5 minutes
¼ cup grated caciocavallo or
  pecorino cheese
Salt and freshly ground
  black pepper

2 ounces fresh caciocavallo or
  primosale cheese
1½ pounds veal or beef
  fillets, cut into twenty-four
  2-by-5-inch slices
1 large onion, cut in wide
  slices (see p. 35)
Bay leaves
2 tablespoons olive oil
½ cup stale white
  breadcrumbs

Sauté the medium-small onion in 2 tablespoons of oil until soft, then stir in 1 cup breadcrumbs, pine nuts, currants, grated cheese, and salt and pepper to taste.

Proceed exactly as in the swordfish *involtini* (see p. 33), putting a teaspoonful of the breadcrumb mixture and a piece of cheese on each slice of meat, rolling it up, and placing it on a skewer, interspersed with slices of onion and bay leaves. When all the slices are rolled and skewered, sprinkle them with oil and coat them lightly on both sides with the remaining ½ cup breadcrumbs.

Broil or grill over moderate coals for about 10 minutes.

———

In the baronial kitchens, these *involtini*, expanded and elaborated upon, became known as *farsumagru*, a puzzling name if taken as the Sicilian for "false lean," more sensible if, as one writer suggests, it comes via a French chef from *farce maigre*, meatless stuffing. Except that once the chefs of the aristocracy got their hands on it, the stuffing was naturally no longer meatless. If the origins of its name cause Sicilian gastronomes to argue, *farsumagru* itself inspires them to wax lyrical:

Behold [as you slice it] how the shining yellow of the egg yolk appears, set in its halo of white, flanked by the nebulae of lard and surrounded by the little green planets of the peas, rotating across the Milky Way of melted caciocavallo, emerging from the infinitely flavorful spaces of the "falso-magro," the undisputed monarch of meat dishes in Sicily.

Pino Correnti, *Il libro d'oro della cucina e dei vini di Sicilia*, 1985

FARSUMAGRU or BRACIOLONE
(Braised Meat Roll)

Serves 8 to 10

1 slice beef weighing 2 to 2½ pounds
¼ pound ground beef
1 egg
⅓ cup grated pecorino or caciocavallo cheese
⅔ cup baby peas (fresh or frozen), blanched in boiling water for 1 minute
Salt and freshly ground black pepper
2 ounces fresh pork fat
2 ounces fresh caciocavallo cheese

4 eggs, hard-boiled
2 spring onions or 1 small red onion
6 sprigs parsley
4 very thin slices of mortadella or cooked ham
1 tablespoon olive oil
1 tablespoon lard
1 cup red wine
2 tablespoons tomato extract (see p. 13) or 3 tablespoons tomato paste
1 bay leaf
Water

To make a *farsumagru*, my butcher gives me the *tasca*, a large, flat muscle known as the "pocket" because it comes from just where their front pockets would be if cattle wore bluejeans. (A flank steak is probably the closest American equivalent, but any large, thick slice from the rump or round would do.) He cuts it almost in half and opens it like a book so that I have a slice about 10 by 14 inches and about ½ inch thick, which is what you're aiming for, wherever you get it from. It should be well pounded, but not to the point of making holes in it.

In a small bowl blend the ground beef, egg, grated cheese, peas, and some salt and pepper.

Cut both the fresh pork fat and the caciocavallo cheese into long, thin strips.

Shell the hard-boiled eggs and cut off the ends up to the yolks.

Trim the spring onions, leaving them whole, or cut the red onion into thin wedges. Trim off the toughest parts from the parsley sprigs.

Line up all the foregoing on your work space, and have a ball of white kitchen twine at hand. Spread out the slice of beef, wider side toward you, and cover it with the slices of mortadella, leaving a 1-inch margin showing all around the edge. Spread the half of the mortadella that is nearest to you with the ground-beef mixure. Line up the eggs end to end on the ground beef (the idea being to arrange them so that the yolk will "shine" in every slice). In rows parallel to the eggs line up the onions, parsley, strips of pork fat, and strips of cheese. Sprinkle it all with a pinch of salt.

Enroll an extra pair of hands if there is one available (it is by no means impossible to do this alone, but it is more difficult), and begin rolling up the meat, rolling away from you so that the half with the ground beef and all the other ingredients is at the center, and the outmost layer is plain beef and mortadella. It should be rolled up quite tight, but not so tight that things start oozing out the ends.

Make a slipknot in the free end of your ball of twine, pass it around one end of the rolled meat, pull tight, and then wrap the rest of the roll up tightly, passing the twine a few times lengthwise around the roll as well. It is better to be liberal with your twine than to lose your stuffing.

Heat the oil and the lard in a heavy casserole big enough to accommodate the rolled meat, and brown the meat on all sides. Then pour the wine over it. Reduce the wine, then add the tomato extract, stirring until it dissolves. Add the bay leaf and enough water to cover about three-quarters of the rolled meat. Bring to a boil and simmer, covered, for about 1 hour. Turn the meat occasionally.

When the meat is cooked, remove it from the pan and allow

it to cool for 20 minutes. Remove the twine and place the meat on a platter. Cut into slices, arranging the slices so the filling shows. Remove the bay leaf from the sauce, correct the seasoning, heat the sauce, and pass it together with the sliced meat.

Note: Farsumagru is also more prosaically known as *braciolone*, especially when executed in smaller rolls, each one an individual serving.

––––––

The Epiphany feast ended with *sfinci* (see p. 247), a fried sweet that is incredibly rich and heavy, and *schiumone*, which was probably a frozen dessert (see p. 297). By the time the young scholars had topped all this off with pastries, cordials, and coffee, they must have found it extremely difficult to stagger as far as the chapel for Vespers.

For an island as rich in fish as Sicily, even the rigors of Lenten fasting were no great problem, although degree and rank were important here as elsewhere in Sicilian life.

> Good Friday was a day of strict fasting: no butter, milk, or eggs, but only food cooked in water or in oil. Fortunately the young were dispensed from this harsh regime. Papà had informed us of the fact that, since our ancestors had fought against the Moors in Spain, we were exempt from respecting the fast except on Good Friday and Ash Wednesday, and that we had the right to hang a golden cauldron above our coat of arms. Mamma, either out of a spirit of contradiction or because she really believed it, had decided that it would have been vulgar to take advantage of such a privilege, and so we fasted like any proletarian family would.
>
> Fulco, *Estati felici: un infanzia in Sicilia*, 1977

Like the blancmange, most dishes come in two versions: *grasso* or fat, i.e., with meat; and *magro*—lean or meatless. Self-denial seems to have been very much a letter-of-the-law affair, to judge by the *pasticcio di magro*, a Lenten version of the *pasticcio di sostanza* that was filled with baby codfish, shrimp, squid, clams, anchovies, cauliflower, and artichokes, and flavored with capers, raisins, and olives.

It is even harder to reconcile one's idea of fasting with *riso nero*, the Holy Week treat for the boys at San Michele. Said to be of Spanish origin, this dessert is now made in honor of the feast of the Black Madonna of Tindari, whose shrine on the northwestern coast of Sicily preserves a much-venerated Byzantine icon. In my opinion, what this pudding proves is that boarding-school fare is universally dismal, but I include the recipe for the curious.

RISO NERO
(Black Rice)

Serves 8 to 10

3 cups short-grain Italian
    pudding rice, preferably
    originario
1½–2 quarts milk
1 cup unsweetened cocoa

1 cup sugar
1 teaspoon ground cinnamon
1 cup almonds, toasted and
    chopped

Put the rice and 1½ quarts of milk in a saucepan and cook over low heat, stirring frequently, until the rice is cooked and has absorbed all the milk. Add more milk from time to time if necessary. Remove from the heat and stir in the cocoa, sugar, cinnamon, and almonds, saving about a third of the almonds to scatter on top. Serve cold.

———

The poorer monasteries and the poorer members of the laity, for whom fresh fish would have been an unattainable luxury, had to make do in Lent with salt fish: some imported cod and herring, but principally the tuna, sardines, and anchovies that Sicily produced in great quantity. An animated description of tuna fishing in Palermo shows how some orders ensured their supply of fish to salt away for Lent.

> The tunnyfish are brought in big boats to the shore, thrown into the sea to wash off the blood, and then pulled up on the shore where they are arranged in rows of ten.
> Then an agent of the Archbishop of Palermo presents the Master of the Tonnara with a purse in which there are ten marbles: nine of these are numbered from one to nine: the tenth has a cross on it; the Master draws

a marble from the purse; suppose it is the marble number three, then the Archbishop's man takes for his share the third fish in each row. If it is the number four or number five marble, then he takes the fourth or fifth fish from each row. The Archbishop insists upon his rights. The three tonnaras of Palermo provide him with an income of six hundred louis.

After the Archbishop, then the Grand Admiral takes his due; it is the right of choosing the best tunnyfish out of every sixty. . . . [While the remaining fish are being chopped up, salted and put in barrels,] a crowd of parasites arrive. These are clouds of Capucines, of Recollects, of other mendicant orders and hermits who rather resemble the hornets who gather

A MONK, *a nineteenth-century engraving by Vuillier*

to pilfer the honey from the beehive. They shamelessly attribute to themselves the success of the fishing: without their prayers it would never have succeeded; the fish would have taken another route, or the mesh of the nets would not have held. The audacity with which they make these assertions and their devout and honeyed tones persuade the poor ignorant fishermen: they announce with prophetic menace that, if no one gives them alms, the heavens in indignation will send tempests to rend the *tonnara*, disperse the fish and capsize the boats; these good souls are frightened by such threats, and thus are parted from a good share of the fruit of their labours.

Jean Houel, *Voyage Pittoresque*, 1784

These were the mendicant orders, however, which ranked very low. First place was held by the Benedictine monks, with the Dominicans close behind. In Palermo there were two great Benedictine institutions, one of them the enormously rich abbey of Monreale, founded by William II in 1180, whose mosaic-lined church, now the Cathedral of Monreale, and adjacent cloisters are among the greatest masterpieces of Sicilian art. The table wasn't bad, either.

The Benedictines [of Monreale] are celebrated for good living, and our bill of fare will not bely their fame; although you will perhaps think the preponderance of sweet dishes somewhat *de trop*. Imprimis—No soup—*piattini* [little plates] of anchovies, ham, olives in sauce, and salame; a sweet dish of *frittelle*; then a large lobster, or rather a fish like a gigantic shrimp, for it has no claws; *Pasticcio di Maccheroni con regaglie*, an *infreddo* (something like brawn) with jelly; roast fowls, and salad; a dish, a sort of sponge cake, adorned with red sweet and white cream, which cake, to my surprise, I learned was made of potatoes; trifle and dessert: the oil was the finest I ever tasted; it was from the immediate neighbourhood, and the choicest part of the olive; being extracted merely by the pressure of men's feet.

Arthur John Strutt, *A Pedestrian Tour in Calabria and Sicily*, 1841

The dessert made of potatoes must have been a version of *sfinci di San Martino* (the only dessert in Sicily made with mashed potatoes), a fried beignet that—nowadays at least—is dipped in honey. This is a ritual sweet for the feast of Saint Martin, who is the patron of the other great Benedictine monastery, San Martino delle Scale, located in the mountains near Monreale.

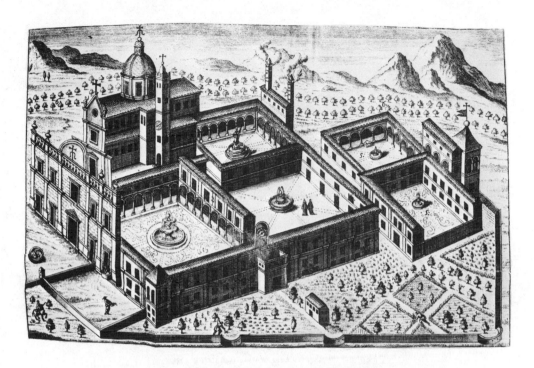

SAN MARTINO DELLE SCALE, *a nineteenth-century engraving by d'Ostervald*

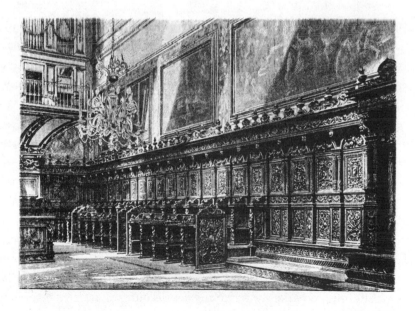

THE CHOIR OF THE MONASTERY OF SAN MARTINO, *a nineteenth-century engraving by Vuillier*

A VIEW OF SAN NICOLA, *a nineteenth-century engraving*

Originally founded by Pope Gregory the Great in the sixth century, and then refounded after its destruction at the hands of the Saracens, this monastery, with its vast church and numerous cloisters dating from the sixteenth century, was reserved for the sons of Palermo's nobility. After seven years of study they either entered the order or took up the cross as Knights of Malta, vowing themselves to celibacy, chastity, and mortifications.

But of all the Benedictine convents, the most famous (or infamous) was that of San Nicola in Catania. Almost every traveler from the North visited this institution, mainly, one would surmise, to seek confirmation of his anti-papist prejudices. For there are many accounts of being gratifyingly scandalized by the splendor of the church ("like all undertakings of priests [it] will cost enormous sums without being executed with the least taste"), the amount of the convent's revenues (derived from fifty-two estates), the number of servants allotted each noble friar (two), the dimensions of the convent itself ("a stupendous building, remarkably terrifying on account of its size"), and by its ill-kempt appearance.

CHOIR OF SAN NICOLA, *a nineteenth-century engraving*

The Prior's apartments, although more spacious, had nothing characteristic about them: they neither looked like the abode of a devotee nor of a man of letters, and the furniture, at once gaudy and shabby, the vases of flowers, and mirrors with tarnished frames, gave them the comfortless air of a ballroom seen by daylight. The inner courts of the buildings are neglected, and overgrown with tall weeds, and contrasted most unfavorably with recollections of the neatly-trimmed grass-plats and well-rolled gravel walks in the quadrangles of the Colleges at Oxford. But the genius of order and activity presides over one spot, while the nightmare of sloth and stagnation broods over the other.

Marquis of Ormonde, *An Autumn in Sicily*, 1832

Just about the only traveler to put in a good word for the monks of San Nicola was a certain J. G. Francis, B.A., who in his 1847 journal concedes that "this princely society keeps the poor of Catania from perishing by famine: a sum of several dollars is disbursed every morning in necessaries to relieve the most pressing cases."

However censorious the foreigners, the most damning criticism came from a Sicilian, the nineteenth-century novelist Federico De Roberto. His major work, a wonderful novel about the Catanese nobility entitled *The Viceroys*, has been unjustly overshadowed by the works of Verga and Lampedusa. It contains a detailed and indignant account of life at San Nicola and a famous description of the monastery kitchen:

> The monks, in fact, had a high old time: eating, drinking, and amusing themselves. On getting up in the morning they each went to say their Mass down in the church, often behind closed doors so as not to be disturbed by the faithful. Then they withdrew to their apartments, to eat something while awaiting luncheon, at which, in kitchens as spacious as barracks, worked no fewer than eight cooks, apart from kitchen-hands. Every day the cooks got four loads of oak charcoal from Nicolosi to keep the ovens always hot, and for frying alone the kitchen Cellerar would consign to them every day four bladders of lard of two *rotoli* each, and two *cafissi* of oil; enough for six months at the prince's. The pots and pans were big enough to boil a whole calf's haunch and roast a swordfish complete; two kitchen-hands would each grasp half a great cheese and spend an hour grating it; the chopping block was an oak trunk which no two men could get their arms around; and every week a carpenter, paid four *tari* and half a barrel of wine for this service, had to saw off a couple of inches or it became unserviceable from so much chopping.
>
> The Benedictines' kitchen had become a proverb in town. The macaroni pie with its crust of short pastry, the rice-balls each big as a melon; the stuffed olives and honey-cakes, were dishes which no other cook could make; and for their ices and fruit drinks and frozen *cassate*, the Fathers had called specially from Naples Don Tino, from the Benvenuto Caffè. All this was made in such quantities that it was sent round as presents to the monks' and the novices' families, and the servitors would sell the remains and get four, and some six, *tari* each for them daily.
>
> Federico De Roberto, *The Viceroys*, 1894

The monks of San Nicola enjoyed Sicilian cooking in its most traditional and at its very best. Their specialties are the great classics of the island's table: the *arancine* and the "macaroni pie" we have already met; stuffed olives, their pits replaced by a caper and a piece of anchovy, have long since entered upon the international cocktail circuit; the ices and the frozen *cassate* are part of a chapter to come. Only the "honey cakes" need be introduced here; they are still a favorite among the people of Catania today.

CRISPELLE DI RISO
(Honeyed Rice Fritters)

Makes about 4 dozen

1 ½ cups short-grain Italian
    pudding rice, preferably
    originario
2 ½ cups whole milk
2 ½ cups water plus
    2 tablespoons
Pinch of salt
Zest of 1 orange

¼ pound fresh ricotta
    (see note p. 18)
⅓ cup flour (see note p. 41)
Vegetable oil for frying
⅔ cup honey
¼ cup superfine sugar,
    or granulated sugar
    ground fine
1 teaspoon cinnamon

Put the rice, milk, 2 ½ cups of water, salt, and orange peel in a saucepan. Bring to the boiling point and cook over low heat, stirring frequently, at least 20 minutes or until the rice is soft and has absorbed the liquid. Pour the rice onto a plate and let it stand overnight.

The next morning, remove the orange peel, add the ricotta and flour, and stir at length until you have a well-blended, firm paste. Let stand for 3 or 4 hours.

Spread the rice on a small wooden chopping board or very flat plate that you can hold in one hand close to the frying pan. The rice should be in a layer ¼ inch thick. Cut into strips ½ inch wide and 2 inches long; as you cut each strip, push or slide it into the oil, which should be very hot and at least 2 inches deep. (If you try to lift the slices from the board and transport them to the oil in any other way, they will break.) Fry the *crispelle* until they are a rich golden brown, lift them out with a slotted spoon, and drain on absorbent paper.

Heat the honey with 2 tablespoons of water in a small saucepan. Dip the *crispelle* in a few at a time, remove, and arrange them

on a platter. Sprinkle with sugar and cinnamon and serve while
they are still warm.

————

It is an anomaly that the monks of San Nicola should be famous for their
crispelle, for in general the production of sweets and pastries was considered
the province of the convents in which their aristocratic sisters dwelled.

A PENITENT, *figure from a religious procession in
a nineteenth-century engraving by Vuillier*

6

Virgins' Breasts, Chancellor's Buttocks, and Other Convent Delicacies

And first 'tis right and justice asks that I
With praising the Origlione sisters should commence,
A convent above them all to hold on high,
Most particular im pomp and in magnificence. . . .
Their *impanatelle* are the awe and wonder
Of all who've tried them, this you may believe;
And should my words give cause to doubt or ponder,
Come, taste, and tell me if I do deceive.

The Martorana, this Eden, paradise on earth,
I wish to praise with verse, with viol and horn.
Blessed the man these sisters deem of worth,
For here the fruits of marzipan are born.
How sweet the chestnut, sweet the carob bean,
The plum, the apricot, the quince so round:
For such as these three Jesuits were seen
To brawl and fight and roll upon the ground.

A month ago I felt my senses fail,
But when a *sfinci* from the Stigmata I was fed,
My face, which first had been so ghostly pale,
To life reborn, became a sanguine red.
In virtue quite elect, a worthy cause for feast,
This convent's *ravazzate* have such fame
That once I heard an ancient Jesuit priest
Say, "*Lapis philosophorum* is their name!"

Abbot Giovanni Meli,
"Li cosi duci di li batii," circa 1790

When the Arabs brought sugarcane to Sicily, they also brought their love for comfits, the sugar-coated "spices for the chamber" that gained rapid popularity among the European nobility of the age of the Crusades. In the thirteenth and fourteenth centuries comfits were imported from the Levant and so made their way into the castles and manors of Europe, where they sweetened courtly dalliance and assuaged pious appetites during the Lenten fasts. Together with almond paste and preserved or candied fruits, they form a particular category of food that, although it became known in England as "banqueting stuff," was not considered as part of the meal, but rather as a refreshment to be served apart.

By the end of the Norman era their production was well established in Sicily, and Frederick II's laws regulated the confectioner's trade. Such was the fame achieved by Sicilian confectionery that together with perfumes and oils and other exotic luxuries it had become part of the popular image of Palermo that is reflected in Boccaccio's description of sex and seduction in Palermo's public baths:

> At this stage the attendants produced graceful silver perfume-bottles, some full of rose-water, and some of orange-blossom lotion, jessamine and extract of citron-blooms, with which they sprinkled the bathers' bodies. Later came boxes of sweets and flasks of precious wines, and for some time the lovers partook of the refreshments.
>
> Giovanni Boccaccio, *The Decameron*, 1353

The production of comfits and confections in Sicily probably kept pace with the production of sugar itself. This was greatly diminished during the turbulent decades following the extinction of the Norman dynasty, reduced perhaps to small plantations scaled to local consumption. Nonetheless, knowledge and techniques survived, ready to accompany the extraordinary expansion in sugar production that began at the end of the fourteenth century, and to satisfy the requirements of the newly established royal court.

Comfits always appeared among the gifts that the city of Palermo presented to royal ambassadors and other VIPs. In 1417 the wife of the viceroy received a tribute of almond, anise, and coriander comfits, as well as *zuccata* and candied citron. Fruits in syrup, marzipan tortes, conserves of apples, pears, quinces, and rose petals were also being produced, both for local consumption and for export. Quince conserves are still very popular in Sicily, and are very easy to make.

COTOGNATA
(Quince Paste)

2 pounds quinces, peeled,   2 pounds sugar
  cored, and quartered   Juice of 1 lemon

Cook the fruit in a heavy saucepan, with just enough water to cover the bottom of the pan, over a low flame for about 20 minutes, or until it is soft. Remove from the heat, and pass through a food mill or ricer. Add the sugar and the lemon juice and return to the flame. Simmer, stirring constantly, until the sugar is completely dissolved and the mixture becomes very dense and comes away from the pan as you stir. Pour into barely oiled saucers or molds to a depth of no more than an inch. Allow to dry in the open air for several days. Unmold and dry on a rack for 2 or 3 days longer, then dust with sugar and store in a dry place. Cut into small squares or strips and serve as candy.

In Sicily, *cotognata* is made in fluted oval molds of tin, similar to those used for a madeleine, or in pretty ceramic molds with designs in the bottom. The same molds are used for another confection that is somewhat similar but made from grape must. Although *mostarda*, as this is called, is usually made in households where there are vineyards and a supply of must is available during the harvest, it can be perfectly well made from the juice of white table grapes, especially the aromatic varieties such as Smyrna or muscatel.

MOSTARDA
(Must Paste)

6 cups of fresh juice from
   white table or wine grapes
¼ cup wood ashes
¾ cup cornstarch
Zest of 1 lemon, orange,
   or tangerine

⅓ cup pine nuts, toasted
⅓ cup almonds, toasted and
   chopped coarse
½ cup raisins
Lemon juice

Put the juice in a stainless steel or enameled saucepan. Stir in the wood ashes (theoretically these should be ashes made from burning the prunings of the grapevines, but I doubt that this is absolutely necessary; it might be wise to avoid ashes from any particularly aromatic woods), bring to a full boil, and remove from the fire. Allow to stand for 24 hours.

Filter this must through very fine muslin or a paper filter, ladling it out from the pot with care so as not to disturb the sediments that the ashes have carried to the bottom. Measure 5 cups of the filtered must, and add them slowly to the cornstarch in a saucepan, stirring to eliminate any lumps. Add the zest and cook over a very low flame, stirring constantly, until the *mostarda* is very thick and comes away from the sides of the pan as you stir. Remove the zest and blend in the nuts and raisins.

Wet the molds (or use plates) with a little lemon juice and pour in the *mostarda*. Allow to dry for twenty-four hours in the sun. Turn the *mostarda* over on the plate or in the mold and allow the underside to dry, turning it from side to side in the sun for several days longer. Put under cover at night to avoid the dew. Store in a cool, dry place (cut into pieces first if you have used plates). It eventually becomes very hard indeed—if, that is, it manages to survive the forays of the family.

Waverley Root says that the *mostarda* he ate in the province of Messina had lots of cinnamon in it, but this is not the custom in the western part of the island. He also says it had mustard in it, but that is quite impossible, since despite the Arabic recipe for wine on page 101, mustard is now totally unknown to Sicilian cooking.

———

Today *cotognata* is a modest treat, but not so in the fourteenth century. According to the accounts of Francesco Datini, a merchant who lived in Prato at this time, a pound of comfits or of powdered sugar cost thirty-six times as much as a pound of beef, and a marzipan torte was more expensive than a brace of peacocks. Such high prices also explain why, in an age in which the chroniclers are usually quite indifferent to what is being eaten, the confectionery is carefully itemized.

The entertainments of this day consisted in diverse dances performed by the Ladies with the Knights, which were opened by the groom and the bride. Said dances were interspersed with pauses for a most excellent refreshment of sweets, brought on in this order.

There appeared at one end of the corridor, through a door that leads to the rooms of the Palace, milord the Marchese della Favara with 25 gentlemen, each carrying a bowl of silver, full of comfits and of diverse sorts of fruit with sugar statues adorned by banners of silver and gold with the coats of arms of the bride and groom; upon these followed milord the Conte di Raccuia with 25 other gentlemen and as many bowls; then came milord the Conte di Cammarata with the third formation, and finally milord the Marchese d'Avola; and these four masters of ceremony were also accompanied by cupbearers with pitchers of drinks.

Don Bernardino Masbelli, *The Wedding of Donna Anna d'Aragona and Don Giovanni Ventimiglia, Marchese di Gerace*, 1574

Sicilian sugar had its heyday in the fifteenth century, when vast fortunes were made from its production and export. The expulsion of the Jews in 1492 meant the loss of both capital and skilled labor, and in the following decades much of the island's remaining capital was immobilized in the creation of feudal holdings. Despite the consequent decline in sugar production, Sicily remained self-sufficient throughout the sixteenth century, and even exported small amounts from mills like the one described by a traveler in 1568:

Whosoever enters in one of these will think to have entered the forges of Vulcan, so great and so steady appear the fires by which the sugar hardens and is refined. And so also those men who work steadfastly here are so sooty, so dirty, so filthy and seared with heat that they seem more demon than human.

Leandro Alberti, *Descrittione di tutta l'Italia*, 1568

Sicily continued to produce sugar with occasionally greater but mostly lesser success until the end of the eighteenth century. But the quantity was insufficient, and from the seventeenth century on, Sicily's sweet tooth had to be satisfied by imported sugar.

Tastes were changing too. The comfits and preserves evolved into something known as *dolci di riposto*, cupboard sweets, which kept well and could be ordered in quantity to provide for unexpected visits. Somewhat like *petits fours* in appearance, *dolci di riposto* are made of almond paste and filled with dates or with quince, fig, or citron preserves, iced in pastel colors and topped with a silvered comfit.

Comfits and sugar statues survive as ritual treats. As in many parts of Catholic Europe, Sicilians still mark the important rites of passage by distributing sugared almonds tied up in little tulle pouches and colored according to the occasion: pink or blue for baptism, white for first communion and marriage, green for engagement, red for a university diploma, silver for the twenty-fifth wedding anniversary. The intricate allegorical centerpieces made of sugar that adorned the banquets of Renaissance and baroque Europe have given way to gaudy sugar statuettes—paladins, ballerinas, carabinieri, and even cowboys and Mickey Mouses—the *pupi di cena* that are sold at the Fair of the Dead. (Claudia Roden describes similar sugar dolls, which she remembers

being sold for the celebration of the sacrifice of the Bride of the Nile when she was a child in Egypt.)

In the eighteenth century "banqueting stuff" disappeared from the refreshment table, be it at princely balls or at public festivities, such as those held in honor of a royal birth:

> In the evening the park was illuminated, in such manner as to appear almost beyond recognition. And without hyperbole it even seemed a theatre of paradise. . . . Add to all this the musical entertainments which could be heard from two orchestras with goodly number of instrumentalists, sitting in circles around the fountains, to the extreme pleasure of the joyful audience; and add the vast number of masked figures who were dancing continuously . . . in the squares about the fountains and in the center of the avenues, and add finally the six public stalls or refreshment stands, whence were offered gratis to the people splendid refreshments of ices, wines, liqueurs, melons and pastries, as if they were so many small *cuccagnas*.
>
> Marchese di Villabianca, *Diario palermitano*, 1772

As sugar was transformed from spice to basic ingredient and began to disappear from the first and second (or first thirty) courses—a development that, as we have seen, was never quite completed in Sicily—the art of pastry making came into its own. In much of southern Italy this art received a convent education. The long and delightful ode that the Abbot Giovanni Meli wrote to celebrate the "sweet things" of Palermo's convents, of which the verses opening this chapter give but a taste, indicates the degree of specialized excellence in pastry to which the nuns of Sicily had attained by the end of the eighteenth century.

No writer whom I have consulted offers any explanation for this phenomenon. The universal if questionable cliché of the frustrated female consoling herself with a box of chocolates or a cream-filled éclair has little application here, since the bulk of the pastries were given away. The pastries that the nuns produced, like the bread made for Saint Joseph's Day, offered women of very restricted lives a rare outlet for creativity, and both would provide interesting material for the study of the relationship between women, food, and religion. I can only venture to suggest that what was originally a humble offering of one's own labor, considered proper to a woman vowed to poverty, maintained this air of suitability and propriety even when it had gotten quite out of hand. For, whatever lay behind its origins, by the nineteenth century the production of pastries within the convents of the island had reached quite startling proportions.

The convents themselves had multiplied in a remarkable fashion. Many of them had been founded in the sixteenth century to provide refuge for "ill-married" women and repentant prostitutes. The Repentite, founded in 1524, was an early example of this, although by 1700 it had become a proper convent in which only virgins were allowed to profess their vows and try their hand at making *cassate* and other sweets.

Others were of much older and more aristocratic origin. One of these was Santa Trinità del Cancelliere, a Cistercian convent that had been founded in 1190 by the Royal Chancellor Matteo d'Ajello, and that admitted only ladies of noble birth. These aristocratic nuns, or rather the servants they supervised, were famous for their *fedde*. In their original version, these pastries must have looked something like clamshells. They were made in oval hinged molds that were lined with *pasta reale* and then filled with apricot jam and egg custard. When the mold was closed the two sheets of almond paste came together and a bit of the filling oozed out: the results, Sicilian writers never fail to observe, bore a remarkable resemblance to female genitals.

This primal version of the *fedde* was replaced sometime during the last century by a completely different one, for which I give the recipe as I found it in two different Sicilian cookbooks. In each case the old-fashioned measures indicated that it had been copied from an older source, possibly without being tried out, and the directions were somewhat vague. The results I achieved were heavy and unappetizing, and it is easy to understand why even with this later version of the confection only the name has escaped oblivion. *Fedde*, in fact, is a Sicilian word that here actually means "slices" (the Italian is *fette*), but it has another meaning, one that has provided great entertainment to generations of Palermitani.

FEDDE DEL CANCELLIERE
(Chancellor's Buttocks)

Makes 12 to 14

BIANCOMANGIARE FILLING

4 cups milk

½ cup cornstarch

1¼ cups sugar

¼ vanilla bean

DOUGH

4 cups milk

1½ cups semolina granules of
the kind used for making
gnocchi (a 250-gram packet)

1¼ cups sugar

4 eggs

½ vanilla bean

2 cups whole shelled
pistachios (about 9 ounces)

1 cup flour

2 eggs, beaten until fluffy

Vegetable oil or lard
for frying

½ cup superfine sugar,
or granulated sugar
ground fine

1 teaspoon ground cinnamon

Prepare the *biancomangiare* filling according to the instructions on page 18, adding the vanilla bean at the beginning. When it is cooked, pour it onto a large plate to cool.

To make the dough: Put the milk, semolina, sugar, eggs, and vanilla bean into a saucepan. Mix well and then heat over a low flame, stirring constantly. Cook until the mixture is very thick and comes away from the sides of the pan as you stir. Allow to cool.

Toast the pistachios in a warm oven (300°F.) for about 15 minutes and chop them very fine, using either a nut grater or a parsley mincer rather than a grinder. Theoretically one should peel off their purple skins, but I find that task both superfluous and thankless, not to mention well-nigh impossible.

Remove the vanilla bean from the cooled semolina mixture and stir in the grated pistachios, blending well. Shape this paste into patties the size of a small hamburger. Dip them in flour, coating thoroughly, and then in the beaten eggs. Fry in ¼ inch of hot oil or lard, turning once, until delicately browned on each side. Drain on absorbent paper.

Cut the *biancomangiare* into 2-inch squares. Split the fried pistachio patties open like hamburger buns, and put a square of *biancomangiare* in each one. Close like a sandwich, then roll in the ground sugar and sprinkle with cinnamon.

For the aristocracy the convents served much the same purpose as the monasteries. The laws regulating the assignment of dowries were so strict and so onerous that most families could not afford to marry off more than one daughter without sacrificing a good part of their property; the others were sent to the convent. Although it spared the property, this was not an inexpensive alternative: the aristocratic orders required that a novice be well-dowered and furnished with a handsome allowance, and each step of her progress toward the veil, from the time she entered to board as a child until she took her final vows, was marked by ceremonies that involved substantial offerings in candles and in cash, as well as generous receptions.

26th November 1781, Monday. The last two daughters, the fifth and sixth of myself, the Count Marquis of Villabianca, by name Rosaria and Anna Michela Emanuele e Vanni, having become nuns of the Order of Saint Benedict in the venerable Monastery of Saint Mary of the Virgins in this capital city on the 23rd of November 1780 last, and having ended the year of their probation and novitiate, made in the aforesaid monastery their solemn profession. . . . The pontifical mass was celebrated by Monsignor the Vicar General Giuseppe Rivarola e Vanni, first cousin to the new nuns. All the nobility of the first rank in the city attended: and in the Parlatory the festivities were concluded with the greatest pomp possible, as was evident in the richness of the decorations and the profusion of the ices and pastries, so as to merit the claim that the function achieved in every way and means a most honorable success.

Marchese di Villabianca, *Diario palermitano*, 1781

THE CONVENT GATE, *a nineteenth-century engraving by Bartlett*

All this must have cost the marchese a pretty penny, although it was restrained compared to one such ceremony in 1755, which a scandalized diarist described as three days of eating and dancing far more suitable to Carnival than to the occasion at hand. Restrained or not, the custom was too much for the king. A mere two months later, he published this proclamation:

> 22 January 1782 . . .
> FERDINANDUS, *Dei gratia, rex utriusque Sicilae, Hierusalem etc.* . . .
>   . . . I find that in four circumstances it is customary to undergo such extravagant expenses, and that is, at the entrance of the maids into the convent, in the vesting of the religious habit, in the profession and in the exercise of the offices . . . for which it is customary to employ considerable sums for that which is called the refreshment with pastries or ices in trays or plates. Since this is an abuse, I have resolved that it be absolutely abolished. And therefore I decree that it is not allowed, on the occasion of this entrance, neither beforehand nor on the day of the entry nor in later times, to honor any individual of the convent with refreshments of ices and pastries, or any other gift of comestible nature, or objects of gallantries or money; and such expenses are to be considered as prohibited even on the part of outsiders.
>   Marchese di Villabianca, *Diario palermitano*, 1782

The marchese makes no comments on this entry in his diary—perhaps he knew that no one would take it seriously. The nuns themselves probably felt that they deserved a good party, meager recompense for all the balls and banquets they were renouncing. Not that convent life, in the aristocratic orders at least, was all that harsh: they were lodged in handsome and richly furnished baroque buildings, equipped with well-designed cloisters and luxuriant gardens, which in some cases even had small lakes where the sisters could go boating. Many institutions had villas in the hills, where the nuns went to escape the summer heat, and while they were in the city it was possible for them to participate, albeit from a distance, in public festivities and religious processions.

> The houses [in the center of Palermo] are all furnished with balconies; and round the upper stories, run long, commodious, but well-barred ones, belonging to the nuns of the various convents; who hire or purchase them, together with the floors to which they appertain, for the purpose of witnessing thence the sumptuous religious processions for which Palermo is

so celebrated. They have usually an underground communication with their convent, constructed in former times; as the usage by which they attain their peeping positions, without passing through the streets, is of great antiquity.

Arthur John Strutt, *A Pedestrian Tour in Calabria and Sicily*, 1841

There appears to have been some suspicion that this privilege was at times abused:

> It should be noted with regard to these festivities [for the birth of the royal princess], that the nuns of the Martorana and of Saint Catherine's were seen to be enjoying them from their loggias until the second hour of the evening, after which time they returned to their cells, which were closed by the superiors, who took the keys away. This measure was thought out and executed by the said good nuns in agreement with our zealous prelate. Nonetheless in the *vista* of Saint Catherine's more than one were still seen to be looking out, but these were believed rather to be the lay sisters and the servants of the lady nuns.
>
> Marchese di Villabianca, *Diario palermitano*, 1772

The sisters were also allowed to receive visits, whether from family or from patronesses. During her exile in Palermo, Queen Maria Carolina was responsible for creating grave financial difficulties among the religious orders: twice each she visited all twenty-one convents in the city, and each felt obliged to be more prodigal in its gifts and more sumptuous in its refreshments than the one before—the Monastero delle Vergini, where the Villabianca daughters had professed their vows, ran up a debt equal to almost ten thousand dollars!

Family visits were very frequent. Palmieri di Miccichè remarks that "the number of carriages drawn up in front of their gates, at all hours of the day, bears witness to the visits of sisters, of mothers, of cousins or aunts: sole and sad indemnity which the latter can pay these unhappy ones."

Although one can hear distinct echoes of anticlericalism in Palmieri's judgments, there must indeed have been unhappy nuns. Some no doubt eventually arrived at a true vocation, even if they had not been so equipped when they took the veil, and for the lucky few who attained the position of Abbess or Mother Superior, the religious life offered possibilities of power and endeavor that were not otherwise available to women. For still others the life of the convent was a peaceful and relatively pleasant alternative to an undesired marriage. Surely these were happier than the undowered girl of minor rank

A RELIGIOUS PROCESSION ON CORPUS DOMINI, *nineteenth-century engraving by Vuillier*

whom the Marchese di Villabianca reports as being picked as a daughter-in-law by a princely family simply because no one with more to offer would have accepted their feeble-minded son.

Yet, despite the visits and the processions, many of the nuns must have suffered dreadfully from the boredom of a closed community, and from the spitefulness and petty rivalry that such an environment engenders. This is the atmosphere described in the autobiography of Enrichetta Caracciolo, the daughter of a cadet branch of the famous Neapolitan family, who was forced to take the veil against her will. A woman of remarkable spirit and intelligence, devout yet passionately patriotic and anticlerical, she fought against her fate for twenty years. Her liberation came in 1860 with the liberation of Naples from Bourbon rule: she risked her life in order to satisfy her ambition to be the first woman in Naples to shake hands with Garibaldi. That same day she lifted the black veil from her head and placed it on an altar in "an act of restitution to the Church that had given it to me twenty years before."

Although hardly unbiased and although it refers to Neapolitan convents (which differed very little, however, from those in Sicily), Enrichetta Caracciolo's account of life in the cloister is firsthand, and it is hair-raising. It also explains to a certain extent why pastry making assumed such importance. As a vent for creativity, competitiveness, and ambition, it was one of the few alternatives to madness that the convent could offer.

> But the principal occupation, the *summa rerum* of the convent, lies in the preparation of sweets . . .
>
> Each nun is the mistress of the pastry oven for an entire day, which begins at midnight on the preceding day; but since at times this is not sufficient, the nun takes recourse to a second and a third, so that the poor lay sisters are dying for want of sleep and some of them actually fall ill. More than one elderly lay sister, grown hoary in the cloister, has said to me that she had never seen the Holy Week services, not having ever had a free minute during that period in which to enter the choir and look into the church. A monk, who with the approach of Easter was holding Lenten services well seasoned with sacred erudition and with eloquence, saw his audience diminish from day to day, and ended up almost alone in the church. The nuns were busy preparing their pastries. One day the monk, seeing fewer than six listeners when he had the right to more than seventy, interrupted the oration and climbed down from the pulpit, muttering over and over to himself: "What a pleasure it is to preach to Saracens!"
>
> Enrichetta Caracciolo, *Misteri del chiostro napoletano*, 1864

The abuse of the convent oven was a perennial problem in Sicily. As early as 1575 the diocesan synod of Mazara del Vallo prohibited the manufacture of *cassate* in the convents, so that the nuns would not be distracted from their devotions during Holy Week, and the same problem crops up in a short story by Pirandello:

> I knew that the nuns of the five abbeys of Montelusa cordially hated Monsignor Partanna, because as soon as he became bishop he had given three dispositions concerning them, each more cruel than the last:
>
> I. *that they should no longer either prepare or sell pastries and cordials* (those delicious cakes of honey and of almond paste, wrapped and tied with silver cord! those delicious cordials, which tasted of anise and of cinnamon!) . . .
>
> Luigi Pirandello, "Difesa di Mèola," 1922

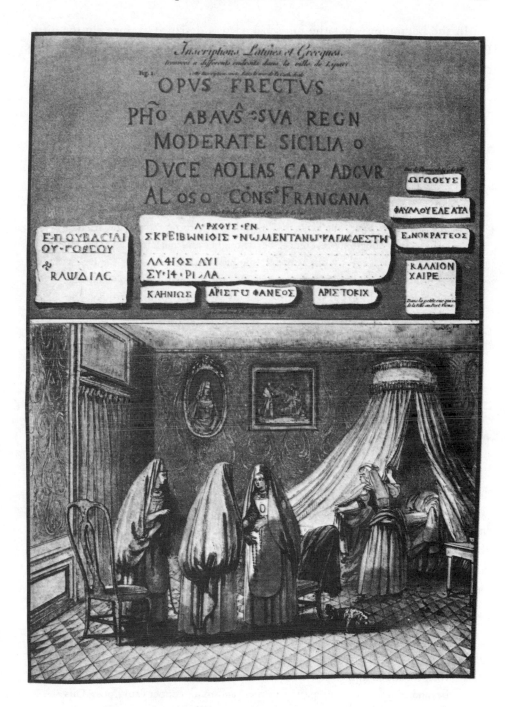

UNCLOISTERED NUNS ON THE ISLAND OF LIPARI, *an eighteenth-century drawing by Houel*

In the beginning what the nuns baked was destined exclusively for gifts. Pitrè describes to us the importance of these pious pastries as a vehicle of communication with the outside world:

> Meanwhile [the newly veiled nun] begins to have the use of a few scudos of her income for certain needs and duties which are not those of food, clothing, laundry and liturgy, for which the convent provides. She cannot do without a maid, or perhaps two, accustomed as she is to being waited on. She cannot be denied a confessor: every nun has one, and she must have one too—her own confessor, exclusively, uniquely hers, since she will not allow, or only very rarely, that her own confessor have other penitents in the same convent. She looks to him, spiritual director, counselor, friend, father, with solicitous reverence: her thoughts and her attentions are all for him. Never a festivity passes but she has some gift for him: for Easter she sends him the most exquisite *pupi cu l'ova*; for Saint Martin's Day the most delicate of filled biscuits. . . . On his saint's day or his birthday, she could not, would not refuse herself the pleasure of sending him a big tray with the special pastries of the convent, or a jar of jasmine conserves, and around them a half dozen handkerchiefs of red and yellow silk, or forks, or silver coffee spoons. Her maid, sent to him with gifts or with a message begging news of his health, well knows that she must study every move of the *padre*, impress upon her memory every word that he pronounces, with the mimic of the accompanying gestures, so that she can immediately repeat them to her lady.
>
> Giuseppe Pitrè, *La vita in Palermo cento e più anni fa*, 1904

If the individual nuns within one cloister strove to outdo each other in the magnificence and the delicacy of their offerings, the same spirit reigned on a larger scale between one convent and the other. Each convent prided itself on the extravagant generosity with which it distributed its handiwork, an extravagance that severely taxed its finances and that, at least on one occasion, caused other and less predictable difficulties.

> It must also be said that these convents all have a patron saint, whose name they often bear and whose feast-day they celebrate with all the magnificence of the Catholic church, distributing to their relatives and their friends an immensity of exquisite sweet dishes, which they are skilled beyond comparison at preparing in their enormous copper cauldrons. This time it was the turn of the Convent della Pietà, and the dish to be distributed *una zuppa alla imprescia*, of which the principal base is milk:

PLATE DECORATED WITH A RELIGIOUS MOTIF,
an eighteenth-century majolica from Trapani

then sugar, chocolate, *zuccata*, pistachios, etc. join to give this dish, one of the most sought-after among the greedy children of Polyphemus, all the flavor and the perfection that one could desire.

But apparently the love of the brides of Jesus Christ for their patron saint, this time too far away, made Jesus Christ jealous: He punished them by making them lose their heads, by making them forget the boiled milk in the cauldrons, and thus He visited his wrath on persons who had no part at all in the loving and mystical flame. Once cooled, this milk imbibed a quantity of verdigris, and changed into violent poison the delicious sweets destined to delight the sensual palaces of the Palermitan nobility, of which almost all the residents were poisoned: and I do not believe that I exaggerate when I bring the total to two or three thousand people, including the abbots, the servants and the nuns: from this one can judge the contents of this new box for Pandora.

The action of the poison did not make itself felt until three or four hours after it had been swallowed, toward the evening and precisely when everyone was gathered in society. The tragicomic effects of this drama were beyond description.

That evening I was at a reception where music was being performed: a lady and a gentleman of my acquaintance were singing a duet, I don't remember which. *"Caro mio bene,"* sang the lady, and then, "Lord, have mercy on me," clutching her hands to her stomach. *"Idolo mio,"* replied the other. "I'm dying!" he added. Sir Caro-mio-bene collapsed in one direction, Madame Idolo-mio in the other, they were carried home, and that was the end of the music.

Michele Palmieri di Miccichè, *Pensées et souvenirs*, 1830

Although Lampedusa also speaks of *zuppa imprescia* (*imprescia* means "in a hurry," a sort of hasty pudding), I can find no adequate recipe for it under that name. Since the sisters of the Pietà were also famous for their *pan di Spagna*, I think it was probably very similar to what some Sicilian cookbooks call *zuppa papale*, which can be made, with all due attention to your copper cauldrons, according to the following recipe.

ZUPPA PAPALE OR ZUPPA IMPRESCIA
(Papal or Hasty Pudding)

Serves 6

EGG CUSTARD

¼ cup plus 1 tablespoon
  cornstarch
5 cups milk
1¼ cups sugar

4 egg yolks
½ vanilla bean or 1 large
  strip of lemon or
  orange peel

1 slice of *pan di Spagna*,
  9 inches in diameter and
  ¾ inch thick (see p. 90)

Zuccata preserves (p. 95),
  apricot jam, or a sweet
  liqueur

Put the cornstarch in a saucepan, add the milk slowly, stirring to dissolve all the lumps, and then add the sugar, egg yolks, and flavoring. Beat together and place over a low flame. Cook, stirring constantly, until the custard begins to thicken a little, but do not boil it. When slightly thickened, remove it from the heat and allow to cool.

Spread the *pan di Spagna* with the preserves or the jam, or sprinkle it liberally with liqueur. Cut into 6 pieces and place each piece on a dessert plate. Ladle the tepid custard over the cake. Serve at room temperature.

If this is indeed the *zuppa imprescia*, then I assume that the chocolate and the pistachios that Palmieri mentions were sprinkled over the top.

The convent of the Origlione was famous, as the Abbot Meli tells us, for the *impanatelle* filled with meat and chocolate that are mentioned in Chapter Four, and also for *amarena 'ncilippati*, a sour-cherry syrup that when diluted with ice water provides an excellent antidote to the heat of the Sicilian summer.

AMARENA 'NCILIPPATI
(Sour Cherry Syrup)

Makes approximately 1 quart

2 pounds sour cherries   Juice of 1 lemon
2 pounds sugar

Pit the cherries and put them in a glass or ceramic bowl. Add the sugar and the lemon juice, mix well, and let stand for 12 hours.

Transfer to a heavy nonreactive saucepan, bring to a boil, reduce the heat, and cook over a gentle flame for 30 to 40 minutes, stirring frequently. Remove the scum that forms on the surface by skimming with a slotted spoon. The syrup is ready when it has become slightly thick (about 220°F. on a candy thermometer) and the cherries are a dark translucent red, no different in color from the syrup around them.

Pour the boiling fruit and syrup into sterilized jars and seal immediately. To serve, put a tablespoon of fruit and a tablespoon of syrup in the bottom of each glass, add ice and cold water and, if you wish, a slice of lemon or a sprig of mint.

THE CHURCH OF THE MARTORANA, *a nineteeth-century engraving by Bartlett*

The Monastery of the Martorana, a convent that has long since disappeared but was once attached to the church of Santa Maria dell'Ammiraglio, one of Palermo's lovely, mosaic-lined Arab-Norman churches, was so closely linked to the production of marzipan fruit that the Palermitani call it *frutta di Martorana*, although elsewhere in Sicily marzipan is known as *pasta reale*. Indeed, they claim that it was invented here: a Mother Superior once planned a little affectionate leg pulling for the Archbishop's Easter visit, and ordered her nuns to fashion the almond paste that they were so skilled in making into different kinds of fruit, which were then hung upon the trees in the cloister garden.

After the convent was torn down the commercial pastry shops took over, and at the end of each October, in preparation for All Souls' Day, when the dead bring marzipan fruit and sugar statues to the children who have prayed for their souls, the pastry shops in Palermo fill their windows with *martorana*.

> Most marvelous of all is the fruit that they exhibit, such as figs just opened from which a crystalline drop is oozing, little strawberries, pears, bananas, walnuts with the shell broken so that the inside is visible, roast chestnuts sprinkled with a faint trace of ashes; nor do they forget the legumes. There are entire collections of peas, of fava beans, of artichokes, of asparagus; I saw even some snails! And all this in almond paste: the shell of the snails and that of the walnuts are sugar and melt in your mouth, true sweets. The imitation is of an amazing exactness.
>
> Gastone Vuillier, *La Sicilia*, 1897

There is a store in Palermo in Via Paternoster, just off the Corso Vittorio Emmanuele, where they make and sell decorative little plaster molds in which the fruit can be shaped before it is painted with food coloring, but the dexterous could do it with their fingers.

PASTA REALE
(Royal or Almond Paste)

Makes about 2 pounds

1 pound shelled and
  blanched almonds
2 cups sugar

1 cup water
1–2 tablespoons
  confectioners' sugar

Grind the almonds to as fine a texture as you can achieve by passing them 3 or 4 times through a meat grinder. If it is available, you may substitute a pound of almond flour for almonds. Almond flour is sold in pastry-supply shops in Sicily, and supposedly gives a much smoother texture than anything one can achieve at home, but it does so at the expense of flavor and moisture.

Heat the sugar and water in a saucepan over a high flame, boiling until the syrup reaches the soft-ball stage (235° to 240°F. on a candy thermometer). Remove it from the fire at once and stir in the ground almonds, blending well. Sprinkle a marble or wooden surface with a little confectioners' sugar, and pour the almond mixture out onto it to cool. When it is cool enough to work, knead the paste as if it were a dough until it becomes smooth and elastic.

Mold the paste into the desired shapes, allow to dry, then paint with food colors. The *frutta di Martorana* is usually brushed with a gum-arabic solution to give it a shine.

Well-wrapped in plastic, almond paste will keep in the refrigerator for several months.

————

We must make a stop at the Convent of the Stigmata, since no book on Sicilian cooking could fail to mention *sfinci*. *Sfinci* supposedly comes from an Arabic word, *sfang*, which means a fried pastry, and is in fact a sort of holeless doughnut. These *sfinci*, which are rich enough to begin with, are sometimes filled with an egg-custard cream, in which case they are called *sfinci fradici* ("thoroughly soaked *sfinci*"), or on Saint Joseph's Day with a ricotta cream, thus becoming *sfinci di San Giuseppe*, heavy enough to undo even the most devout. The sisters of the Stigmata did well to limit themselves to honey.

There are any number of *sfinci* recipes to choose from, including the potato-based ones from Monreale. The one that follows is traditional, and may be similar to the one the nuns used.

SFINCI AMMILATI
(Honey Puffs)

Makes about 30 small sfinci

1 cup water	5 eggs
¼ cup lard	Vegetable oil for frying
Pinch of salt	½ cup honey
1 ½ cups flour (see note p. 41)	

Bring the water, lard, and salt to a boil in a saucepan. While the pan is still on the heat, sift the flour into the water, stirring as you go. Stir until well blended, remove from the heat, and allow to cool.

When the flour mixture has cooled, add the eggs one at a time, and beat at length until the mixture is smooth and lumpless.

Drop one tablespoon at a time into very hot oil (375°F.) and fry slowly until the *sfinci* are puffed and a deep golden brown in color. Drain on absorbent paper.

Heat the honey in a saucepan and dip the *sfinci* into the hot honey. Serve immediately.

Finally it should be noted that while the Origlione, the Martorana, and the Stigmata were all wealthy convents, which probably produced a great many of the ingredients for all these pastries on their own farmlands and could count on the allowances of their aristocratic residents to defray the expenses of the remaining ingredients, culinary fame was not denied the less privileged:

> There were monasteries of inferior order, which could not allow themselves such luxury: and even they, in their modest spheres, enjoyed renown, be it for their *scàcciu*: roasted chickpeas, almonds, fava beans, and pumpkin seeds (the Cappuccines); be it for their stuffed olives (the Assumption).
>
> And, since next to evil stands good, so, almost as a remedy for the inevitable indigestions provoked by so many pastries, cakes, cannoli, marzipans, creams, fritters, pizzas, olives and almonds, the Abbey of Saint Rosalia performed the merciful office of preparing a medicinal antacid, of guaranteed effectiveness.
>
> Giuseppe Pitrè, *La vita in Palermo cento e più anni fà*, 1904

In the wake of Garibaldi's expedition in 1860 and Sicily's union with the Kingdom of Italy, the property of the Church, which amounted to one tenth of all the land in Sicily, was confiscated. Many of the religious orders were closed and those that survived were greatly impoverished. The scale on which the convents distributed their pastries was reduced in proportion to their circumstances—perhaps only at Christmas and Easter and only to close relatives or benefactors, such as the family of Fulco di Verdura, who remembers them arriving "on trays covered with multicolored tissue paper and decorated with a tinsel fringe and gold and silver sugar pills." It must have been at about this time that it became possible to order the various specialties for a fee or, in the beginning perhaps, a discreet donation to the convent's coffers. Thus the Convent delle Vergini, stronghold of aristocratic splendor a century earlier, had become by the end of the nineteenth century a purveyor of sweets to aristocratic households.

> Scorning the table of drinks, glittering with crystal and silver on the right, he moved left toward that of the sweetmeats. Huge blond *babas, Mont Blancs* snowy with whipped cream, cakes speckled with white almonds and green pistachio nuts, hillocks of chocolate-covered pastry, brown and rich as the topsoil of the Catanian plain from which, in fact, through many a twist and turn they had come, pink ices, champagne ices, coffee ices, all

parfaits, which fell apart with a squelch as the knife cleft them, melody in major of crystallized cherries, acid notes of yellow pineapple, and those cakes called "triumphs of gluttony" filled with green pistachio paste, and shameless "virgins' cakes" shaped like breasts. Don Fabrizio asked for some of these and, as he held them in his plate, looked like a profane caricature of St. Agatha. . . . Why ever didn't the Holy Office forbid these cakes when it had the chance? St. Agatha's sliced-off breasts sold by convents, devoured at dances! Well, well!

Giuseppe di Lampedusa, *The Leopard*, 1960

First made in Palermo's Monastero delle Vergini, "virgin cakes" are more commonly and more outspokenly known as *minni di virgini*, or "virgins' breasts." From Palermo they have spread as far as Catania, where they are dedicated to the patron saint Agatha, who is always depicted holding the symbol of her martyrdom on a plate. The most notorious of all the convent pastries, *minni di virgini* owe their fame above all to their name, which so delights the Sicilians that they will apply it indiscriminately to almost any cake, provided it is small and rounded. The following recipe is, I believe, for virgins' breasts as they were originally made in Palermo. The Catanians take things one step further and place a small red cherry on top.

MINNI DI VIRGINI
(Virgins' Breasts)

Makes 1 dozen

PASTA FROLLA CRUST (see note p. 94)

1½ cups almond flour	¾ cup lard
2 cups flour (see note p. 41)	1 egg
¾ cup sugar	1 tablespoon milk if necessary
Pinch of salt	

Zuccata preserves (see p. 95) or ½ recipe *biancomangiare* (see p. 18)	1 egg white, beaten

Prepare the crust by mixing the dry ingredients, cutting in the lard, and working in the egg and, if necessary, enough milk to hold the dough together. Shape into a ball and refrigerate for at least 2 hours.

Roll the dough out to an ⅛-inch thickness. Using cookie cutters or glasses, cut out approximately a dozen circles 2½ inches in diameter, and an equal number of circles 4 inches in diameter.

Transfer the 2½-inch circles to a greased cookie sheet, and on each circle place a small heap of *zuccata* preserves or *biancomangiare*. The filling should be sufficient to make a mound about 1 inch high. Brush the rim of each circle with the beaten egg white, cover it with one of the larger circles, and seal the edges. Brush the outside of each pastry with egg white and bake in a moderate oven for about 15 minutes or until delicately browned.

Prince Fabrizio really wasn't at all hungry, or he would have succumbed to the "triumph of gluttony." This is another of the great convent specialties, but each order of nuns seems to have had its own idea of Waterloo, for the number and content of the different layers changes from place to place. One recipe I have seen called for a bottom layer of *pan di Spagna* soaked with rum, on which were spread pistachio preserves, followed by a layer of *pasta frolla*, then a layer of egg-custard cream covered with more *pasta frolla* and still more custard, each layer slightly smaller than the one below. Once this basic cone was formed, its entire surface was spread with apricot jelly, covered with a thin sheet of *pasta reale*, and decorated with candied fruit and chopped pistachios.

The only triumph of gluttony that I have actually tasted, one made by a convent in Palermo, was quite different but equally irresistible. There were five layers of *pan di Spagna*, each less than ½ inch thick, which alternated with deep layers of what seemed to be just enough of a rather liquid *biancomangiare* to hold together coarsely chopped pistachios and candied *zuccata*. The cone-shaped cake was covered with preserves—possibly pistachio—with a patterned decoration of candied fruit and frills and curlicues fashioned of *pasta reale*. A large green almond of marzipan was balanced on the top of the cone.

If its outward appearance was touchingly naïve, within the golden stripes of *pan di Spagna* framed bright green chips of pistachio and greeny-gold cubes of glistening *zuccata*, which floated in the pale *biancomangiare* like so many tesserae from the mosaic wall of an Arab-Norman chapel. This harmony of color was echoed by equal sophistication in the balance of the flavors: the *zuccata* was a miracle of delicacy; the pistachio was present yet not obtrusive; the faint suggestion of jasmine gave context to an affirmation of stick cinnamon, crushed in a mortar and sprinkled over every layer.

Even if I were fortunate enough to have it, a recipe for this triumph of gluttony would be useless without the secret of the sisters' *zuccata*. The best I can offer is a recipe for pistachio preserves, which are very simple to make. If you were to use them in a *zuppa imprescia* that was sprinkled with abundant crushed stick cinnamon, you would be brought close enough to a triumph of gluttony to feel that you were succumbing in style.

CONSERVA DI PISTACCHIO
(Pistachio Preserves)

Makes about 1 pint

½ pound shelled pistachios   ¼ cup water
1 cup sugar

Chop or grate the pistachios to a fine grain. The preserves will have a nicer color if you remove the purple inner skins from the nuts before chopping them, but again, it's asking a great deal when you haven't a refectory's worth of nuns to give you a hand.

Heat the sugar and the water until the sugar dissolves into a syrup. Add the chopped pistachios and cook, stirring, until thick.

————

Not all the pastries heaped so tantalizingly on the sweetmeat table at Prince Fabrizio's ball were of holy provenance. During the nineteenth century commercial pastry stores were opened in Palermo. One of these was the Gulì firm, which started out as a basement candy factory and had grown by the turn of the century into an elegant tearoom and pastry shop in Piazza Marina, glittering with chandeliers and candy vases of imported Bohemian crystal, and famous for its multitiered *cassate*. This was also the period in which Swiss *patissiers* were establishing themselves throughout Europe, and in Sicily too: the Caflisch family in Palermo and the Caviezels in Catania. Besides making babas and brioches and chocolate pastries unlike anything that Sicily had seen before, they also copied the traditional convent pastries. But their efforts appear to have been considered strictly *parvenu* by the aristocracy, who "with ancestral snobbery preferred the convent ones, even though their appearance was archaic by comparison."

The nuns of Palermo were by no means the only nuns on the island who produced sweets. The macaroons offered to Prince Fabrizio by the Abbess at Palma di Montechiara were really *biscotti ricci*, and they are still being made there today.

BISCOTTI RICCI
(Almond Curls)

Makes 4 dozen

5 cups whole blanched almonds	8 egg whites
4 cups sugar	½ teaspoon ground cinnamon
	Grated rind of 1 lemon

Grate the almonds to a fine meal in a nut grater or a blender, and mix in the sugar. Beat the egg whites until soft peaks form, and then fold them into the almonds together with the cinnamon and the lemon rind. Mix well and put the dough into a pastry bag with a large notched nozzle. Preheat oven to 300°F. Squeeze the dough out onto a greased and floured cookie sheet in 3-inch S-shaped curlicues, spacing them about 1 inch apart. Bake until the ridges on the cookies begin to color.

The Badia dello Spirito Santo in Agrigento still accepts orders for a much-admired *cuscus dolce* tasting of almonds and of pistachios. The original recipe is said to have called for equal weights of wheat and pistachios.

At Erice the nuns were famous for their *dolci di riposto*. Carlo Levi describes buying some right after the last world war:

> We wanted to taste the famous cakes of almond paste and the *mustazzoli* made by the nuns of a cloistered convent. We entered the atrium and expressed our wishes to a sort of shadow behind a double grate and shortly, without any accompanying words, the pastries appeared on the wheel, tender flowers of green and pink and violet and azure, and we left our money in their place.
>
> Carlo Levi, *Le parole sono pietre*, 1951

The nuns of this convent of San Carlo have since died or gone elsewhere, and the convent is now a gallery, but Maria Grammatico, who was a lay worker

A VIEW OF THE CONVENT OF THE BENEDICTINES AT SCIACCA,
a nineteenth-century engraving by d'Ostervald

in their kitchens for fifteen years, has opened her own pastry shop. She continues to make exquisitely iced *dolci di riposto* filled with homemade citron preserves, and a bewilderingly large assortment of delicious almond cakes and cookies.

The nuns of Santa Chiara in Noto, inspired perhaps by the *putti* that swarm about the churches and palaces of this most baroque of towns, invented a cake of marzipan and sponge covered with chocolate icing, on which they placed a pink-cheeked cherub's face cut out of colored tinfoil.

It is only a few years since the nuns of the Badia Grande at Alcamo stopped selling *bocconetti*. When I first came to Sicily, my mother-in-law would send her eldest son to the abbey with a bag full of almonds from our farm, and he would go back a few days later and bring home a tray of almond *bocconetti*, each one stuffed with *zuccata*, sprinkled with powdered sugar, and wrapped in tissue paper.

The complicated bookkeeping that became necessary when the value added tax was introduced in Italy discouraged the nuns from their commerce, but they still make small quantities of *bocconetti* as gifts, and the recipe survives.

BOCCONETTI DI MANDORLA
(*Almond Kisses*)

Makes 3 dozen

3 cups shelled and blanched almonds	3 egg whites
2 cups sugar	*Zuccata* preserves (see p. 95) or any other fairly firm preserves
½ teaspoon vanilla	

Grind the almonds to a fairly fine meal. Stir in the sugar and then the vanilla. Beat the egg whites until soft peaks form, then fold them into the almonds. Mix well enough to have a workable paste. Shape a tablespoon of the mixture into a ball, poke a hole in it, and fill the hole with ½ teaspoon of preserves. Cover the hole with a little more of the almond mixture, and roll gently between the palms of your hands until it is a well-sealed ball little more than 1 inch in diameter. Repeat with the rest of the almond mixture. Bake on greased and floured cookie sheets in a 300°F. oven for about 25 minutes or until delicately browned.

———

Twenty years ago there were still two or three convents in Palermo that sold pastries. Today only the Benedictine sisters at the Monastero delle Virgini still do so, a handful of elderly sisters who work at the ovens that the younger nuns have deserted in favor of more socially useful activities. In a small room in Piazza Venezia it is still possible to order cannoli, virgins' cakes, and triumphs of gluttony through a grate and watch them come round on the wheel. It was there that I ordered the "bunch of grapes" that I described in my book *On Persephone's Island*, a magnificent baroque monument in almond and pistachio paste, lovingly fashioned in the shape of a cluster of pale-green grapes, glistening with a silver bloom, curling with leaves and tendrils, and hiding a filling of *zuccata* preserves flavored with cinnamon. It was so beautiful that we could hardly bear to eat it, and so delicious we could hardly bear to stop.

Just as I started to write this chapter a friend of mine went to order a bunch of grapes to take with her to the north as a hostess present, but the lay worker behind the grate told her that the nun who had made them had died suddenly, at the age of sixty-one. There is no one else in the convent who knows her secrets, so the bunch of grapes is gone forever. Another chapter in Sicilian culinary history has come to a close.

7

Street Fare

The quantity of fruit-stalls is innumerable, and the women and boys walking up and down with pomegranates, olives, medlars, oranges, pistaccio-nuts, figs, and other fruits are equally so; all of them have such potent voices that they never cease one minute to extol their merchandise with an intolerable, and almost deafening bawl. To these you may add droves of country people with asses and mules, laden with all kinds of potherbs, crying out likewise in a manner which must affect the strongest nerves. At this time the sailors flock from the port to purchases provisions. The police officers, secretaries, clerks, and apprentices, hasten to their daily occupations, taking their breakfast on the road, which consists in some bread or biscuit, and a little fresh fruit just gathered in the neighbouring gardens and covered with a luxuriant bloom.

T. Bingham Richards, *Letters from Sicily Written in the Year* 1798

There was a remarkable contrast between the streets of Palermo and Catania, so alive with vendors and cookshops and stalls selling every type of edible ware, and what the foreign traveler found once he ventured beyond the walls of the big cities. Well into the nineteenth century Sicily lacked roads suitable for wheeled traffic, and the tourist was obliged to proceed by mule—either astride or in a litter—accompanied by a hired guide and a pack mule loaded with provisions for the journey. It was often impossible to procure food en route, and the only bed available in many small towns was at the monastery.

During the early nineteenth century the number of hotels and inns operating in Sicily increased, thanks in part to the presence of the British navy and to an ever greater flow of foreign visitors. A few of these hotels, such as the Albergo del Sole in Syracuse, met with constant approval on the part of the travelers, usually because the innkeeper had served as cook or manservant with the British forces, and knew how to win the hearts of his guests by

TRAVELING BY LITTER, *a nineteenth-century engraving by Bartlett*

presenting them with their beloved beefsteak. But these were rarities; elsewhere accommodations were rustic.

Four hours and a half . . . brought me to Fiume Di Nisi, eighteen miles from Messina; where the muleteer informed me there was an excellent inn. It consists of an immense range of open stalls for the mules, and wretched lofts above, they call rooms. The supper room you are shewn into, is a division of the stable; with a fire on the ground, or rather, bare earth—a bed for the family—some casks full of wine—a pig lately killed, swinging from the rafters—and a table and bench. Upon the ashes they toast you a slice from the pig; with two or three eggs, and a bottle of wine: and that forms your supper; while the muleteer stalks in with a satisfied air from having told you the truth. The chamber for sleeping is a wretched-looking garret, with a mattress, *en suite*; shutters, for windows; and a door that won't shut. Were an English lady's maid shewn into such a place, at the worst inn on the road, she would immediately *swoon*. And take this for a picture of every locanda in Sicily, except in great towns, or the immediate beaten tract from one English post to another.

Thomas Wright Vaughan, *A View to the Present State of Sicily*, 1811

And in still other establishments, the supper was truly self-service:

The poor wretch [of an innkeeper] was without means of buying us provisions, and we had to go ourselves the evening before in quest of them, returning at last in triumph, the master with a beefsteak upon a skewer, and the man with an enormous bunch of broccoli under his arm.

W. H. Bartlett, *Pictures from Sicily*, 1853

Nor could the foreign traveler be sure of getting a decent meal in a private house. Those who had letters of introduction to the local nobility would in most cases be received with sophisticated ease and lavish hospitality, but those whose only hope lay in a middle-class host soon discovered that in Sicily dining was a private affair.

Castelvetrano.

After dinner I called upon Don J. B. Genaro Consiglio, a well-known merchant; he was at table. Every Sicilian of good rank must sit down at noon precisely, and does not receive anyone while he dines; the house itself is closed and shuttered as if it were midnight. . . .

Don Consiglio covered me with honor; he obtained a lodging for me at the [Monastery of the] Recollects, to which he had one of his sons guide me, and he sent to my room some wine, some fish, and a pyramid of macaroni for my first meal. . . . Sicilians do not willingly have people to dine in their houses; but they will send you much more food than they would have offered you at a meal.

Jean Houel, *Voyage pittoresque en Sicile*, 1784

When Houel did get invited inside a middle-class household, that of a French vice-consul who obviously could not avoid making the gesture, he found that the women of the house were not present since, he claims, "a husband would seem to be lacking in self-respect were he to expose his wife to the glances of strangers."

Such provincial attitudes were much rarer in Palermo, of course, but they were part of that Saracen imprint on the organization of public and private

AN INN! . . . I REMAIN SPEECHLESS, *a nineteenth-century engraving by Vuillier*

TRAVELERS PICNICKING IN THE GROTTO OF THE GOATS, *an eighteenth-century drawing by Houel*

life which was to survive until the middle of the twentieth century. Sicily remained Levantine in her eating establishments: hundreds of cookshops selling Sicilian-to-go but no restaurants except those connected to hotels that served the tourists and travelers. It was only in the years following World War I that the first restaurants catering to a local trade were opened in Palermo, and these, with exotic names like The Phoenix or The Gardens of Armidda, were patronized by the gay blades of Palermo society and their mistresses. No respectable Sicilian woman, maiden or matron, would have cared to be seen in one of those ambiguous establishments.

The restaurant scene has changed totally in the last fifty years, yet there is still nothing startling about seeing a kettle of macaroni being trundled through the streets. The street markets and the cookshops still flourish, though work clothes and army-navy surplus are now on sale in Via dei Lattarini, once the Suk-el-Attarine, the market of perfumes, where attar of roses and essence of jasmine were sold. The markets of the Capo, the Vucciria and Ballarò, are still a motley jumble of dry goods, housewares, and foodstuffs—heaps of green and black olives; sacks of dried beans and chickpeas; sides of pork and milk lambs still in their wool; entrails and whole beef livers hanging from hooks; yellow nets filled with mussels and clams; pink shrimp and rosy mullets arranged on beds of dark-green seaweed; mackerel and sardines glinting turquoise and silver; whole swordfish pointing skyward; vegetables in stalls glowing red and yellow and green.

> Abundance of vegetables—piles of white and green fennel, like celery, and great sheaves of young purplish, sea-dust-coloured artichokes, nodding their buds, piles of big radishes, scarlet and bluey purple, carrots, long strings of dried figs, mountains of big oranges, scarlet large peppers, a last slice of pumpkin, a great mass of colours and vegetable freshnesses. A mountain of black-purple cauliflowers, like niggers' heads, and a mountain of snow-white ones next to them. How the dark, greasy, night-stricken street seems to beam with these vegetables, all this fresh delicate flesh of luminous vegetables piled there in the air, and in the recesses of the windowless little caverns of the shops, and gleaming forth on the dark air, under the lamps.
>
> D. H. Lawrence, *Sea and Sardinia*, 1921

In addition to the raw vegetables, the greengrocer's stall usually has a couple of copper cauldrons, one in which new potatoes have been cooked in their skins, another in which, in wintertime, boiled artichokes float among slices of lemon. Spring brings steamed string beans and large pans of roasted onions and sweet peppers, ready for a summery salad.

PEPERONI ARROSTITI
(*Roasted Sweet Peppers*)

Serves 6

2 pounds large sweet peppers
Olive oil

Salt and freshly ground
pepper

Pick the smoothest, most regularly shaped peppers, as those that curl over on themselves are difficult to roast evenly. Wash them carefully and place them in a roasting pan in a hot oven, or immeasurably better, on a rack over hot coals. Cook, turning them, until the skin is black and blistered all over. Cool, peel off the blistered skin, scrape out the seeds and the white membranes from the inside, and cut the peppers into strips. Add olive oil, salt and pepper to taste, and serve as a salad or in a mixed antipasto.

———

While you have your barbecue lit, you really ought to take advantage of the coals to roast some artichokes.

CARCIOFI ARROSTITI
(Roasted Artichokes)

2–6 small artichokes per person (according to occasion and appetite)	1 or 2 garlic cloves per person
	Salt and freshly ground black pepper
Abundant fresh mint	Olive oil

Wash the artichokes, then trim about ½ inch from the top of each and all but ½ inch from the stem. Wash and dry the mint leaves and chop them very fine together with the peeled garlic cloves and the salt and pepper (a pinch and a grind per artichoke).

Bang the artichokes one by one, tip downward, on a chopping board or other hard surface until the leaves loosen up and you can open them enough to stuff a teaspoon of the mint and garlic mixture down into the heart. Pour about a tablespoon of oil into each artichoke and set them upright on a bed of medium-hot coals for about 20 to 30 minutes. The tough outer leaves will char while the inner leaves and the heart roast slowly. They are done when a leaf comes away at a gentle tug. Eat leaf by leaf with your fingers, as you would a steamed artichoke, discarding the choke when you come to it. Messy but marvelous.

———

A YOUNG VENDOR, *a nineteenth-century engraving by Vuillier*

Although in Sicily the greengrocers usually do sell olives, these are also sold by specialized vendors:

> Piled in pyramids upon the counters, they form a range of barren moun-
> tains, black olives, brown and green, shiny-smooth or wrinkled, as they
> come off the tree or stuffed with a piece of anchovy or sweet red pepper,
> dried or salted, preserved in oil or in a brine. Each type has its own
> mountainous silhouette, rendered less harsh by sprigs of rosemary and tufts
> of sage, which seen in scale become trees growing upon the mountainsides.
> Often the mountain range is flanked by plates of artichokes *alla cacciatore*,
> or artichokes *alla contadina*, with parsley and garlic.
> A. Denti di Pirajno, *Siciliani a tavola*, 1970

Artichokes *alla contadina*, better known perhaps as *alla villanella*, is the recipe most commonly used for artichokes in Sicily.

CARCIOFI ALLA VILLANELLA
(Artichokes Peasant-style)

Serves 6 to 8

12–15 small artichokes, cleaned and cut into wedges (see recipe for *frittedda*, p. 19)
¼ cup olive oil
¾ cup water
4 garlic cloves, sliced

½ cup parsley leaves, chopped coarse
A few mint leaves, chopped coarse (optional)
Salt and freshly ground black pepper

Put the artichokes in a heavy saucepan, add all the other ingredients (except the pepper, which should be added after cooking), cover tightly, and cook over low heat for 10 to 15 minutes. Serve either hot or cold.

CHILDREN WITH CART, *a nineteenth-century engraving by Vuillier*

Very often the olive sellers sell green olives dressed in a sort of salad.

OLIVE CUNZATI
(Dressed Olives)

Makes enough for 6 to 8 as part of a mixed antipasto

1 pound green olives in brine,
   well rinsed and pitted
2 ribs celery, cut in ½-inch
   pieces
2 carrots, sliced
2 garlic cloves, sliced
½ sweet green pepper, cut
   into small pieces

1 tablespoon dried oregano
A few flakes of crushed
   red pepper
½ cup olive oil
1 tablespoon white wine
   vinegar (see note p. 20)

Mix all the ingredients together and allow to stand for several hours before serving. You may want to increase the amount of oil if, as in my household, there is going to be a lot of surreptitious dipping of bread into the dressing. In the street markets the olives are rarely pitted, but it is worth the effort to pit them yourself.

———

Brightly painted stalls sell fruit to eat on the spot: slices of watermelon in the summertime, the big globe cut open to show how red and sweet it is (the pale ones rouged up with the aid of a tomato), and prickly pears in the fall (at the turn of the century an English writer noted that the stalls selling prickly pears also sold "tiny iron tweezers, costing a halfpenny each").

The principal source of ready-to-eat food has always been, however, the cookshops, which were common in classical Rome and throughout Western Europe in the Middle Ages and after, but in Sicily have been remarkably long-lasting.

For the Arabs, street food was a very consistent part of the daily menu: travelers to medieval Cairo speak of ten to twelve thousand cookshops, in which almost all of the city's food was prepared. The habits that the Saracens brought

NEAR THE PALERMO MARKET, *a nineteenth-century engraving by Vuillier*

with them when they invaded Sicily have persisted long after their departure, encouraged by a variety of factors. In the seventeenth and eighteenth centuries, government policies aiming at a fair distribution of food in times of famine forbade that bread should be baked at home. This meant that an oven rated as a luxury, especially in a climate so mild that a small charcoal brazier was considered an adequate source of winter heat. Above all, fuel was expensive, especially after all the forests in the vicinity of the big cities had been devoured by the furnaces of the sugar mills.

> Coal is such a scarce commodity that the coal-carts are drawn by tiny Sardinian asses, and the shops show a piece of coal hung on a string across the door.
>
> Douglas Sladen, *Sicily, the New Winter Resort*, 1910

Friends in my neighborhood tell me that in the early 1960s the last of these charcoal sellers was still to be seen in our streets, a figure so familiar that he could limit his cry to the strictly essential, prophetic *"Minni vaiu, minni staju ennu, min'ivi"* ("I'm going, I've gone, I went!"). Bottled gas has almost completely replaced charcoal since World War II, but it is still possible to find cookshops that have maintained their original aspect despite the change in fuel:

> [They have] long, beautifully clean stoves covered with rich old tiles and dotted like a cribbage board with little holes to contain charcoal embers. Then there is a fine array of glittering brass and copper cooking vessels, often some good old plates, and sometimes an old brass lamp of fine design, though flares are taking their place. These cookshops are generally mere cupboards open to the busy thoroughfare, without glass.
>
> Douglas Sladen, *Sicily, the New Winter Resort*, 1910

The best-known kind of cookshop is the *friggitoria*, the fryshop, which sets out before the hungry passer-by a wide variety of fried delights, each wrapped in a golden-brown crust, to eat on the spot or take home as a quick first course: slices of breaded eggplant, *arancine*, and trays of finger-shaped potato croquettes also known, with what the reader will recognize by now as typical Sicilian humor, as *cazzilli*—"little pricks."

CROCCHÈ DI PATATE
(Potato Croquettes)

Serves 6

2½ pounds potatoes
2 egg yolks
⅓ cup grated caciocavallo or pecorino cheese
1 garlic clove, minced very fine
2 tablespoons fresh parsley, minced very fine
Salt and freshly ground black pepper

Pieces of anchovy fillets, fresh caciocavallo, diced salami (optional)
½ cup flour
2 egg whites, beaten lightly
1 cup dried breadcrumbs (see p. 12)
Vegetable oil for frying

Peel the potatoes. Cook in boiling salted water until tender, then pass through a ricer or food mill. Mix in the egg yolks, grated cheese, garlic, parsley, and salt and pepper to taste. Blend well, and shape the potatoes into small finger-shaped croquettes about ¾ inch in diameter and 2 inches long. Although it is a deviation from the classic *cazzillo*, my mother-in-law used to hide a piece of anchovy or cheese or salami in the middle of each croquette, an innovation that everyone approved of.

Dredge the croquettes in flour, then dip in the egg whites, then in the breadcrumbs, binding them well. Fry, a few at a time, in abundant and very hot (375°F.) vegetable oil until they are a deep golden brown.

———

A much more delicate version of these—perhaps the fruit of a *monzù's* elaboration—and not to be found in the fryshops, should be served together with calf's brains and rice croquettes in an aristocratic *fritto misto*.

CROCCHÈ DI LATTE
(Milk Croquettes)

Serves 6

½ cup sweet butter	Pinch of grated nutmeg
1½ cups flour (see note p. 41)	½ cup flour
4 cups milk	2 egg whites, beaten lightly
2 egg yolks	1 cup dried breadcrumbs
½ cup grated parmesan	(see p. 12)
cheese	Vegetable oil for frying
Salt and freshly ground	
black pepper	

Make a very thick béchamel by melting the butter in a saucepan, adding the flour, and cooking it for about 5 minutes, stirring constantly and taking great care that the flour doesn't brown. Scald the milk and stir it into the butter and flour. Cook over low heat, stirring constantly, until the mixture is very thick. Remove from the heat and add the egg yolks, the cheese, and the seasonings. Pour onto a greased plate and allow to cool.

Cut the béchamel into small pieces—somewhat smaller than a *cazzillo*—although this will be perforce an approximate and sticky business, and dip them in the flour, then the egg whites, then the breadcrumbs. Fry in very hot (375°F.) oil until golden brown.

AN OLD LADY SELLING EGGS, *a nineteenth-century engraving by Vuillier*

No fryshop would be complete without *panelle*, a flat fritter probably of Arab origins, which is one of the very few dishes in Italian cooking to use chickpea flour.

PANELLE
(Chickpea Fritters)

Makes about 40 panelle

4 cups chickpea flour

6 cups water

2 tablespoons finely chopped
   parsley

Salt and freshly ground
   black pepper

Vegetable oil for frying

Put the chickpea flour in a saucepan, and add the water slowly, stirring carefully to avoid the formation of lumps. Add the parsley, salt and pepper to taste, and cook over a medium flame, stirring constantly, about 15 minutes or until the mixture is very thick and just begins to stand away from the sides of the pan as you stir.

Working rapidly, pour the mixture out onto a lightly oiled marble or wooden surface, and spread it out with an oiled spatula into a thin sheet, less than a quarter of an inch thick. When cooled, cut into 2-by-3-inch rectangles.

An alternative and easier method is to pour the mixture into an empty, clean, and oiled tin can (the squared cans that olive oil comes in are perfect). When it is cool, turn the can upside down, open the bottom with a can opener, push the loaf of *panelle* paste out a little at a time, cutting off very thin slices with a sharp knife or a length of dental floss stretched taut.

Fry the slices a few at a time in hot oil deep enough to float them, turning once, until both sides become pale golden brown. Drain on absorbent paper and serve hot.

Another fryshop favorite is *quaglie*, small eggplants cut so that when they are fried they fan out like the tail feathers of a quail.

QUAGLIE
(Eggplant Quails)

Serves 6

6 small eggplants   Vegetable oil for frying
Salt

Wash the eggplants, trim off the stems, and then make a series of parallel lengthwise cuts, about ½ inch apart, from the bottom toward the stem end, taking care to stop at least an inch from the stem end. Turn 90 degrees and repeat the operation, so that the eggplant is cut into sticks for about three-quarters of its length, but remains in one piece, held together at the stem end.

Put the eggplants into heavily salted water with a weight on them to keep them submerged, and soak for several hours. Rinse well, drain, and dry as well as possible with paper toweling.

Fry the eggplants in hot (375°F.) oil deep enough to cover them until they are a golden brown.

Sfincione (see p. 127) is usually on sale as well, cooked in long black tins in the oven of the neighborhood bakery and delivered to the fryshop by a young boy who balances them precariously on his head as he pushes his way through the crowds.

All of these when eaten in the street are served in a large roll, and they fill much the same function that hotdogs or fish and chips do elsewhere. But it has recently become popular among Palermo restaurateurs to serve a few *panelle* and a few *crocchè di patate*, together with a little *caponata*, as an antipasto. While they are no doubt less ruinous to the health when prepared in the home or in a fancy restaurant, they inevitably lack the special flavor of the *friggitoria*, which is said to depend on frying oil that is often replenished but never replaced.

A big *friggitoria* would offer all of these plus the *pituni* described in Chapter

Three, and other forms of fried bread dough. Still other odds and ends, both animal and vegetable, would be presented, unrecognizable beneath a crust of crumbs or batter, in a glorious spread of *fritto misto*, a mixed fry, more appropriately translated, by a young American girl touring at the turn of the century, as "fried mysteries."

A smaller enterprise might be itinerant, specializing in one or two different items, such as the *panellari* who sell *panelle* and *cazzilli*, which they fry up over bottled gas on the back of their Vespa pickups, parked in strategic locations near high schools or construction sites. There is still at least one *panellaro* to be seen in Palermo who does his cooking on a donkey-drawn cart that is black with years of accumulated grease but beautifully planned and constructed like a ship's galley, with lurch-proof compartments for each ingredient and implement.

The common denominator of most of this street food is the low cost of its ingredients, and this is certainly true of the meat dishes. One such delicacy is *quaruma*, which is tripe and all the parts of calf or cow you thought no one would ever want to eat—mainly gristle and callus and other pale and translucent bits—boiled up together and served with a squirt of lemon. The *quarumaru*'s stall has large pans heaped with these bits and pieces, and then a row of heavy white crockery plates, each with a knife and fork crossed upon it, awaiting the customer's pleasure. I have yet to succumb to *quaruma*, but I do like *stigghiole*, the fatty intestines from lambs and kids, which are carefully washed, soaked in wine, then wrapped around a few stalks of parsley and grilled by the roadside on portable barbecues that fill the air with greasy and pungent smoke.

Better still is *pani cu' la meuza*, soft buns known as *guasteddi* filled with sautéed beef spleen, either *schiettu* (nubile) if all by itself, or *maritatu* when wedded to fresh ricotta and grated caciocavallo cheese. That is how Garibaldi ate it at the Antica Focacceria di San Francesco after his triumphal entry into Palermo. The Antica Focacceria still operates in the piazza of that name, still makes excellent and dependable *pani cu' la meuza*, and is a good place to see how a cookshop has inched itself toward being a restaurant by the addition of a few marble-topped tables and cast-iron chairs.

As might well be expected, fish also have an important place on the street. The stalls of the fishmongers are among the most colorful and most fascinating, both for the wares and—in the past at least—for the stalls themselves.

> Strange fish can be sometimes seen in the old market in the Piazza Nuova. But the best place to see them is at the fish sales on the Borgo, where the salesmen have queer booths shaped like Greek temples and with curious devices and religious mottoes. One is inscribed "Dio solo è grande" (Only God is great), and another, with a sort of mermaid for its device, has "Viva Maris SS della Provvidenza."
>
> Douglas Sladen, *Sicily, the New Winter Resort*, 1910

There are separate booths selling seafood to eat on the spot: dark purple sea urchins cut in half to expose the vivid orange roe, which is eaten raw with lemon; raw mussels, although these have fallen from favor since the cholera outbreak in Naples some years ago; and above all *purpu*—octopus boiled to a dark pink and sitting on the counter with its tentacles curled up about it. Along the waterfront at Mondello, the summer resort just outside Palermo, there is a long row of booths selling octopus. The Palermitani out to catch the cool breezes off the sea love to break their stroll here for a plateful of *purpu*. Current Palermo mythology relates that at least one of these *purpari* sells so much octopus each summer that come winter he treats his whole family to a month of skiing in Switzerland.

BOY SELLING CRABS, *a nineteenth-century engraving by Vuillier*

WATER! . . . WATER! . . . , *a water seller in a nineteenth-century engraving by Vuillier*

In the past the figure who most intrigued the foreigners wandering through the Sicilian streets was the water seller. Visitors to the island marveled at the Sicilians' inordinate passion for drinking ice water, although their surprise usually melted as soon as the scirocco, the hot, dry wind from off the Sahara, began to blow. For a Sicilian, cold water is the only truly effective thirst quencher.

> From then on until my school days, I spent all my afternoons in my grandparents' apartments at Via Lampedusa, reading behind a screen. At five o'clock my grandfather would call me into his study to give me my afternoon refreshment—a hunk of bread and a large glass of cold water. It has remained my favorite drink ever since.
>
> Giuseppe di Lampedusa, *Two Stories and a Memory*, 1962

I have seen a desperate look come over the faces of my own thirsty children when they have opened an American refrigerator, filled with Coca-Cola and grape juice and lemonade, only to discover that there was no bottle of plain tap water placed there to cool.

The water sold in the streets and the markets usually had a splash of *zammù* added to it, anise extract, which sweetened it and hid, I imagine, whatever odd flavors it had acquired on its travels. Originally the water seller's equipment was very elementary: slung about his neck was a small barrel or an amphora of terra cotta, so porous that some water would seep through and evaporate, thus cooling what remained inside, while in one hand he carried a glass, in the other a bottle of *zammù*. In the late nineteenth century some inspired craftsman designed a small table with a handle to carry it by, brightly painted and decorated with silver and brass and, in some cases, with ships' lanterns. On the top of the table there was a rack to hold the glasses and the *zammù* bottle. The fancier of these tables were much admired and occasionally purchased by foreign tourists, and even today the souvenir shops sell dollhouse-sized models.

Perhaps it was the good fortune of selling one's table to a tourist that allowed upward mobility in the water trade.

> The aristocracy of watersellers are the people who have second-hand church canopies painted in the brightest colours. The most fascinating thing about these stalls are the sinks with the jet of water always running. The *padrone*

SICILIAN POTTERY, *ceramic jugs and water jars in a nineteenth-century engraving by Vuillier*

positively provokes the thirst of passers-by with the ostentatious way in
which he rinses out his glasses. You hear the cool plash and look up. You
see a canopy as bowed and picturesque as a Japanese temple. Its brass
counter glitters like gold. All round hang festoons of lemon boughs, so
cool with their dark green foliage and pale yellow fruit. To show how
familiar he is with water, he has a big bowl of goldfish; and to show how
rich he is in it, he plays with his sink—a pleasant sight in a thirsty land.

Douglas Sladen, *Queer Things About Sicily*, 1913

Some of these kiosks exist today, although the branches hung with oranges
and lemons that decorate their façades are usually made of plastic. The sound
of running water is still an attraction in a land that is still thirsty, and the
young boys in white aprons who work in them are proud of their art. They
halve the lemons and flip them into the juicer with an economy of motion so
studied that it becomes ostentatious flourish.

One type of itinerant vendor has not survived the twentieth century:

> Another particularly Palermitan type was the candy man. This vendor, always surrounded by a group of greedy youths, stood with a stopwatch in his left hand, while from his right hand dangled a string about a foot and a half long, with a large oval piece of hard candy on the end. This allowed the client who had paid an infinitesimal fee to suck the candy for exactly one minute, after which, as soon as the stopwatch sounded, the sticky sweet was torn from his mouth and immediately inserted into that of his neighbor. Naturally there were always scenes and discussions which ended in fights. The slogan of this hygienic industry was "a penny a lick."
>
> Fulco, *Estati felici*, 1977

The candy man was not the only one to have a slogan. The street markets were and still are as colorful to the ear as they are to the eye, each vendor trying to drown out the competition and employing all his poetic powers of persuasion to convince the clientele of the freshness and the inimitable delicacy of his wares.

> *Haju pipi e mulinciani!*
>   *Vo friitivi i cucuzzi;*
>   *haju cucuzzi longhi comu sciabulmazzi!*
> I've got peppers and eggplants!
>   Go fry yourselves some squash;
>   I've got squashes long as sabers!
>
> *La zzà munachiedda mi li scippàu,*
>   *ccu li manuzzi fatti di cira,*
>   *'sti catalaneddi veri!*
> The holy sister grabbed them from me,
>   with her little waxy-white hands,
>   these real Catalonian figs!
>
> *Alivi cunzàti belli,*
>   *'u cala-pani, sbrogghia pitittu!*
> Beautiful dressed olives,
>   they slide the bread down, unleash the appetite!
>
> Catanian street cries, twentieth century

Industry and ingenuity are constantly challenged by the changing of the seasons—figs give way to oranges, slices of watermelon to roasted chestnuts—

FESTINO DI SANTA ROSALIA, *an eighteenth-century drawing by Houel*

and by the requirements of the church calender, since each saint's day or other religious feast is accompanied by special foods and special demands upon the market.

For the street vendors of old Palermo the heyday came in July with the Festino, the festival dedicated to Saint Rosalia, the city's patroness. For five days the city was (and still is) given over to processions, fireworks, concerts, horse races, and other celebrations, and with all this going on who ever would want to stay at home cooking! Moreover, the city was filled with people from the provinces—the *regnicoli*, as the Palermitani disdainfully called those who lived in the rest of the Regno—who flocked wide-eyed and open-mouthed to see the goings-on in the big city. A visit to the Festino was an event so tantalizing that it was often written into marriage contracts.

Those whose chefs had to cook willy-nilly ate *sarde a beccafico* for Saint

Rosalia's feast day, but the special street food of the Festino has always been *babbaluci d'u festinu*, snails much smaller than escargots, sautéed in oil with lots of parsley and garlic. Sucking the *babbaluci* out of their shells is very laborious and time-consuming, so it seems you are getting a good deal of eating for your money.

The candy sellers did great business too, not only the ones with the stopwatches but the booths where *torrone* and *cubaita* were sold, together with crystallized almonds and a kind of nougat that is made in large loaves and cut into slices. Striped in bilious pink, white, and chartreuse, this colorful addition to the street scene resembles a serving of multiflavored ice cream, but since it doesn't need to be refrigerated, it is known as *gelato di campagna* ("country ice cream").

THE "NAVE" OF SILVER, *scene from a religious procession in a nineteenth-century engraving by Vuillier*

The *siminzari*, or seed sellers, did such good business for Saint Rosalia that they had special carts used only for the Festino, shaped like sailing ships and decorated with multicolored paper flags. The decks were spread with *semenza e càlia*—pumpkin seeds and toasted chickpeas—and with peanuts, hazelnuts, and dried chestnuts, which the vendors weighed out on a brass scale and poured into brown paper cones. Even today a Sicilian does not feel that he has taken a proper walk or watched a proper procession unless he has done so clutching a cone of *semenza e càlia* in one hand and leaving a trail of shells behind him.

But he who came to the Festino with only one penny in his pocket would neither spend it on *babbaluci* nor squander it on *semenza*. Shoving his way through the heat and the dust of the crowded streets, he would save it until he arrived at a booth belonging to one of those vendors who had elected Saint Rosalia as their patroness, the vendors who did more business than anyone else during the Festino, the vendors who satisfied the inordinate Sicilian craving for ice cream.

8

I Scream, You Scream, We All Scream for Ice Cream

The bishop's revenues are considerable, and arise principally from the sale of snow and ice not only to the whole island of Sicily, but likewise to Malta, and a great part of Italy, and make a very considerable branch of commerce; for even the peasants in these hot countries regale themselves with ices during the summer heats, and there is no entertainment given by the nobility of which these do not always make a principal part: a famine of snow, they themselves say, would be more grievous than a famine of either corn or wine.

Patrick Brydone, *A Tour through Sicily and Malta*, 1773

The bishop in question was bishop of Catania; the snow, that which fell on the slopes of Etna. Etna is a natural freezer—the snow that the winter winds blow into her crevices often lasts through the summer, insulated by a blanket of the fine volcanic ash that the volcano emits together with her gases even when she is not in eruption.

In the relentless heat of the Sicilian summer, such a source of refreshment was to be treasured. The Greeks and Romans employed lumps of Etna's snow to chill their wine; the Arabs used it instead to chill their *sarbat*. The Italian word *sorbetto* and the English *sherbet* come from these sweet fruit syrups that the Arabs drank diluted with ice water. The passage from *sarbat* and water, chilled in a container of ice, to *granita* was only a question of time, perhaps the chance invention of a housewife distracted by a passing vendor or a crying child.

Sicilians always claim an Arabic origin for their ices, although in her book on Middle Eastern food Claudia Roden cites neither an Arabic name nor a Levantine history for the *granita* recipes she gives. In any case, whether it was in Damascus or in Catania that the *sarbat* stayed too long on ice, Sicily is the home of ices as far as the Western world is concerned, and Araby their inspiration.

The flavors most common to the western part of Sicily are those that by now are famous elsewhere in Italy and in America as well, lemon and coffee. The first is served all by itself in a glass or a metal sherbet cup, its very color— the palest yellow possible—speaking of ice and freshness and the coolness of it gliding down your throat. Many bars in Sicily have the lovely habit of putting a scoop of lemon *granita* into each glass of iced tea as it is served.

GRANITA DI LIMONE
(Lemon Granita)

Serves 8 to 10

1½ cups sugar	1 cup freshly squeezed
4 cups water	lemon juice

(You will need about 9 small lemons, which should ideally consist of 5 yellow lemons and 4 *verdelli*, which are small green summer lemons.)

Make a syrup of the sugar (add ½ cup more if you want a very sweet *granita*; subtract ½ cup if you prefer it sour) and 1 cup water, bringing it to the boiling point and cooking just long enough to be sure the sugar is completely dissolved. Allow to cool and add the remaining water and the lemon juice. Stir well and pour into a shallow aluminum pan (a cake pan is perfect for this). Place in the freezer.

Remove from the freezer after half an hour and scrape down the sides and bottom of the pan, breaking up the part that has solidified and blending it into that which is still liquid. Repeat this every half hour, until the *granita* becomes a fairly firm, flaky slush. Remove the *granita* from the pan and serve at once, or return it to the freezer in a sealable glass or plastic container. If left too long in the metal pan it will "burn"—i.e., the water will separate and form ice crystals.

Note: The ice-cream parlor near my house makes a much stronger *granita di limono*, using 2 parts juice to 4 parts water, but for pure refreshment I prefer the weaker version.

GRANITA DI CAFFÈ
(Coffee Granita)

Serves 6

1 cup water	1 cup triple-strength
½ cup sugar	Italian-roast coffee
	Whipped cream

Bring the water and the sugar to the boiling point, stirring until the sugar is completely dissolved. Allow to cool.

Add the coffee, chill, pour into an aluminum pan and proceed as in *granita di limone* (see preceding recipe). Serve in small glasses liberally crowned with dollops of whipped cream.

———

If you can't cope with the whipped cream and you are in a Sicilian bar, you'd do just as well to order *caffè freddo*, which is coffee a little less concentrated and a little less frozen than that used for *granita*.

A rarer type of *granita* (and one that also benefits from the addition of whipped cream) is made from the fruit of the black mulberry. If you have a black mulberry tree at your disposal it is well worth trying, but be warned that it is a colorful business. This fruit is so swollen with intensely scarlet juice that by the time we have picked the mulberries and converted them into *granita* I, my kitchen, my children, and even my Dalmatian dog are stained a most startling shade of crimson.

GRANITA DI GELSO
(*Mulberry Granita*)

Serves 12 to 15

3 quarts fresh black mulberries	2 cups sugar
7 cups water	Whipped cream

You cannot wash mulberries without losing all the juice, but since they are not grown commercially I doubt that they ever get sprayed.

Put the mulberries in a saucepan with 3 cups of water, bring to a boil, and simmer for about 30 minutes. Allow to cool.

Meanwhile, make a syrup by simmering 2 cups of sugar with 4 cups of water for 30 minutes and then allow this to cool too.

Pass the mulberries, with all their juice, through the fine disk of a food mill, and add the resulting liquid to the sugar syrup. When everything has cooled to room temperature, pour into a shallow aluminum pan, and proceed as in *granita di limone* (p. 284). Serve with whipped cream—in this case less really isn't more! This will keep a month or more in the freezer.

———

The *sarbat* of the Saracens was behind all of these, but one kind of ice, very difficult to find nowadays unless you make it yourself, is a concentrate of the Arabian Nights. It is often called *granita di scurzunera*, but a more accurate name would be *granita di gelsomino*.

GRANITA DI GELSOMINO
(Jasmine Ice)

Makes 12 small servings

3 cups freshly picked jasmine flowers	1½ cups sugar
	Pinch of cinnamon
5 cups water	Juice of 1 small lemon

Pick the flowers in the evening when they have just opened (you need a good-size jasmine vine to get this many flowers) and put them to soak for 12 hours in 4 cups of water, weighting the flowers down with a saucer or small plate on the surface to keep them submerged.

The next morning make a syrup of the sugar and 1 cup of water, then allow it to cool. Filter the jasmine water through a

fine sieve and blend it into the syrup, together with the cinnamon and the lemon juice. Pour into a metal pan and proceed as in *granita di limone* (p. 282). A little of this highly perfumed *granita* goes a long way.

———

On the eastern coast, *granita* is more often known as *cremolata*, and the most popular flavor is that made from almond milk.

CREMOLATA DI MANDORLA
(*Almond Granita*)

Makes 8 to 10 small servings

6 cups *latte di mandorla* (see p. 207)

You may use either homemade almond milk or the commercial syrup. In the latter case dilute the syrup with slightly more water than you would to make *latte di mandorla* to drink (I use 6 cups water to 1 cup syrup). Put the *latte di mandorla* into a metal pan and proceed as in *granita di limone* (p. 284). Although I am told that in Syracuse they use a different and more complicated procedure, this *cremolata* is as refreshing as it is easy, and has won a permanent place in my freezer.

———

Sicilian documents mention such odd facts as a shipload of snow from Etna being sent as a gift to the pope, but ices and sherbets as such go unmentioned until the middle of the sixteenth century. One can only hypothesize a logical progression from *sarbat* to *granita* and then to the *sorbetto*, which is churned constantly during the freezing so that no large flakes of ice form, and then again from sorbet to the milk-based ice cream with which we are most familiar today.

By the middle of the sixteenth century a sorbet had become a dish fit for a queen: in the retinue of Italian cooks that followed Catherine de' Medici to Paris there was a Sicilian whose task it was to make milady's ices. A century

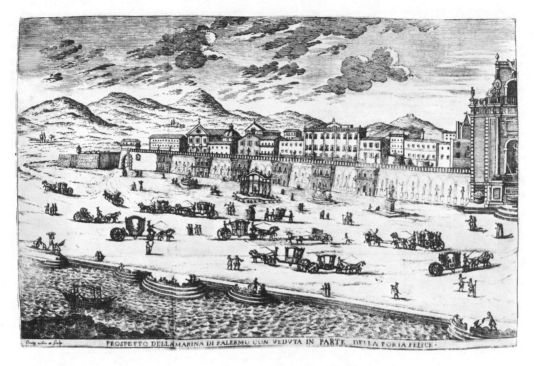

PROSPETTO DELLA MARINA DI PALERMO CON VEDVTA IN PARTE DELLA PORTA FELICE·

THE WATERFRONT WITH THE MARINA AND THE FORO ITALICO, *an eighteenth-century engraving showing Palazzo Butera, by Orstij*

later another Sicilian emigrated to France, a man by the name of Francesco Procopio de' Coltelli, who opened the first coffeehouse in Paris, where he served preserved fruits, ices, and other drinks as well as coffee. The Café Procope, which still exists today, was an enormous success, and counted Voltaire and his friends among its most faithful customers.

In eighteenth-century Sicily ices and sorbets were ubiquitous; together with pastries they had taken the place of the confections of Renaissance taste as the suitable refreshment for every occasion. Unable to persuade the Sicilian nobility to accept reforms, Vittorio Amedeo of Savoy referred to the Sicilian assembly as an "ice cream and sorbet parliament," which preferred eating ices to legislating. The servings must have been large as well as frequent: for a ball at Palazzo Butera in 1799, perhaps in honor of Ferdinand and Maria Carolina, three hundred and some guests were served dinner and supper and "constant servings of ices," so constant that eleven thousand pounds of snow

THE SNOW CAVES, *an eighteenth-century drawing by Houel*

were consumed in the preparations. Pleasant indeed it must have been to stroll, between one quadrille and another, upon the terrace of Palazzo Butera, with its majolica tiling and its wrought-iron railings entwined with jasmine vines and roses, and to look out across the waterfront to the sea and savor the cool sweetness of a *granita di limone* or a cinnamon sorbet.

Obviously a demand of this magnitude was not going to be met by snow that just happened to survive into summer: the preservation of snow had become a proper industry. Houel describes a grotto on Etna used for this purpose:

> This grotto was rented, or sold, to the Order of Malta which, finding neither ice nor snow on the barren rock on which it is situated, has rented on Etna several caverns, where people in their employ are careful to heap up and conserve the snow, which they send to Malta as it is needed.
>
> The grotto has therefore been arranged at the expense of the Order: stairways have been built: two wells have been carved, through which the

snow is thrown down, and which serve to illuminate the grotto. On the ground above the grotto a large extension of land has been leveled, and surrounded by high walls, so that when the winds, which are very strong at this altitude, bring down the snow from the higher peaks into this enclosure, it is retained and piled up into a heap. It is then thrown down into the grotto through the wells, where it is compressed and can be conserved without melting in the summer heat. The thickness of the lava which serves as a ceiling to the grotto guarantees this.

When the shipping season arrives, the snow is put into great sacks, which are forcibly filled: the snow is beaten down, and this compression gives it consistency and makes it very heavy: the men transport it out of the grotto, as I have shown in my drawing, and load it on mules, which carry it to the shore where small boats are waiting. . . .

In these climates the lack of snow is feared as much as the lack of grain, wine, or oil. I was in Syracuse in 1777; no snow was to be had: it became known that a little ship that was passing was loaded with snow; without a moment's deliberation everyone ran down and demanded that the ship be unloaded, and when the crew refused, the ship was attacked, and taken, and the Syracusans lost several men in the battle.

Jean Houel, *Voyage pittoresque en Sicile*, 1784

The dramatic incident with which Houel concludes his account is evidence that in the eighteenth century the taste for ices had spread throughout the population. It seems hardly likely that it was princes and marquises who were brawling on the docks for ice, and in any case the universality of its appeal was remarked upon by almost all foreign visitors. In 1813 William Irvine wrote that "wretches whose rags have scarse adhesion enough to hang upon their bodies, yet find a 'baioc' (a small coin equal to ⅗ penny) to spend in the ice shop."

Sicilians were not only passionate about their ice cream, they were extremely serious as well. Palermo's supply came mainly from the mountains behind the city, near Piana degli Albanesi, but when, as in 1774, that failed, it was a matter for government action. If Vittorio Amedeo had been around at the time, he would no doubt have been amused by the alacrity of the parliamentary response.

November 10, 1774. Thursday. By determination of the deputies of the newly installed Pretorial Council . . . the Senate of Palermo was charged with sending upon the instant Corradino Romagnuolo e Texiera Albornoz, presently Senator, in mission to Mount Etna, with the object of providing snow for this city, which for some time now has deplored with universal suffering the lack thereof. Therefore the aforesaid di Romagnuolo departed on the 11th of November in the company of a captain of arms and a following of twenty or more dragoons.

Marchese di Villabianca, *Diario palermitano*, 1774

One foreign visitor was particularly captivated by Sicilian ice cream, and his delight in it captivated the Sicilians in turn. This was a young Moorish prince who had accompanied his father, the ambassador of the King of Morocco, on an official visit to the court at Naples. On his way home he stopped at Palermo.

The unexpected arrival of such a personage in Palermo put the whole city into an uproar for the novelty of dealing with such a singular nation, never seen and most curious in its customs. . . . And it is to be noted that he liked the city greatly, and above all the cordial manners of our people were pleasing to him, and he thought them very courteous and graceful. He never accepted invitations to meals at the houses of these friends, however, in order not to eat butchered meat and the other foods prohibited by his sect, since he was a follower of the Mohammedanism of Efurcan, which is the most religiously observant of the laws. He attended instead and with the greatest pleasure receptions where confections and iced sweets were served, and was never able to satiate his taste for the latter. And this signifies that in his country they do not count snow to be precious, and that because of their barbarity they lack confectioners who know how to use it to such taste and such advantage, while over there iced beverages would be even more pleasant and suitable than for us Europeans, because there they must breathe a much hotter air, those countries being further south than ours. . . .

It is furthermore to be noted that this Moorish prince wanted to take home with him from Palermo both confectioners and coachmen, the first for the usage of ices, and the second for the commodity of carriages, which he wanted to introduce into his country. None of our people wanted to go, however.

Marchese di Villabianca, *Diario palermitano*, 1782

For all its universality, "taking an ice" remained something of an occasion. For Lampedusa's ancestors, it was even something to be immortalized on the walls of the dining room in the villa at Santa Margherita Belice.

There were another two pictures, but I can only remember the subject of one of them, for it was always facing me: this was the children's afternoon refreshment. Two little girls of ten and twelve years of age, powdered and tightly laced into their pointed bodices, sat facing a boy of about fifteen, dressed in an orange-colored suit with black facings and carrying a rapier, and an old lady in black (certainly the governess); all were eating large pink ices of an odd pink color, maybe of cinnamon, rising in sharp cones from long glass goblets.

Giuseppe di Lampedusa, *Two Stories and a Memory*, 1962

Bless Lampedusa for the sensual delight he took in describing food: there are so many writers who would never have bothered to guess at the flavor. Cinnamon ice has disappeared from today's ice-cream counter, but I am told that a scoop of cinnamon ice and a scoop of jasmine ice were one of the classic combinations of old-fashioned ice creamery.

GRANITA DI CANNELLA
(Cinnamon Granita)

Serves 8 to 10

4 sticks of whole cinnamon	4 cups water
4 to 5 inches in length	1 cup sugar

Soak the cinnamon sticks in the water overnight. The next morning bring the water and sticks to a boil, remove from the heat, and strain. Add the sugar and return to the heat until the sugar dissolves. Allow to cool, then pour into a metal pan and proceed as in *granita di limone* (p. 284).

I must admit I found this *granita* to be a sort of frozen penny candy, a confection of literary rather than culinary interest.

———

On other days the children who sat for their portrait might have been served chocolate ice cream—always an eighteenth-century favorite—or perhaps hazelnut, which is the ice cream that everyone in my family would choose to be painted with if they had to settle for enjoying only one flavor for the rest of time.

Ice cream is not really the proper translation for *gelato*, since unlike American ice cream Sicilian *gelato* is not made with cream at all, but with a *crema rinforzata*, which is nothing other than the omnipresent *biancomangiare* in a particularly liquid form. One old recipe calls for goat's milk, but I do not know whether this is because goat's milk is considered to be more delicate or simply because goat's milk was once the most readily available form of fresh milk in Sicily, at least outside the big cities. (The goatherds would drive their nanny goats through the towns and milk them on the spot into the clients' receptacles.)

Modern Sicilian ice-cream parlors have abandoned goat's milk, but it is still not easy to duplicate their efforts at home. I myself tend to stick to making *granita* when I am in the country, and run around the corner when I am in Palermo to Gelato 2, where Angelo La Mattina makes some of the best ice cream in the city. Mr. La Mattina has kindly explained some of his secrets to me, and although I cannot claim to come anywhere near his results, I now know how to survive when he closes down for his winter vacation.

While the *gelati* made from fresh fruit require cold processing that involves stabilizers that are not available on a retail basis, the chocolate and nut-flavored ice creams, made with a *crema rinforzata* that needs no exotic ingredients, can be satisfactorily duplicated in domestic ice-cream machines.

GELATO SICILIANO
(Sicilian Ice Cream)

Serves 8

CREMA RINFORZATA BASE

5 cups milk	1½ to 2 cups sugar
4 tablespoons corn or wheat starch	

Heat 4 cups of milk to the boiling point. Remove from the heat, and add the remaining cup of milk, in which you have carefully dissolved the 4 tablespoons of starch and the sugar. (I like to use vanilla sugar in all these ice creams.) Stir, and return to the heat. Bring once more to the boiling point, stirring constantly, then remove from the heat and allow to cool.

When the *crema* is at room temperature, add one of the flavorings listed below. Refrigerate, and when well chilled, put in your ice-cream machine and process according to instructions.

ALMOND ICE CREAM

2 cups almond flour or very finely ground blanched
almonds (about ½ pound)

HAZELNUT ICE CREAM

2 cups very finely ground toasted and peeled
hazelnuts (about ½ pound)

PISTACHIO ICE CREAM

1 ½ cups very finely ground
pistachios

½ cup very finely ground
almonds

CHOCOLATE ICE CREAM

7 ounces semisweet chocolate   ½ cup milk

Use only 1½ cups sugar in making the *crema*. Melt the chocolate in the milk over a very low flame. Add the chocolate to the *crema* when both have cooled.

VANILLA ICE CREAM

This is an exception; make the *crema rinforzata* as follows:

1 cup heavy cream	1½ cups sugar
1 vanilla bean	4 tablespoons cornstarch
4 cups milk	1 egg yolk

Heat the cream, the vanilla bean, and 3 cups of milk to the boiling point. Remove from the fire, then add the sugar and the starch dissolved in the remaining cup of milk. Return to the flame and bring once more to the boiling point. Cool, remove the bean, and, if you want a stronger vanilla taste, add a few drops of vanilla extract. Beat in the egg yolk, then chill. Process in your ice-cream machine.

Note: Mr. La Mattina makes his *gelati* using industrially prepared nut pastes that are milled to complete smoothness. There is no way that I know of to grind nuts that well at home, but with the help of a little patience and a meat grinder or an electric blender one can achieve a fairly fine texture.

————

Patrick Brydone reports that the eighteenth century also favored molded ices. At the magnificent banquet ("We were just thirty at table, but, upon my word, I do not think that we had less than a hundred dishes of meat") to which he was invited by the Bishop of Agrigento,

> The dessert consisted of a great variety of fruits, and a still greater of ices: these were so disguised in the shape of peaches, figs, oranges, nuts, &c., that a person unaccustomed to ices might very easily have been taken in.
> Patrick Brydone, *A Tour Through Sicily and Malta*, 1773

I have never seen anything like that today, but orange and lemon ices are often served in the hollowed-out skins of the fruit.

The eighteenth century also saw the introduction of *pezzi duri,* "hard pieces," which generally speaking are multiflavored wedges of ice cream sliced from a bombe and served as individual portions. Each town had its own specialties. In Catania the *spongato,* a name now used to indicate any ice cream served in a cup, was once made of ice cream layered with *pan di Spagna* (sponge cake). *Schiumone* was also from eastern Sicily, a bombe of one or more layers of ice cream hiding a center of egg yolks whipped with sugar and rum into a frozen zabaglione. One of Palermo's classics, almost impossible to find nowadays, was the *giardinetto* ("little garden")—layers of lemon, strawberry, and pistachio or peach ice cream in the shape of a brick, which was topped with finely diced multicolored candied fruit.

The *pezzi duri* tradition culminated in the *cassata gelata,* which, since it requires cream, may have been developed as a result of the increased availability of cream from the Crown dairy.

CASSATA GELATA
(*Frozen Cassata*)

Serves 12

1 ¾-inch layer of *pan di Spagna* (see p. 90)	½ recipe vanilla ice cream (see p. 296)
½ recipe pistachio ice cream (see p. 295)	½ recipe chocolate ice cream (see p. 296)

FROZEN CHANTILLY

4 egg whites at room temperature	¼ cup diced *zuccata* (see p. 94) or candied citron
1 cup sugar	½ cup rum or sweet liqueur
2½ cups whipping cream	Whipped cream
¼ cup semisweet chocolate bits	Candied fruit
	Chocolate shavings

Prepare the *pan di Spagna* and cut it across to form a ¾-inch layer that is slightly smaller in diameter than the mold that you intend to use for the *cassata*. (The remaining *pan di Spagna* will keep in the freezer.) A proper *cassata* mold is at least 6 inches deep, and must be made of aluminum or tin (stainless steel, plastic, and glass do not allow the dessert to freeze rapidly enough). The quantities given in this recipe will fit into a mold that is 9 inches in diameter and 6 inches deep, or into a cake pan that is 12 inches in diameter and 2 inches deep.

Prepare the various ice creams, and chill the mold by placing it in the freezer.

Prepare the frozen chantilly: Whip the egg whites until stiff, at the end incorporating one-half of the sugar. Put in the freezer while you whip the cream and the rest of the sugar until soft peaks form. Fold the cream into the beaten whites and place the mixture in the freezer. When the chantilly is well chilled and beginning to stiffen, stir in the chocolate bits and the *zuccata* (they will fall to the bottom if you do it sooner).

Cut out a disk of wax paper the same diameter as the mold and place it in the bottom. You must assemble the *cassata* layer by layer, allowing each kind of ice cream time to soften enough so that you can spread it (the layers need not be even, but every wedge of *cassata* when you cut it should have at least a taste of each flavor), and then time enough in the freezer to harden again; otherwise it will all melt into a mud-colored mess.

The proper order is as follows: pistachio at the bottom, then vanilla, then the *pan di Spagna* sprinkled with the rum, followed by the chantilly and on top the chocolate ice cream. This will not work, however, if you are using the 12-inch mold. In that case you should ring the sides of the mold with ice cream, first pistachio and then chocolate, with the vanilla ice cream, the cake, and the chantilly in the center.

Freeze for 5 or 6 hours. Turn the *cassata* out onto a cake platter, remove the paper, and decorate with whipped cream, candied fruit, chocolate shavings, and, as the Italians would say, *chi più ne ha, più ne metta* (whatever your cupboard offers or your fancy suggests). Return to the freezer until 15 minutes before serving.

———

VIEW OF PALERMO HARBOR AND THE MARINA FROM THE TERRACES OF THE HOTEL VICTORIA,
a nineteenth-century engraving by Bartlett

Unlike the various sorbets and *granitas* that itinerant vendors used to sell in the streets by the glass, or even—in the same "a penny a lick" economy as that of the candy seller—by the spoonful, the *pezzi duri* require greater cere mony, ideally a table to sit at and perforce the leisure to allow the "hard piece" to soften a bit, lest it shoot from the plate under the pressure of the spoon. Eating a *granita di limone* in order to cool off can be a mere expedient: ordering a *pezzo duro* is an occasion.

> When, in honor of the Festino or some other rare occasion, *'a pigghiata di ielati*—the "taking of an ice"—was decided upon, no one slept the night before and the hours never passed.
>
> Youth was inevitably destined to a half portion, and this left such an impression on the child that he aspired to adolescence solely in order to acquire the right to a whole piece.
>
> Oreste Lo Valvo, *La vita in Palermo 30 e più anni fa*, 1907

Even for those who could afford from birth to eat all the ice cream that common sense would allow, the occasion was governed by an elaborate set of rules:

But our favorite ice cream seller was Mommo ai Leoni, located next to the gate of the Park of the Favorita, near the two stone lions that gave the square its name. How many times we stopped there on our way home, to enjoy a delicious strawberry spumone with whipped cream. It wasn't even necessary to get down from the carriage because the waiter brought them to us on a tray and we ate them in the carriage, while the coachman had his on the box. To descend and go sit at a table on the sidewalk was unthinkable. The same rule held true on the Marina, but if it was a hired carriage, then it was considered very bad taste not to sit at the tables. Only women of ill repute remained in a hired carriage.

Fulco, *Estati felici*, 1977

The accelerated tempo of modern life has worked against the *pezzi duri*. In Palermo in particular there are very few sidewalk cafés, and the noise and fumes of the city's chaotic traffic have robbed the survivors of much of their appeal. Sicilians have by no means lost their passion for ice cream, but they prefer it on the run, in a cone or in a *brioscia*, a small brioche-like roll cut almost in half and filled with a large scoop of ice cream and a ruffle of whipped cream on top. Ice cream in a brioche is summertime breakfast for thousands of Sicilians on their way to work or to the beach.

Generally ice cream here is still made on the spot, and it is absolutely delicious—far better than any of the industrial products from northern Italy that are also available. The modern specialists exercise their fantasy in inventing new flavors to add to the traditional repertoire: innovations such as kiwi and mango, inspirations of questionable worth such as sea urchin or prickly pear, or something that has recently made a hit in Palermo called *baci baci*, which is essentially Baci Perugina candies made into ice cream, a mixture of chocolate and hazelnut with pieces of peanut and hazelnut strewn in.

The take-home ice cream cakes and rolls that show the influence of industrial products can be excellent but have little to do with the old traditions. These do survive in some places, however: Avola and Acireale, to mention only two, are towns where cafés of renown offer a large selection of traditional *pezzi duri* together with modern flights of fancy.

Just about the only place in Palermo where one can still find the old *pezzi duri* is at one of the two ice-cream parlors that still operate at the Foro Italico, on what is known as the Marina. The Marina is one of the tragedies of contemporary Palermo: once the playground of the city, it is celebrated in countless letters and diaries as one of the most beautiful waterfronts in Europe, "whither in summer nights the inhabitants resort to enjoy the fanning breeze, take refreshments, and listen to the serenades that enliven the still hour." The poor arrived on foot, the gentry by carriage: "a long line of handsome equipages, issuing from every part of the city, completely occupy the road."

The ring of elegant palaces that formed a backdrop to the Marina was badly damaged by Allied bombs in 1943, and today traffic roars past on a six-lane throughway leading out of the city toward Messina. Between the traffic lanes and the sea a desolate stretch of bare earth is occupied in part by a noisy and gaudy fun fair, in part by rubbish. There are plans to restore it to its former beauty, just as there are plans to save the rest of Palermo's monuments, but here as elsewhere decay is proceeding faster than bureaucracy.

Yet the trees are still there, a handsome row of *eritrina* trees, which in the early summer are afire with scarlet blossoms, and on the far side of the road the Mediterranean still glitters. It is possible to sit out at a table, to order a piece of *cassata gelata*, and to wait for a pause in the traffic, when the soft sea breeze rustles the leaves and brings a whiff of jasmine from the terrace of Palazzo Butera.

The clientele sitting around the tables is mixed. Here a group of upper-middle-class intellectuals chat languidly over their wedges of pistachio and hazelnut. There sit a group of northern tourists from the Jolly Hotel down the road, their pale skin, sunburnt to the color of their strawberry *spongato*, glowing painfully under pastel-colored, no-iron clothing; next to them a working-class family, dressed up for 'a pigghiata di gelatu and bent on keeping the drips of chocolate ice cream off the clean shirts of the children, and on stopping the smallest child from getting down from his chair and running out into the road. But even he has an entire "piece" all for himself, and his family is not celebrating anything more rare or special than the pleasure of an evening's outing.

Now Carnival comes every day in Sicily. The terrible hunger that tormented centuries of Sicilians survives only in isolated pockets of the Palermo slums. My children's contemporaries, the first generation of Sicilians to be raised on powdered formula and homogenized baby foods, tower over me, even though I was once the tallest person on the street.

The enormous class distinctions in the island's diet have also disappeared in the swell of postwar prosperity, which has blotted out many of the ancient traditions and imposed a lifestyle in the place of a culture. People whose mothers and fathers counted themselves lucky to have *lasagne cacate* now eat pasta with smoked salmon and caviar on New Year's Eve, and when my cleaning woman's elderly aunt, down from their mountain village to have her bronchial tubes examined, wanted to present the doctor with a couple of chickens or a dozen eggs, her niece advised a bottle of Chivas Regal instead.

Most of these changes have taken place during the twenty-five years that I have lived in Sicily. For me, sitting here in this motley crowd, next to the traffic and across from the fun fair, the sight of these children enjoying their ice cream is a small but significant symbol of the island's progress. Yet at the same time I can taste, as always in Sicily, a faint flavor of regret for all that has been lost.

> The bay is silvered over, the mountains stand around in shade like giant sentinels, freshness breathes from the water, perfume is in the air, everything around is steeped in beauty, and the heart and senses open to the tenderest and most contagious emotions. Hour after hour is thus passed away, the spot is abandoned with regret, and it is often midnight before the throng reluctantly separate, and the Marina is deserted until the following evening.
>
> W. H. Bartlett, *Pictures from Sicily*, 1853

THE FORO ITALICO ON A SPRING EVENING, *a nineteenth-century engraving by Vuillier*

Appendix:
A Few Suggestions About
Eating in Sicily Today

In the past thirty years Sicilian cooking has emerged from the home and from the cookshops of the street and acquired an active public life. The number of restaurants has increased by geometric progression, and tourists can now find excellent opportunities for tasting authentic Sicilian cooking when they visit the island. It is necessary to pick and choose, however. Without a long tradition behind them, Sicilian restaurateurs are often unable to avoid the pitfalls of pretentiousness, and either cater to the newly acquired purchasing power of their compatriots by sprinkling cream and caviar over everything, or camouflage slipshod cooking by festooning their menus with dialect and their ceilings with puppets and bits of painted Sicilian carts.

The following pages contain some suggestions about places where I or trusted friends have had pleasant experiences. This selection certainly does not offer a complete coverage, and is biased in terms of geographic distribution. I hope my readers will find many favorites of their own to add to it.

Palermo offers a wide choice of restaurants in every category. I am not a habitué of luxury restaurants, but I have enjoyed eating at La Scuderia (Via del Fante 9, closed Sunday evenings), which has a very pleasant location near the entrance to King Ferdinand's hunting reserve, La Favorita. La Scuderia's large menu has a permanent section devoted to Sicilian classics, including a good *formaggio all'argentiera*, which might be difficult to find elsewhere.

My personal favorite is a much simpler trattoria in the dilapidated courtyard of an ancient palazzo in the heart of the old city, the Trattoria Stella, commonly called "Hotel Patria" (Via Aragona 6, closed Sundays). In summer the tables are out in the courtyard, shaded by a palm tree and with oleanders in bloom. *Panelle*, *cazzilli*, and pickled eggplants are the house antipasto, and it was here that I first tasted an *insalata di arance e aringhe*.

The Trattoria Primavera (Piazza Bologni 4, closed Fridays) always serves reliable and unpretentious versions of such standard Sicilian classics as *sarde a beccafico*, *pasta con le sarde*, and *pasta con i broccoli arriminati*. The Cucina Papoff (Via Isidoro La Lumia 28/B, closed Sundays) specializes, despite the Russian name, in lesser-known Sicilian dishes, and in wintertime offers the chance to taste *maccu*.

For a smaller, if not necessarily lighter, meal, the Antica Foccacceria San Francesco (Via Paternoster 58, closed Mondays) is to be highly recommended, both for its turn-of-the-century décor and for its *pani cu la meuza*. This restaurant is also a dependable place in which to experiment with *sfincione* and other kinds of street food that one might hesitate to try in the street itself.

Anyone with a passion for vegetables and a desire to see the mosaics at Cefalù might like to plan a day trip that includes a stopover for lunch in the small town of Cerda, at the Trattoria Nasca (Piazza Merlina, closed Saturdays except by appointment and on Sunday evenings), which has a reputation for excellent food in rather dismal surroundings. Cerda is artichoke country, and I am told that in the winter and the early spring Mr. Nasca serves them in every possible manner, while in the summer he turns his talents to eggplants.

Picnic enthusiasts departing from Palermo can contemplate two possibilities. Superrefinement in the way of cold cuts and cheeses is centrally available at Mangia (Via Principe di Belmonte 17), and right across the street the Spinnato bakery offers a wide variety of breads and rolls. A more adventurous picnic, including many different kinds of olives, could be put together in the Vucciria or the Ballarò street markets. No one interested in food should pass up the chance to visit one of these, but like all the food stores, they are closed on Sundays and on Wednesday afternoons, and in this case I would put off buying the bread until outside the city. In general the smaller the town the better the bread, and one should look for signs saying *pane casareccio* (home-style bread) or *forno a legno* (wood oven) or even for a pile of logs heaped on the sidewalk.

Incidentally, if you are interested in decorative bread in addition to edible bread, you should try to plan a spring trip that would bring you to Salemi for Saint Joseph's Day (celebrated both on March 19 and the following Sunday). The local tourist office prints up a list each year of the families who are preparing altars, and tourists are more than welcome. There is also a bakery in Syracuse (right behind the Cathedral in the Via Roma) that makes spectacular sunbursts of bread all year round. If you can get one home in one piece, a coating of insecticide and shellac will preserve it for several years.

Seafood lovers who are planning to spend several days in the Trapani area during the summer months (late May to late September) would do well to take the ferry or the hydrofoil to Favignana, at least for a day. This island just off the Trapani coast has a special tradition of cooking, inspired by wonderfully fresh fish and by the thyme, mint, oregano, and other herbs that grow wild on the island. Most people consider the finest restaurant on the island to be that run by the Guccione sisters at the Albergo Egadi, but it is only open in the evening and by reservation. If you are there at noon, you would do well to try Da Matteo or El Pescador, and to pop in a little ahead of time to reserve a table, as both are very popular. All of these restaurants are near the main square of the town of Favignana, just a few blocks from the port.

A friend with a professional palate called me up long distance to rave about a country restaurant that she had discovered near Cammarata, to the north of Agrigento. Both the setting and the food were rustic; when she was there in April, *stigghiole* and roasted artichokes were being served as an antipasto. The Ristorante Filici, as it is called, is on the road that goes from Cammarata to Santo Stefano Quisquina, about four kilometers from Cammarata on the right side of the road. It is closed on Wednesdays. I'm planning a pilgrimage soon.

I have already made a special trip to eat at a restaurant that is a mecca for Sicilian food lovers: this is the Ristorante Majore (Via Martiri Ungheresi 12, just off the Piazza del Duomo, closed Mondays) in Chiaramonte Gulfi, near Ragusa. Known as the Paradise of the Pig, this restaurant raises its own acorn-fed pork, which it serves in a variety of ways, including an excellent stuffed pork chop. It is the ideal place to try a *ragù* or sausage, and you can buy a salami to take away with you.

I am told by many sources that the best place to sample the cooking of Syracuse is at the Ristorante Don Camillo in Via Maestranze 96, near Piazza Archimede. Wonderful pizza and spinach pies and *scaccie* of different kinds are available in Piazza Archimede itself, in a little pizzeria and *tavola calda* on the corner of the Via Dione.

Sicily is rich in between-meal indulgence. Pastries are available both at convents and in commercial establishments, and ice cream is to be found in abundance all year round. In Palermo only one convent pastry kitchen has survived, that of the Benedictine convent in Piazza Venezia 38A: it has excellent cannoli in the cold season and will make a triumph of gluttony on twenty-four-hour notice. The Badia del Santo Spirito in Agrigento still sells its sweets, including a sweet couscous made with chopped pistachios that must be ordered ahead, while a convent of the same name in Palma di Montechiaro is famous for its pistachio-filled marzipan Paschal lambs. None of the convents is open for business on Sundays.

The Paschal lamb made by Maria Grammatico of Erice is filled with homemade citron preserves, and it is not the more common seated version made in a mold, but the slaughtered lamb that was traditionally made by the nuns in the local convent before it closed. The nuns also taught her to make *dolci di riposto* and delicious almond cakes. All of these are on sale in her pastry shop in Erice, in Via Vittorio Emanuele 14.

Those who are traveling in the vicinity of Enna are advised to make a stop at the Bivio Sant'Anna, the crossroads at the southern foot of Enna's mountain, where the modern city is spreading. There the Bar Nocilla (Piazza Antonello da Messina, closed Tuesdays) sells *lunette*, half-moons of *pasta frolla* filled with chocolate and almonds, chewy chocolate pastries known as *rami di Napoli*, and wonderful Christmas cakes as well.

Two famous pastry chefs in eastern Sicily are Giuseppe Chemi, whose masterly marzipan and nougat are on display at the Pasticceria Etna in Taormina (Corso Umberto 112, closed Mondays), and Corrado Costanzo, who sells *cassate* and sugar engagement hearts (which would make a very special Valentine) at his shop in Noto (Via Silvio Spaventa 7–9).

There are good commercial pastry shops in Palermo, too. My favorite is the Pasticceria Scimone (Via Imera 8, closed Tuesdays), which is a short walk from the flea market; it makes a wicked *buccellato*. The Pasticceria La Preferita (Via Villareale 47, closed Tuesdays) is a little more centrally located, and has very good marzipan and candied fruit.

Always last but never least, the ice cream: My beloved Gelato 2 (Via Alcide de Gaspari, closed Wednesdays) is excellent but far off the tourist track. The Palermitani are fond of the ice cream at Cofea (Via Villareale 18) and at the Bar Mazzara (Via Generale Magliocco 15). The latter is the *caffè* at whose tables Lampedusa is said to have written *The Leopard*, but fancy redecoration has destroyed the air of shabby gentility in which he found inspiration.

The Gelateria Ilardi (Foro Umberto Primo 6, open June through September) is still the place to go for *pezzi duri* if you are in Palermo. On the eastern coast the Gelateria Costarelli-Maugeri in Acireale is famous, as is the Bar Avola Finocchiaro in the main piazza of Avola. Syracuse has a bar, the Bar Viola in Corso Matteotti, that is renowned for its *gianduia* (chocolate and hazelnut) ice cream, and would also be a good place to try *cremolata di mandorla*.

My apologies to all the places I have yet to discover, and *buon appetito!*

Bibliography

SICILIAN COOKBOOKS

Alliata, Enrico, duca di Salaparuta. *Cucina vegetariana e naturismo*. Palermo, 1977.

Cascino, Francesco Paolo. *Cucina di Sicilia*. Cefalù, 1982.

Cascino, Mimmo. *La cucina palermitana*. Cefalù, 1985.

Colonna Romana, Franca. *Sicilia in bocca*. Palermo, 1974.

———. *Sicilia nel cuore*. Palermo, 1977.

Consoli Sardo, Maria. *Cucina nostra*. Palermo, 1978.

Coria, Giuseppe. *Profumi di Sicilia: Il libro della cucina siciliana*. Palermo, 1981.

Correnti, Pino. *Il Libro d'oro della cucina e dei vini di Sicilia*. Milan, 1985.

D'Alba, Tommaso. *La cucina siciliana di derivazione araba*. Palermo, 1980.

Denti di Pirajno, Alberto. *Siciliani a tavola: Itinerario gastronomico da Messina a Porto Empedocle*. Milan, 1970.

De Simone, Giovanni. *La cucina di Sicilia*. Caltanissetta, 1974.

Grasso, J. C. *The Best of Southern Italian Cooking*. New York, 1984.

Pisa, Antonella, and Anna Chines. *Cucina di putiri fare: Cucina d'un putiri fare*. Palermo, 1970.

Pomar, Anna. *La cucina tradizionale siciliana*. Rome, 1984.

Sapio Bartelletti, N. *La cucina siciliana nobile e popolare*. Milan, 1985.

Uccello, Antonino. *Del mangiar siracusano: itinerari gastronomico-letterari e anche archeologici*. Syracuse, 1979.

OTHER SOURCES

Alberti, Arturo. "Appunti sull' organizzazione domestica nell'abbazia di San Michele Arcangelo il Nuovo a Troina (1795–1866)," in *La cultura materiale in Sicilia*, Palermo, 1978.

Alberti, Leandro. *Descrittione di tutta Italia*. Venice, 1568.

Alciphron. *The Letters of Alciphron, Aelian and Philostratus*, trans. A. R. Benner and F. H. Fobes. Cambridge, Mass., 1949.

Alessandro, Abbate di Telese. "De' Fatti di Ruggiero Re di Sicilia (1127–35)," in G. Del Re, *Cronisti e scrittori sincroni della dominazione normanna del regno di Puglia e Sicilia*. Naples, 1845–65.

Amari, Michele. *Biblioteca Arabo-Sicula: Raccolta di testi arabici che toccano la geografia, la storia, la biografia e la bibliografia della Sicilia*. Turin, 1880.

———. *Storia dei Musulmani di Sicilia*, abbreviated version. Catania, 1977.

Angiuli, Emanuela. "L'altare del pane," in *La Gola*. April 1983, p. 4.

Anonymous diarist in Gioacchino Di Marzo, ed., *Diari della città di Palermo dal secolo XVI al XIX*, Vol. I. Palermo, 1871.

Apicius. *Cookery and Dining in Imperial Rome*, trans. Joseph Dommers Vehling. New York, 1977.

Aristophanes. *The Wasps*, trans. Douglass Parker. Ann Arbor, 1962.

Arnott, Margaret L., ed. *Gastronomy: The Anthropology of Food and Food Habits*. The Hague, 1974.

Athenaeus. *The Deipnosophists*, trans. C. B. Gulick. Cambridge, Mass., 1949.

Aymard, Maurice. "Une famille aristocratique sicilienne aux XVIe et XVIIe siècles: les ducs de Terranova," in *Revue historique*, No. 501 (1972), pp. 29–66.

——— and Henri Bresc. "Nourritures et consommation en Sicile entre XIVe et XVIIIe siècle," in *Mélanges de l'école française de Rome, Moyen Age/Temps Modernes*. Tome 87 (1975), 2, pp. 535–81.

Balsamo, l'Abbate Paolo. *Giornale del viaggio fatto in Sicilia e particolarmente nella Contea di Modica*. Ragusa, 1969.

Bartlett, W. H. *Pictures from Sicily*. London, 1853.

Battaglia, Aristide. *L'evoluzione sociale in rapporto alla proprietà fondiaria in Sicilia* (1895). Palermo, 1974.

Bautier, G., and H. Bresc. "*Maramma*: I mestieri della costruzione nella Sicilia medievale," in *I Mestieri: organizzazioni, tecniche, linguaggi*. Palermo, 1984.

Beccaria, Giuseppe. *Spigolature sulla vita privata di Re Martino in Sicilia*. Palermo, 1894.

Beck-Bossard, C. "L'alimentazione in un villaggio siciliano del XIV secolo, sulla scorta delle fonte archeologiche," in *Archeologia medievale*, Vol. VIII, 1981, pp. 311–20.

Bingham Richards, T. *Letters from Sicily written in the year 1798*. London, 1800.

Boccaccio, Giovanni. *The Decameron*, trans. Frances Winwar. New York, 1955.

Bonaviri, Giuseppe. *L'incominciamento*. Palermo, 1983.

Bozzo, Stefano Vittorio. "Una poesia siciliana del XIV secolo inedito. Studio paleografico, letterario e storico," in *Archivio Storico Siciliano*, Nuova Serie 1877, Anno II, fasc. II, pp. 173–94.

Braudel, Fernand. *The Structures of Everyday Life*, Vol. I. New York, 1981.

Bresc, Henri. "Les jardins de Palerme (1290–1460)," in *Mélanges de l'école française de Rome, Moyen Age/Temps Modernes*. Tome 84 (1972), No. 1, pp. 55–127.

Brown, Linda K., and Kay Mussell, eds. *Ethnic and Regional Foodways in the United States: The Performance of Group Identity*. Knoxville, 1984.

Brydone, Patrick. *A Tour Through Sicily and Malta*. Edinburgh, 1840.

Camporesi, Piero. *Il pane selvaggio*. Bologna, 1980.

———. *Alimentazione, folclore, società*. Parma, 1980.

———. *Il paese della fame*. Bologna, 1978.

Cancila, Orazio. *Baroni e popolo nella Sicilia del grano*. Palermo, 1983.

Caracciolo, Enrichetta. *Misteri del chiostro napoletano* (1864). Florence, 1986.

Carini, Isidoro. "Sul Monastero di San Giovanni degli Eremiti," in *Archivio Storico Siciliano*, Anno I, pp. 61–78, 1985.

Cavalcanti, Ottavio. "Le feste del grano nel Sud" in *La Gola*, November 1982, p. 3.

Clark, J. A., and S. A. Goldblith. "Mense di Roma Antica," in *La Gola*, April 1983, p. 20.

Colonna Romana, Franca. "Il pane in Sicilia," in *Sicilia*, 1970, No. 83.

Columella, Lucio Giunio. *L'arte dell'agricoltura*. Turin, 1977.

Cordaro, Bianca. "A tavola dal barone," in *Il Giornale di Sicilia*, Sept. 21, 1968.

———. "Il coniglio dell'argentiere," in *Il Giornale di Sicilia*, Oct. 3, 1968.

———. "Con i complimenti della principessa," in *Il Giornale di Sicilia*, Oct. 6, 1968.

———. "Alla ricerca dei sapori perduti," in *Il Giornale di Sicilia*, Oct. 10, 1968.

Correnti, Pino. *La gastronomia nella storia e nella vita del popolo siciliano*. Milan, 1971.

Correnti, Santi. *La Sicilia del Seicento: Società e cultura*. Milan, 1976.

D'Andrea, Jeanne. *Ancient Herbs in the J. Paul Getty Museum Gardens*. Malibu, Calif., 1982.

De Borch, le Comte. *Lettres sur la Sicile et sur l'ile de Malte*. Turin, 1782.

De Roberto, Federico. *The Viceroys* (1894), trans. Archibald Colquhoun. New York, 1962.

Detienne, M. "La coscienza gastrologica," in *La Gola*, October 1982, p. 3.

d'Ostervald, J. F. *Voyage pittoresque en Sicile*. Paris, 1826.

Duby, Georges. *L'economia rurale nell'Europa medievale*. Bari, 1972.

Emanuele e Gaetani, F. M., Marchese di Villabianca. "Diario palermitano," in Gioacchino Di Marzo, ed., *Diari della città di Palermo dal secolo XVI al XIX*, Vols. XIX–XXVIII. Palermo, 1871.

Fazio, Beppe. "Di Archestrato, gastronomo siciliano," in *Sicilia*, 1960, No. 25.

Field, Carol. *The Italian Baker*. New York, 1985.

Fileccia, Salvatore. "Per la storia dello zucchero siciliano in età moderna: il trappeto della Milicia nei primi anni del '600." Università di Palermo. Facoltà di Agraria, Thesis, 1977–78.

Finley, M. I. *Ancient Sicily to the Arab Conquest*. London, 1968.

Flandrin, J. L., and O. Redon. "Les livres de cuisine italiens des XIV et XV siècles," in *Archeologia medievale*, Vol. VIII, 1981, pp. 393–409.

Francis, J. G., B.A. *Notes from a Journal kept in Italy and Sicily during the years 1844, 1845 and 1846*. London, 1847.

Frati, Ludovico, ed. *Libro di cucina del XIV secolo*. Livorno, 1899.

Freeman, E. A. *The History of Sicily from the Earliest Times*. Oxford, 1891–94.

French Angas, George. *A Ramble in Malta and Sicily in the Autumn of 1841*. London, 1842.

Fulco. *Estati felici: Un' infanzia in Sicilia*. Milan, 1977.

Galt, John. *Voyages and travels in the years 1809, 1810 and 1811, containing statistical, commercial and miscellaneous observations on Gibralter, Sardinia, Sicily, Malta, Serigo & Turkey*. London, 1812.

Gattuso, Ignazio. *Economia e società in un comune rurale della Sicilia (secoli XVI–XIX)*. Palermo, 1976.

Giuffrida, Antonino. "Considerazioni sul consumo della carne a Palermo nei secoli XIV e XV," in *Mélanges de l'école française de Rome MA/TM*. Tome 87, 1975, 2, pp. 583–94.

Goethe, J. W. *Italian Journey (1786–1788)*, trans. W. H. Auden and Elizabeth Mayer. San Francisco, 1982.

Guastella, Serafino Amabile. *L'antica carnevale nella Contea di Modica* (1887). Palermo, 1969.

Henisch, Bridget Ann. *Fast and Feast: Food in Medieval Society*. London, 1976.

Homer. *The Odyssey*, trans. Robert Fitzgerald. New York, 1961.

Houel, Jean. *Voyage pittoresque des isles de Sicile, de Malte et de Lipari* . . . Paris, 1782–87.

Hugo Falcandus. "Praefatio ad Petrum," in G. Del Re, *Cronisti e scrittori sincroni della dominazione normanna del regno di Puglia e Sicilia*. Palermo, 1845–65.

Ibn Idrisi. *Il Libro di Ruggiero* (1150), trans. Umberto Rizzitano. Palermo, 1966.

Ingrassia, Giovanni Filippo. *Informatione del pestifero et contagio morbo*. Palermo, 1576.

Irvine, William. *Letters on Sicily*. London, 1813.

Isgrò, Giovanni. *Festa, teatro, rito nella storia della Sicilia*. Palermo, 1981.

————. *Feste barocche a Palermo*. Palermo, 1981.

Istituto Nazionale di Sociologia Rurale. *Gastronomia e società*. Milano, 1984.

Jacob, H. E. *Six Thousand Years of Bread: Its Holy and Unholy History*. Westport, Conn., 1970.

Lampedusa, Giuseppe di. *Two Stories and a Memory*, trans. Archibald Colquhoun. New York, 1962.

————. *The Leopard*, trans. Archibald Colquhoun. New York, 1960.

La Rosa, Don Giovanni Battista. "Alcune cose degne di memoria 1330–1632," in Gioacchino Di Marzo, *Diari della città di Palermo dal secolo XVI al XIX*, Vol. II. Palermo, 1871.

Lawrence, D. H. *Sea and Sardinia*. London, 1981.

Levi, Carlo. *Le parole sono pietre*. Torino, 1964.

Levi, Mario Attillo. *Roma antica*. Torino, 1963.

Lodato, Gaetano. "Antichi gastronomi siciliani," extract from *Realtà*, Dec. 1, 1927.

Lo Presti, Salvatore. "Gli ultimi gridatori delle vie di Catania," in *Sicilia*, No. 40, 1963.

Lorenzoni, G. *Inchiesta parlamentare sulle condizioni dei contadini nelle province meridionali e nella Sicilia*, Vol. VI: *Sicilia*. Rome, 1910.

Lo Valvo, Oreste. *La vita in Palermo 30 e più anni fa in confronto a quella attuale*. Palermo, 1907.

————. "La vita palermitana del '700," in *Studi su Giovanni Meli*. Palermo, 1942.

Mack Smith, Denis. *A History of Medieval and Modern Sicily*. London, 1968.

Maggiore-Perni, F. *Delle condizioni economiche, politiche e morali della Sicilia dopo il 1860*. Palermo, 1896.

————. *La popolazione di Sicilia e di Palermo dal X al XVIII secolo*. Palermo, 1892.

Martial. *Epigrams*, trans. W. C. A. Ker. Cambridge, Mass., 1948.

Meli, Giovanni. *Opere poetiche*, ed. Eduardo Alfano. Palermo, 1915.

Mennell, Stephen. *All Manners of Food: Eating and Taste in England and France from the Middle Ages to the Present*. Oxford, 1985.

Montanari, Massimo. *Campagne medievali: Strutture produttive, rapporti di lavoro, sistemi alimentari*. Turin, 1984.

————. "L'arrosto dei forti," in *La Gola*, April 1986.

Nicolosi, Pietro. *Palermo fin de siècle*. Milan, 1979.

Norwich, John Julius. *The Kingdom in the Sun*. London, 1970.

Origo, Iris. *The Merchant of Prato*. London, 1957.

Ormonde, Marquis of. *An Autumn in Sicily (1832)*. Dublin, 1850.

Palmieri de Miccichè, Michele. *Pensées et souvenirs historiques et contemporains*. Palermo, 1969.

————. *Costumi della corte e dei popoli delle Due Sicilie*, trans. Preziosa Loveto. Milan, 1987.

Papa, Sebastiana. *La cucina dei monasteri*. Milan, 1981.

Papa Algozino, Rosaria. *Sicilia araba*. Catania, 1977.

Paruta, Filippo, and Niccolò Palmerino. "Diario della città di Palermo 1500–1613," in Gioacchino Di Marzo, *Diari della città di Palermo dal socolo XVI al XIX*, Vols. I and II. Palermo, 1871.

Peri, Illuminato. *Uomini, città e campagne in Sicilia dall'XI al XIII secolo*. Bari, 1978.

Peter of Blois. Letter to the Archbishop of Messina, quoted in John Julius Norwich, *The Kingdom in the Sun*, London, 1970.

Pirandello, Luigi. *Novelle per un anno*. Milan, 1924.

Pitrè, Giuseppe. *Feste patronali in Sicilia*. Palermo, 1900.

————. *La famiglia, la casa, la vita del popolo siciliano*. Palermo, 1913.

————. *La vita in Palermo cento e più anni fà*. Palermo, 1904.

————. *Palermo nel Settecento*. Palermo, 1906.

————. *Proverbi siciliani*. Palermo, 1880.

————. *Usi e costumi, credenze e pregiudizi del popolo siciliano*. Palermo, 1889.

Platina, Bartolomeo. *Il piacere onesto e la buona salute (1475)*, trans. Emilio Faccioli. Turin, 1985.

Plato. *The Epistles*, trans. R. G. Bury. Cambridge, Mass., 1946.

Prezzolini, G. *Maccheroni e Co*. Milan, 1957.

Raffiotti, G. *Gabelle e dogane di Palermo nel I° trentennio del '700*. Palermo, 1962.

Revel, Jean François. *3000 anni a tavola*. Milan, 1980.

Riedesel, Baron von. *Travels through Sicily and that part of Italy formerly called Magna Graecia, and a tour through Egypt*, trans. J. R. Forster. London, 1773.

Roden, Claudia. *A New Book of Middle Eastern Food*. London, 1986.

Rodinson, Maxime. "Romania et autres mots arabes en Italien," in *Romania*, Vol. LXXI (1950), pp. 433–449.

———. "Sur l'étymologie de 'losange,' " in *Scritti in onore di G. Levi Della Vida*. Rome, 1956, Vol. II, pp. 425–35.

———. "Ghidha'," in *Encyclopédie de l'Islam*, Leyde-Paris, 1965, Vol. II, pp. 1081–1094.

Root, Waverley. *The Food of Italy*. New York, 1977.

Rossi, Annabella. "Ex voto di pane," in *Esso Rivista*, Vol. XXIII, No. 3, pp. 8–13.

Rosso, Valerio. "Varie cose notabili occorse in Palermo ed in Sicilia 1587–1601," in Gioacchino Di Marzo, *Diari della città di Palermo dal secolo XVI al XIX*, Vol. I. Palermo, 1871.

Saint-Non, l'Abbé J. C. *Voyage pittoresque ou description du royaume de Naples et de Sicile*. Paris, 1781–86.

Salamone-Marino, Salvatore. *Costumi ed usanze dei contadini della Sicilia*. Palermo, 1879.

———. *La vita dei contadini siciliani del tempo andato descritta da essi*. Palermo, 1894.

———. *Una festa nuziale celebrato nel 1574 in Palermo e descritta da un contemporaneo*. Palermo, 1877.

Sampolo, Luigi. "Istoria degl'istituti femminili di emenda della città di Palermo dal secolo XVI al XIX," in *Archivio Storico Siciliano*, Anno II, 1874, pp. 289–344.

Scarlata, Marina. "L'approvvigionamento alimentare di una nave negli scali mediterranei del XIV secolo," in *Archeologia medievale*, Vol. VIII (1981), pp. 305–310.

Schifani, Carmelo. *Redditi e consumi nell'agricoltura siciliana*. Palermo, 1960.

Schirò, Giovanni. *Topografia medica*. Palermo, 1846.

Sciascia, Leonardo, ed. *Delle cose di Sicilia: Testi inediti o rari*, Vol. I. Palermo, 1980.

Sereni, Emilio. *Terra nuova e buoi rossi e altri saggi per una storia dell'agricoltura europea*. Turin, 1981.

————. *Storia del paesaggio agrario italiano.* Bari, 1982.

Simond, L. *A Tour in Italy and Sicily.* London, 1828.

Sladen, Douglas. *In Sicily.* London, 1901.

————. *Queer Things About Sicily.* Edinburgh, 1913.

————. *Sicily, the New Winter Resort: An Encyclopedia of Sicily.* London, 1904.

Smyth, W. H. *Memoir descriptive of the resources, inhabitants and hydrography of Sicily and its Islands . . .* London, circa 1820.

Sonnino, Sydney. "I contadini in Sicilia," in *La Sicilia nel 1876,* Vol II. Florence, 1877.

Starke, Mariana. *Travels in Europe between the years 1824–28, adapted to the use of travellers, comprising an historical account of Sicily . . .* London, 1828.

Strutt, Arthur John. *A Pedestrian Tour in Calabria and Sicily.* London, 1841.

Swinburne, Henry. *Travels in the Two Sicilies in the Years 1777, 1778, 1779 and 1780.* London, 1790.

Teti, Vito. "Carnevale abolito dall'abbondanza," in *La Gola,* Feb. 1984, p. 84.

————. "Carni e maccarruni assai," in *La Gola,* February 1985, pp. 9–10.

Thompson, W. H., Esq. *Sicily and its Inhabitants: Observations made during a residence in that country during the years 1809 and 1810.* London, 1813.

Titone, Virgilio. *La società siciliana sotto gli spagnoli e le origini della questione meridionale.* Palermo, 1978.

————. *Riveli e platee del regno di Sicilia.* Milan, 1961.

————. *Storia, mafia e costume in Sicilia.* Milan, 1964.

Trasselli, Carmelo. *Siciliani fra quattrocento e cinquecento.* Messina, 1981.

————. *Storia dello zucchero siciliano.* Caltanissetta, 1982.

Uccello, Antonino. *Pani e dolci di Sicilia.* Palermo, 1976.

Verga, Giovanni. *I Malavoglia* (1881). Milan, 1965.

Viollet-Le-Duc, Eugène. *Lettres sur la Sicile.* Paris, 1860.

Vittorini, Elio. *Conversazioni in Sicilia.* Turin, 1941.

————. *Le città del mondo.* Turin, 1969.

Vuillier, Gastone. *La Sicilia: Impressioni del Presente e del Passato.* Milan, 1897.

Watkins, Thomas. *Travels through Swisserland, Italy, Sicily, the Greek Islands . . . in the years 1787, 1788, 1789.* London, 1792.

Wright Vaughan, Thomas, Esq. *A View to the Present State of Sicily . . .* London, 1811.

Zambrini, ed. "Il Libro della cucina del secolo XIV," in *Scelta di curiosità letterarie.* Bologna, 1863.

Index

Note: Page numbers in *italics* refer to recipes.

ILLUSTRATION CREDITS

Grateful acknowledgment is made to the following people and organizations for providing artwork included in this volume:

Archivio Fotografico, Soprintendenza Beni Culturali ed Ambientali, Palermo, for detail from *The Holy Family* by Pietro D'Asaro, from Church of the Matrice, Cammarata (page 63); an eighteenth-century wine flask (page 162) and an eighteenth-century plate (page 241) from the Pitrè Museum, Palermo.

Biblioteca Comunale di Palermo, for an engraving from l'Abbé de Saint-Non, *Voyage pittoresque ou description des Royaumes de Naples et Sicile*, Naples, 1781 (page 178); and engravings by J. F. d'Ostervald from J. F. d'Ostervald, *Voyage pittoresque en Sicile*, vols. I and II, Paris, 1826 (pages 217 and 254).

Biblioteca Comunale di Palermo and Società per la Storia Patria, Palermo, for engravings by Jean Houel from Jean Houel, *Voyage pittoresque en Sicile*, vols. I–IV, Paris, 1783–1787 (pages 6, 14, 30, 47, 83, 109, 130, 239, 261, 280, and 290.

Biblioteca Regionale Siciliana, Palermo, for engravings by W. H. Bartlett from W. H. Bartlett, *Pictures from Sicily*, London, 1853 (pages 8, 100, 102, 234, 244, 258, and 299); engravings by Antonino Bova from A. Leanti, *Lo stato presente della Sicilia o sia breve e distinta descrizione di essa*, Palermo, 1761 (pages 86, 185, 206, 289); an engraving by Antonino Bova from P. La Placa, *La felicità della Sicilia per la fausta nascita del regal principe Filippo Antonio*, Palermo, 1748 (page 152); an engraving by Antonino Bova from P. La Placa, *La regia in trionfo per l'acclamazione e coronazione della Sacra Real Maestà di Carlo, infante di Spagna, re di Sicilia . . . ,* Palermo, 1736 (page 191); engravings from Gustavo Chiesi, *La Sicilia illustrata*, Milan, 1892 (pages 145, 218, 219); and engravings from G. F. Ingrassia, *Informatione del pestifero et contagio morbo*, Palermo, 1576 (pages 107 and 112).

Istituto di Economia e Politica Agraria, Palermo, for engravings by Gastone Vuillier from Gastone Vuillier, *La Sicilia*, Milan, 1892 (pages 25, 33, 43, 45, 65, 74, 129, 142, 149, 158, 171, 175, 189, 203, 215, 217, 222, 237, 260, 264, 265, 267, 270, 275, 276, 278, 281, and 302).

Mandralisca Museum, Cefalù (photograph copyright © Melo Minnella), for Sicilian Greek vase (page 26).

Photographs by Angelo Provenzano: pages 37, 41, 49, 53, 61, 69, 80, 88, 92, 95, 117, 133, 134, 139, 147, 160, 166, 168, 187, 192, 210, 225, 227, 229, 246, 250, 273, 282, 285, 287, and 295.

Publifoto, for mosaic floor detail (pages 56–57) and detail from *The Last Supper* by Pietro D'Asaro, from the collection of Galleria Regionale Palazzo Abatellis, Palermo (page 115).

Società per la Storia Patria, Palermo, for an engraving by P. Dewint from Major William Light, *Sicilian Scenery from Drawings by P. Dewint*, London, 1823 (page 208).